Shakespeare in the Theatre: Mark Rylance at the Globe

SHAKESPEARE IN THE THEATRE

Series Editors
Bridget Escolme, Peter Holland and Farah Karim-Cooper

Shakespeare in the Theatre: Mark Rylance at the Globe

Stephen Purcell

Bloomsbury Arden Shakespeare
An imprint of Bloomsbury Publishing Plc

B L O O M S B U R Y

LONDON · OXFORD · NEW YORK · NEW DELHI · SYDNEY

Bloomsbury Arden Shakespeare

An imprint of Bloomsbury Publishing Plc

50 Bedford Square	1385 Broadway
London	New York
WC1B 3DP	NY 10018
UK	USA

www.bloomsbury.com

**BLOOMSBURY, THE ARDEN SHAKESPEARE and the Diana logo
are trademarks of Bloomsbury Publishing Plc**

First published 2017
Reprinted 2017

British Library Cataloguing-in-Publication Data
A catalogue record for this book is available from the British Library.

ISBN: HB: 978-1-4725-8172-3
PB: 978-1-4725-8171-6
ePDF: 978-1-4725-8174-7
ePub: 978-1-4725-8173-0

Library of Congress Cataloging-in-Publication Data
Names: Purcell, Stephen, 1981- author.
Title: Shakespeare in the theatre : Mark Rylance at the Globe / Stephen Purcell.
Other titles: Mark Rylance at the Globe
Description: London ; New York : Bloomsbury Arden Shakespeare, 2017. | Series: Shakespeare in the
theatre | Includes bibliographical references and index.
Identifiers: LCCN 2016056085 | ISBN 9781472581716 (paperback) | ISBN 9781472581723 (hardback)
Subjects: LCSH: Shakespeare, William, 1564-1616--Dramatic production. | Shakespeare, William,
1564-1616--Stage history. | Rylance, Mark--Appreciation--Great Britain. | Globe
Theatre (Organization : London, England) | BISAC: DRAMA / Shakespeare. | LITERARY
CRITICISM / Shakespeare.
Classification: LCC PR3091 . P86 2017 | DDC 792.9/5--dc23 LC record available at https://lccn.loc.
gov/2016056085

Series: Shakespeare in the Theatre

Series cover design: Dani Leigh
Cover image: Hamlet, Mark Rylance; at Shakespeare's Globe Theatre,
London, UK, 2000; Credit: Marilyn Kingwill/ArenaPAL www.arenapal.com

Typeset by Fakenham Prepress Solutions, Fakenham, Norfolk NR21 8NN
Printed and bound in Great Britain

To find out more about our authors and books visit www.bloomsbury.com.
Here you will find extracts, author interviews, details of forthcoming events
and the option to sign up for our newsletters.

For Jan, John and Anna Purcell, with whom I first enjoyed many of these productions.

CONTENTS

LIST OF
ILLUSTRATIONS

ACKNOWLEDGEMENTS

This book has benefited from the help and support of many people. First, I should like to thank Mark Rylance himself, who made time in his busy schedule to talk in great depth about his work at the Globe. He and Claire van Kampen kindly welcomed me into their home for this conversation. Our interview, much of which is transcribed in this book, was invaluable, but so too were our informal conversations before and afterwards, and our exchanges of emails. Rylance was very generous in allowing me access to his personal archives, both at the Globe and at his home. Thanks are also due to his assistant, Meryl Robertson, for her help in facilitating this.

I am indebted to the numerous Globe practitioners who have shared their thoughts with me over the years, especially to Tim Carroll, Marcello Magni and James Garnon, whose conversations with me are quoted in this book. The Globe has always been very open in sharing its artistic processes with the public, and this book has benefited hugely from the post-show talks and online material offered by the theatre. Globe Education's freely accessible archive of 'Adopt an Actor' interviews (1998–) was enormously helpful, as were the Research Bulletins published by the Globe's Research team. Between 1995 and 2002, Pauline Kiernan, Chantal Miller-Schütz, Jaq Bessell, Jessica Ryan and Sam Howey-Nunn documented the rehearsal processes of over twenty productions and interviewed scores of Globe practitioners, providing a rich archive of Globe practice. The past and present staff of the Globe's Library and Archive, especially Victoria Lane and Miki Govedarica, have been very supportive in helping me to access those parts of the theatre's archival material that are not publicly available.

I am grateful to the series editors, and especially to Farah Karim-Cooper for our many conversations about the Globe's work and her generous and helpful feedback on my first draft. I am also indebted to Margaret Bartley and all at Arden/Bloomsbury for their support. Thanks, too, to my colleagues and students at the University of Warwick, whose conversations about the Globe have helped me to formulate the arguments in this book. A period of research leave from Warwick gave me time to finish writing it. Thanks, as always, to my friends at The Pantaloons, whose practical work and willingness to experiment always inform my research into Shakespeare in performance. Finally, and most importantly, thank you to Zoe, who has lived and breathed this book with me for three years, and whose patience, interest and support has never wavered.

SERIES PREFACE

Each volume in the *Shakespeare in the Theatre* series focuses on a director or theatre company who has made a significant contribution to Shakespeare production, identifying the artistic and political/social contexts of their work.

The series introduces readers to the work of significant theatre directors and companies whose Shakespeare productions have been transformative in our understanding of his plays in performance. Each volume examines a single figure or company, considering their key productions, rehearsal approaches and their work with other artists (actors, designers, composers). A particular feature of each book is its exploration of the contexts within which these theatre artists have made their Shakespeare productions work. The series thus considers not only the ways in which directors and companies produce Shakespeare, but also reflects upon their other theatre activity and the broader artistic, cultural and socio-political milieu within which their Shakespeare performances and productions have been created. The key to the series' originality, then, is its consideration of Shakespeare production in a range of artistic and broader contexts; in this sense, it de-centres Shakespeare from within Shakespeare studies, pointing to the range of people, artistic practices and cultural phenomena that combine to make meaning in the theatre.

Bridget Escolme, Peter Holland, Farah Karim-Cooper

Introduction

It is 23 April 2005. I have spent much of the day in London at Shakespeare's Globe for the celebrations marking Shakespeare's birthday. It is St. George's Day too, of course, but so far, the day has defied my expectations of flag-waving patriotism and taken a more irreverent, even subversive tone. Throughout the day, before a crowd of hundreds, members of the public have been performing brief passages from Shakespeare on the Globe stage; every few minutes, somebody would start yet another 'To be or not to be' with an apologetic smile, and the crowd would laugh along at what was rapidly becoming the in-joke of the day. Costumed musicians and whiteface clowns have been interacting with spectators. Three Shakespeare 'lookalikes' in bald wigs and false beards have been put through their paces in a series of improvisational games. A bearded Anne Hathaway has burst from a giant birthday cake.

Now, as the sun sets, I am watching an evening of Shakespeare-themed improvised comedy on the Globe stage. The show is called *Shall We Shog?*, and its Master of Ceremonies is the legendary theatrical maverick Ken Campbell. Three teams of actors representing London, Liverpool and Newcastle are competing in a series of mad performance tasks to accrue the highest number of apples and oranges, these items of fruit being awarded indiscriminately by Campbell after each exercise and skewered onto each team's wooden pole by the Elizabethan-costumed 'Goader', Josh Darcy. Some games are played by members of all three teams, others by only one. They include a trade-off of Shakespearean-style insults, judged by the audience; improvised songs and sonnets, based on audience suggestions; competitive quibbling; an extempore re-enactment of the 'famous' scene from Shakespeare's lost play *Cardenio*; three attempts to fit the word 'honorificabilitudinitatibus', the longest word in Shakespeare, into an improvised scene; and a series of games based on Patrick Tucker's eccentric *Secrets of Acting Shakespeare* (2002). The performers are wearing a vague approximation of Elizabethan dress, but regularly incorporate references to their surroundings and to modern popular culture – one sonnet is on the theme of Sony Playstations, another composed in praise of a blushing audience member. They know their stuff: Campbell won't tolerate any deviations from the strict metric and rhyme structure of an English sonnet. He introduces us to the tradition of the 'nub', a short piece of meaningless blank verse that can be used by a Shakespearean actor who has momentarily forgotten his lines, the name for which derives from the actor's use of the word 'nub' at both the beginning and the end of the diversion so as to alert his fellow actors to his departure from, and imminent return to, the script. Competitive improvised nubbing follows.

Standing at the side of the stage though most of this, leaning against its rim and watching the anarchic goings-on with a broad smile on his face, is a quiet, bearded figure. Many of the spectators will recognize him as Mark Rylance. He is about to embark upon his final season as the theatre's Artistic Director, but unlike most Artistic Directors, he is visually conspicuous – he has played main roles on this stage for each of the last nine seasons. A three-man production of *The Tempest*, in which he will play Prospero, goes into previews in two weeks. Tonight, he stands paradoxically as both a symbol of Shakespearean authority and an icon of puckish subversion. During the interval, he throws an apple at a tutu-wearing clown and gets dragged up onto the stage before being rugby-tackled to the floor. When the performance resumes, he comes on stage to deliver Hamlet's advice to the players as a kind of prologue to a set of games that Campbell has devised around this speech; upon his entrance, the entire company prostrate themselves before him in mock-deference. The audience laugh. He begins:

'Speak the speech, I pray you, as I pronounced it to you – trippingly on the tongue ...' (3.2.1–2). He speaks softly, his eyes darting around the auditorium; he is sharing an idea with us, clear and quick, extending that idea and playing with it, playing with *us*, every bit as interactively as the improvising comedians. The atmosphere is electric – this theatre, so full of noisy activity only moments earlier, is now filled with the hush of focused concentration. Midway through the speech, Rylance falters for a second. A laugh starts to build, and just in time, Rylance seizes the opportunity for a quick 'nub'. Somebody throws an apple at him. The laughter explodes like a crashing wave, and there are ripples of applause.

Over a decade later, I find that my memory of this moment – reconstructed with the aid of some handwritten notes I took at the time – encapsulates much of what I continue to find fascinating about the period of Rylance's Artistic Directorship at Shakespeare's Globe. It reminds me of the Globe's position at an intersection between high art and popular culture, and of the powerful effects of a transition from laughter to silence and back again. It makes me think about the conversation between actor and audience for which the theatre has become famous, about the almost imperceptible dividing line between success and failure, and about the thrill that the possibility of failure can bring. It reminds me of the symbolism of the building itself, half sacred and half profane; a house in which irreverence becomes almost a form of reverence, in which mockery and subversion claim a kind of Shakespearean authority; a building in which the past is invoked in quotation marks, and reconstruction moves in and out of pastiche. As I remember that night, I picture the playhouse as a crucible of spectators directing their attention and their laughter, from all angles, towards that central spot on the stage at which the actor can seem, for a moment, almost superhuman.

Mark Rylance at Shakespeare's Globe

Mark Rylance's Artistic Directorship of Shakespeare's Globe
Theatre was officially announced on 1 August 1995 and took
effect the following January. He remained in the position for a
decade, finally handing over to Dominic Dromgoole in 2005.
During that period, he oversaw the Globe's transformation
from a project that was initially widely dismissed as an eccentric
exercise in heritage tourism to one that profoundly changed
the modern British theatrical landscape. While the Globe
was generally understood, and indeed often presented itself,
as an investigation of the historical conditions under which
Shakespeare originally produced his plays – architecture, music,
clothing, cosmetics and so forth – Rylance's Globe pioneered
approaches to acting, directing and even spectatorship that did
not so much recreate the conditions of original performance
as blaze a trail for modern Shakespearean theatre, unsettling a
number of received ideas about what it is that we do when we
produce and watch Shakespeare on the modern stage.

It is for this reason that this book will not concern itself
primarily with the Globe's status as a historical reconstruction.
This aspect of the Globe's work has been covered extensively
in the two excellent academic studies that neatly bookended
the Rylance era. J. R. Mulryne and Margaret Shewring's
collection *Shakespeare's Globe Rebuilt* was published just
before the theatre's official Opening Season in 1997, and
detailed much of the archaeological and archival research that
had gone into the reconstruction. In 2008, Christie Carson
and Farah Karim-Cooper's *Shakespeare's Globe: A Theatrical
Experiment* surveyed the some of the discoveries of the first
decade of the Globe project shortly after Rylance's Artistic
Directorship came to an end, compiling a selection of essays
by both academics and Globe practitioners. Carson and
Karim-Cooper's book highlights the experimental nature of
the Globe enterprise, and this is the aspect under scrutiny in
the current volume.

In keeping with the ethos of the Globe project, this book will focus on the theatre's practices rather than its productions. The Globe did not provide any particularly groundbreaking 'readings' of Shakespeare's plays over its first decade, but to judge its success or failure by this measure would be to misunderstand the nature of its contribution to modern Shakespearean performance. Productions at the Globe were rarely fixed, and Rylance encouraged his creative teams to keep experimenting (and in some cases, go into re-rehearsals) well into a production's run.[1] Over the course of rehearsals for the thirty-eight in-house productions that took place during Rylance's Artistic Directorship, the Globe amassed over a thousand pages of actor interviews and Research Bulletins that detailed its wide-ranging investigations into the use of space, direct address, improvisation, verse speaking, voice, movement, characterization and other practices. Indeed, Carson and Karim-Cooper conclude their 2008 book with the observation that,

> despite the existence of a great deal of writing critical of the Globe, much of the practical work produced in this initial crucially important ten-year period has not been thoroughly or rigorously interrogated, although the Theatre has given unprecedented access to its own creative processes. (2008: 228)

The present volume is an attempt to redress this imbalance. Chapter 1 considers the numerous experiments staged at the theatre over its first four seasons, and the ways in which critics in academia and the press attempted to make sense of them. Chapter 2 examines the ways in which practice at the Globe challenged the role of the director and pioneered a more collaborative way of working, while Chapter 3 takes as its subject the actor/audience relationship for which the Globe has become famous, arguing that the theatre allowed its audience a radically active role in the creation of theatrical meaning. Academic writing has tended to focus on the politics of performance at the Globe, especially in relation to gender and national identities, and Chapter 4 will survey some of this writing in light of the arguments of Chapters 2 and 3. Chapter 5 is an interview with Rylance himself, while the Epilogue looks at the legacy of Rylance's era, drawing attention to some of the ways in which the Globe's work between 1995 and 2005 influenced modern Shakespearean theatre-making.

Despite its title, this book does not focus exclusively on Rylance himself. Rylance's style of leadership was to lead from within an ensemble of actors and craftspeople, and his influence on practice at the Globe lay more in his fostering of a radically collaborative artistic environment than it did in the imposition of any ideas or techniques unique to Rylance himself. In a period of modern theatre history when critics and theatre professionals alike tended to assume that the director was the primary figure in the creation of theatrical meaning, the appointment of a 35-year-old actor as Artistic Director of a project like the Globe was itself a provocative move. Rylance's Globe was the site of a gradual displacement of the director from this position of artistic and indeed ideological control, and as this book will show, this challenge, while gentle, had far-reaching implications. Rylance was not only the theatre's Artistic Director during its first decade but also its most prolific actor (he was the only actor to play all ten seasons), and though this book's analysis will range across the contributions of numerous actors to the Globe project, examples from Rylance's own performances will be discussed throughout. Rylance's artistic leadership, in fact, often resided in his own practice as an actor, a practice that he shared and developed in the rehearsal room with his fellow actors and one that often provided a model for them in performance. One of the keynotes of Globe actor interviews is the observation that they had learned about performance at the Globe by watching Rylance do it.

The background

The Globe project began many years before Rylance's appointment. Barry Day's book *This Wooden O* (1996) provides an entertaining if rather partisan overview of the decades leading up to the Globe's official opening, tracing the story from Sam Wanamaker's initial encounter with the Globe site in 1949 and his inception of the reconstruction project in 1969, through its financial and legal difficulties in the 1970s and 1980s, to the design and completion of the building in the 1990s. Day casts Wanamaker as the hero in a tale of a lone maverick realizing a lifelong dream in the face of seemingly insurmountable obstacles: an apathetic theatre community, critical sniping, a hostile local council, and persistent problems with fundraising events that ended up costing more money than they raised. Though Day defends Wanamaker against the charge frequently levelled at him during the early years of the Globe project – that it was heading towards becoming a kind of Disneyland for Shakespeare tourists, or, as a leader article in *The Times* put it, a 'Falstaffland theme park' (21 April 1993) – the book does show something of the theme park in Sam Wanamaker's early pitch for the Globe, which apparently included a 'mixed media entertainment building', a 'period restaurant', 'adventure playgrounds' and 'authentic reconstructed Tudor and Elizabethan buildings' (1996: 31–2).

The project had involved performances at the Globe site for more than two decades before the theatre's official opening, and these performances had started to set the agenda for what artistic practice at the finished playhouse might look like. In his essay on Wanamaker, Paul Prescott argues that the festival seasons staged in a tent on the Southwark site in the early 1970s 'represent the nearest thing we have to a repertoire and an artistic policy for Bankside as curated by Wanamaker himself, a demonstration of what he thought it worthwhile to accomplish' (2013: 188). The 1972 and 1973 seasons hosted performances of Shakespearean plays by the official Globe company alongside productions of non-Shakespearean drama from major regional theatres: as well as the Globe company's own *Hamlet* in 1972 and *Twelfth Night* and *Antony and Cleopatra* in 1973, productions included the Crucible Theatre Sheffield's production of Dekker's *The Shoemaker's Holiday* (1972), the Northcott Theatre Exeter's *Cornish Passion Play* (1972), the National Theatre's touring *'Tis Pity She's a Whore* (1972), a production of Marston's *The Malcontent* by the Nottingham Playhouse (1973), and a co-production with the Belgrade Theatre, Coventry, of Ionesco's *Macbett* (1973). Wanamaker was staking a claim for classical theatre as part of a popular tradition, framing these productions within a wider festival of discos, films, public art and street theatre in what was then, as Prescott reminds us, 'a run-down borough in the heart of London' (2013: 189). Anticipating the sort of critical discourse that would eventually greet the Globe company's performances in the finished playhouse, Michael Billington called *Macbett* a 'joyously funny, anarchic Shakespearean pantomime … pitched half way between Palladium panto and the Old Vic' (*Guardian*, 10 August 1973); the *Sunday Telegraph*'s Frank Marcus likewise noted the Globe company's 'improvisational, barnstorming style' in a review headlined 'Summer Panto' (19 July 1973; quoted in Prescott 2013: 190–1). It is striking that the Globe's own Shakespearean productions during these early 'Tent' seasons made no attempts towards historical 'authenticity': *Twelfth Night* was set in the 1920s, while both *Hamlet* and *Antony and Cleopatra* were modern-dress. The latter starred Vanessa Redgrave and Julian Glover, both of whom would go on to act at the Globe during the Rylance years; Day's account shows that the production was not without its own offstage dramas, and it was finally cancelled mid-run as rain threatened the structure of the tent in which it was being performed (1996: 69–75). The financial losses incurred meant that Wanamaker had to scale back the 1974 and 1975 seasons; for the rest of the 1970s there were no more performances on the site, and only occasional fundraising performances during the 1980s.

Rylance brought his own company, Phoebus Cart, to the Globe site in 1991, performing their touring open-air production of *The Tempest* in what was still at that time a building site. Though nobody knew it at the time, the production had been put together by many of the people who would become key figures in the theatre's first decade: Rylance directed, and played Prospero, while the music was by his wife Claire van Kampen, the design by Jenny Tiramani, and the choreography by Sue Lefton (it also featured as Caliban the actor John Ramm, who would return to the Globe for the 2001 and 2002 seasons). It is perhaps not too much of a stretch to claim that *The Tempest* was a foretaste of the aesthetics of the Rylance-era Globe. The actors were flexible and responsive, having to contend with the debris of a building site, unpredictable weather and noisy distractions. *The Tempest* was a promenade production, moving between four stages around the perimeter of the space, each of which represented a different one of the four elements: Rylance explained in an interview with the *Evening Standard* that the aim was 'to heighten the quality of liveness of the event' and 'to make it more something that happens around you and is more of an experience' (7 June 1991). The mystically-themed production was, by all accounts, strangely well-suited to the building site in which it found itself for its London run. The set looked to the *Evening Standard*'s Annalena McAfee as though it had been 'collected from the thrift shops and rubbish tips of Britain' (1 July 1991), while for Andrew St George in the *Financial Times*, the production worked against its setting: 'the vision of cloud capped towers and gorgeous palaces seems all the more poignant when raised from a waste of concrete' (21 June 1991). It was as a direct result of his dealings with Wanamaker on this production that Rylance was invited to join the Globe's Artistic Advisory Board.

Wanamaker set up the Artistic Advisory Board (later the Artistic Directorate) in 1990. It was composed largely of actors, writers and directors whom Wanamaker admired, and by the time of his death in 1993, it numbered around fifty. It seems that membership was granted relatively informally, at Wanamaker's invitation. Its chairman, Michael Birkett, told Barry Day that he could 'never be quite sure who Sam had invited to be a member of the Directorate': 'He'd see some production that had impressed him and then say to So-and-So – "Oh, you must be a member of our Artistic Directorate ..."' (1996: 268). A draft policy document from August 1993 indicates the importance of the Artistic Directorate in determining the Globe's future during the crucial years leading up to the building's completion:

> The Directorate will appoint [handwritten: or dismiss] the artistic leadership of the theatres. [...] The artistic leadership may be chosen from amongst the membership of the Directorate and will be answerable to it. (Shakespeare's Globe 1993a)

Following Wanamaker's death from cancer in December 1993, the matter of the theatre's artistic leadership became a pressing one, and the Board immediately set about looking for an Artistic Director. According to Rylance, the Artistic Directorate campaigned vociferously for their right to nominate somebody. The chairman of the Board, Sir Michael Perry, agreed to suspend his discussions with other potential candidates and listen to the advice of the Directorate, who elected Rylance; Rylance has attributed his nomination to the fact that he 'spoke very angrily at times about what was happening to the project after Sam died' (*Independent*, 27 April 2003). Rylance's appointment was subsequently ratified by the Board.

A young actor rather than an established director, Rylance was not a typical choice for a role of this sort. Born in the UK in 1960, he had grown up from the age of two in the US, moving back to England in 1978 to train as an actor at the Royal Academy of Dramatic Art (RADA). His early roles with the Royal Shakespeare Company (RSC) included Ariel in Ron Daniels's *The Tempest* (1982) and the title role in

John Caird and Trevor Nunn's 1983 production of *Peter Pan*.
Frustrated with the primacy of the director in modern British
theatre, he and six other actors formed the London Theatre
of Imagination in 1984, working on productions including
Othello (1985) and *Much Ado About Nothing* (1986) without
a director and using an ensemble-based system of casting; the
group was to become the 'parent company' of Phoebus Cart,
which Rylance founded with van Kampen in 1990 (Rylance
1997a: 169). In 1988, he played the title role in Ron Daniels's
RSC *Hamlet*, returning to the role on and off over the next
four years for both national and international tours. By the
time of his appointment at the Globe, he was firmly established as one of the most exciting actors of his generation,
having just won the 1994 Olivier Award for Best Actor for his
performance as Benedick in Matthew Warchus's *Much Ado
About Nothing*. News of his appointment was generally met
by the theatre community with a combination of surprise and
delight: Terry Hands, who had directed him as Romeo in 1989
at the RSC, called the choice 'brilliant', describing Rylance as
'a visionary' and noting that 'normally visionaries don't get
jobs like this' (*Independent*, 28 July 1995).

Rylance's honeymoon period did not last long. A few
weeks after his appointment was announced, Phoebus Cart's
production of *Macbeth*, for which Rylance was both the
director and principal actor, opened at the Greenwich Theatre.
It was an experimental production, recontextualizing the play
as the story of a power struggle within a modern religious
cult. While the critical reaction was mixed, several well-
known reviewers took a particularly brutal line, describing
the production variously as 'ridiculous and bizarre' (Nicholas
de Jongh, *Evening Standard*, 26 September 1995), 'prepos-
terous' and 'ill-conceived' (Benedict Nightingale, *Times*, 27
September 1995), and 'witless, shambolic and tedious' (John
Peter, *Sunday Times*, 1 October 1995). Underlying much of
this criticism was an anxiety, sometimes stated overtly, that
Rylance had proven himself a dangerously eccentric choice
for the Globe's artistic directorship; 'one begins to fear for

his future plans as the newly appointed Artistic Director of the rebuilt Elizabethan Globe Theatre', wrote Maureen Paton (*Daily Express*, 26 September 1995), while Charles Spencer opined that the Globe was 'already in trouble' and that if Rylance continued to offer work like this, 'we can look forward to a fiasco of monumental proportions' (*Daily Telegraph*, 27 September 1995). This critical savaging led the Greenwich Theatre's artistic director Matthew Francis to defend Rylance in a right-of-reply piece for the *Independent*:

> The Globe is in good hands. The unholy *schadenfreude* to which some of you gave vent in your reviews, predicting disaster for London's newest theatre, could not be more misplaced. Rylance is a director of outstanding vision, diligence, commitment and audacity. The Globe is lucky to have him. (3 October 1995)

The episode marked the beginning of a strained relationship between Rylance and many of the major press critics, which is explored further in Chapter 1.

The cultural context

The Globe's Workshop and Prologue Seasons of 1995 and 1996 took place during the dying years of John Major's Conservative government. By the time of the theatre's official opening in June 1997, Britain had just elected its first centre-left government in eighteen years, Tony Blair's New Labour having achieved a landslide victory in the previous month's general election. Later the same year, as a direct result of Labour's election, referendums were held on the establishment of a Welsh Assembly and a Scottish Parliament; the pro-devolution campaigns were victorious in both, paving the way for the formation of these new legislatures in 1999. The Northern Ireland Assembly was re-established following the Good Friday Agreement in 1998.

The British handover of Hong Kong to China in July 1997 was a defining moment in Britain's declining colonial power. The unexpected death of Diana, Princess of Wales in August 1997 was met with an unprecedented and heavily mediatized public outpouring of grief in which ideas about nation, citizenship and monarchy were both affirmed and tested. Following the Maastricht Treaty of 1992, the decade was also a period of ever-closer European integration – a project that was the subject of fierce debate both in Britain and elsewhere.

The Globe thus opened during one of the most rapid periods of change in British politics for a generation. Mark Leonard of the think-tank Demos saw this moment of 'flux' in British identity as an opportunity to 'rebrand' the country, capitalizing on a 'renewed national confidence in the arts, fashion, technology, architecture and design' (1997: 1). In a publication titled *Britain™: Renewing Our Identity*, Leonard suggested that the nation was perceived internationally 'as a backward-looking has-been, a theme park world of royal pageantry and rolling green hills', and argued for the need to 'project a coherent forward-looking image' of the country as opposed to 'presenting Britain as a nation of heritage' (1997: 1–2). Demos's ideas are thought to have influenced New Labour's decisions to associate itself with cultural figures such as pop musicians and fashion designers both before and after the 1997 election, and, in 1998, to set up a committee of politicians, business people and celebrities called 'Panel 2000' with the aim of promoting 'Cool Britannia' abroad. Under the previous Conservative government, the rationale for arts funding had often been stated in terms of tourism and heritage; the 1995–7 National Heritage Secretary Virginia Bottomley, for example, saw her role as being in part 'to encourage tourism and our great traditions' (*Observer*, 16 May 1996), and looked to fund 'institutions which affect tourism and our national pride' (*The Times*, 17 October 1995). One of the Blair government's first interventions in the nation's arts culture was to rebrand the Department for National Heritage as the Department for Culture, Media and Sport.

The Globe project could thus be considered somewhat out of step with the prevailing cultural mood, since on one level it was clearly a heritage-based exercise in reconstructing the past. Indeed, some of its earliest commentators criticized it on these grounds. Theatre reviewer David Roper was quoted by *Reuters News* in 1995 complaining that the Globe was 'a building of absolutely no practical use' and 'an experiment in reconstituting the past', aimed more at tourists than it was at Londoners (1 August 1995). The academic Terence Hawkes argued in 1992 that the project's backward-looking search for 'authenticity' masked a desire to 'forget about change and about the history and politics which produce it'; the reconstruction of the Globe, '[t]hat firmest of rocks on which the true unchanging English culture is founded', offered, he suggested, 'a peculiarly satisfying bulwark against change' (1992: 142).

But it would be a mistake to assume that the project was understood exclusively in such terms. The Shakespeare film boom of the 1990s had begun to associate Shakespeare with modern popular culture rather than exclusively with the past or with elite audiences. Kenneth Branagh's *Henry V* (1989) and especially *Much Ado About Nothing* (1993) had proved that there was a huge popular audience for Shakespeare, while Baz Luhrmann's *Romeo + Juliet* (1996) was an even bigger worldwide hit, using an urban setting, young cast, pop soundtrack and MTV-style editing to reposition Shakespeare as part of modern youth culture. The film's success spawned a sub-genre of Shakespearean high-school movies including *10 Things I Hate About You* (1999), *Never Been Kissed* (1999), *O* (2001), *Get Over It* (2001) and *She's The Man* (2006). In 1998, John Madden's *Shakespeare in Love* reconstructed two more Elizabethan playhouses, presenting both the Rose Theatre and the Curtain as sites of rough, rambunctious popular theatre. The film was a major international hit, and won seven awards, including Best Picture and Best Actress, at the following year's Academy Awards; naturally it also became a frequent reference-point in popular discourse about the new Shakespeare's Globe. As I have argued elsewhere, the 'popular Shakespeare' phenomenon tended to construct modern Shakespearean performance as both a return to an imagined 'authentic' popular Shakespeare of the past, and a subversion of 'high culture' Shakespeare today (Purcell 2009).

The Globe project should also be understood, despite its status as a historical reconstruction, as an example of modern theatre design. Thrust stages had been gaining in popularity since the 1950s, partly due to the impact of Tyrone Guthrie, whose Festival Theatre at Stratford, Ontario (1957) and Guthrie Theatre at Minneapolis (1963) influenced the designs of the Chichester Festival Theatre (1962), The Crucible in Sheffield (1971), the Olivier Theatre (1976) and the Quarry Theatre in Leeds (1990). Modern British theatre architecture had made particular use of galleried spaces: the Young Vic (1970), the Royal Exchange Manchester (1976), the Cottesloe (now the Dorfman, 1977), the Tricycle (1980), the Swan in Stratford-upon-Avon (1986), the Courtyard Theatre in Leeds (1990) and the Orange Tree (1991) are just a handful of notable examples of theatre buildings that stack their audiences around a large central playing space. Many of these spaces also seat their audiences on benches, fostering a more interactive relationship between playgoers than might be the case at a Victorian proscenium arch theatre; Nicolas Kent, director of the Tricycle from 1984 until 2012, apparently claimed that the absence of arms between seats at his theatre had led strangers 'to talk and in six cases to marry' (Mackintosh 1993: 24). Productions at some of these buildings, alongside those at theatres such as the Bouffes du Nord and the Cartoucherie in Paris, had experimented with putting their audiences in shared light with the actors. The Globe, then, was not just a reconstruction, but a manifestation of an increasingly collective, non-illusionistic tendency in contemporary theatre architecture.

The theatre was also part of a much more local trans-formation. For much of the reconstruction's history, Southwark had been one of London's most deprived boroughs, and the

Globe project was instrumental in bringing about a period of rapid change. Globe Education, which was founded in 1989, worked regularly with students and teachers from the local area and brought in visitors from much further afield, helping to pave the way for the subsequent development of the rest of the Globe project. The completed building brought a great deal of investment and tourism to the area, and other cultural attractions were developed on the neighbouring regions of the South Bank around the same time. The *Golden Hinde II*, a working replica of Sir Francis Drake's famous ship, found a semi-permanent home in St Mary Overie Dock in 1996. The same year, the refurbished Oxo Tower Wharf opened on the riverside, housing a range of arts, craft and design shops. The completion of both the Tate Modern art gallery and the Millennium Bridge in 2000 placed the Globe at the centre of London's newest cultural hub; the Tate's cavernous Turbine Hall would play host to numerous large interactive artworks in a gesture towards public engagement and popular art analogous to the Globe's. The Globe, built with a combination of public money and private and corporate sponsorship, both a tourist destination and a serious artistic and educational enterprise, was in many ways emblematic of the uneasy tensions of the emergent new Southwark.

It was possible, then, for all its trappings of heritage tourism, to see the Globe as part of the wave of cultural renovation that came with New Labour's election. Rylance himself argued as much in 2008:

To be a theatre our plays had to reflect the world outside. In the first season, *Henry V* (1997) was about a group of people earning a new land for themselves with words, encountering the fate they have inherited and risking everything, and *The Winter's Tale* was about the rebirth of something that had been lost. These ideas coincided with both the reopening of the Globe and New Labour returning to power. They were hopeful days. (Rylance et al. 2008: 195)

Rylance's nostalgia for those 'hopeful days' is tinged, perhaps, with a sense of regret. As the Blair era progressed, the British public grew increasingly disillusioned with a government widely perceived as being more interested in 'spin' than substantial political change. Following the September 11 attacks on New York and Washington in 2001, the Blair government's foreign policy became much more hawkish, involving the British military in the invasions of Afghanistan in 2001 and Iraq in 2003. Rylance was among the signatories of a letter to the *Guardian* objecting to the Iraq war on 8 March 2003, and later the same year, he told Paul Taylor that he felt Blair's course was 'murderous and terrible' (*Independent*, 27 April 2003). He titled the Globe's 2003 season the 'Season of Regime Change', and if its all-male productions of *Richard II* and *Edward II* and all-female productions of *The Taming of the Shrew* and *Richard III* seemed less overtly political than Nicholas Hytner's concurrent *Henry V* at the National Theatre, it was because Rylance's team understood the politics of performance rather differently than Hytner, and not because of any absence of political intent. Chapter 4 will explore this in more detail.

The Globe experiment

From the start, the Globe project was seen by its participants as an experiment. Its Chief Executive, Michael Holden, used the term 'laboratory' to describe the theatre in 1997 – a word, according to Robert McCrum, that was 'echoed by several people on the new Globe site' (*Observer*, 1 June 1997). Two of the books about practice at the Globe during the Rylance years feature the word 'experiment' in their titles: Carson and Karim-Cooper's *Shakespeare's Globe: A Theatrical Experiment* (2008) and David Crystal's *Pronouncing Shakespeare: The Globe Experiment* (2005). The same word crops up repeatedly in virtually all of the Globe's Research Bulletins. What kind of experiment, then, was it?

The Globe's earliest academic participants tended to see the project as an exercise in retrieving lost meanings. For Andrew Gurr, the chief academic advisor to the Globe project since 1981, the new Globe was 'no more than a test-tube, the basis for experiments aimed at getting a better idea of how Shakespeare expected his plays to be staged' (1997: 159). A recreation of the physical conditions of original performance, argued Gurr, would enable practitioners to test things like 'the locations of the entries in the Folio or quarto texts', and his early writings on the Globe tended to make assertions about original practice which were to be tested by modern performance (1997: 161). Pauline Kiernan, one of the Globe's two Leverhulme Research Fellows from 1995 to 1998, likewise saw the Globe project as 'an opportunity to recover something of the dynamic which existed in the theatrical space for which Shakespeare and his contemporaries wrote many of their plays' (1999: xi). The first three chapters of her book *Staging Shakespeare at the New Globe* are very invested in proving that the new Globe partially recovered the dynamics of the Shakespearean one, quoting Elizabethan and Jacobean sources at length and comparing them with modern actor testimony and experiences at the new playhouse. She concludes the book with the assertion that 'playing the Globe space is able to produce research findings about original staging', arguing that actors' 'experiential evidence' ought to be weighed alongside 'archaeological evidence and academic scholarship' (1999: 123).

This concept of the Globe experiment has been treated rather sceptically by others in the scholarly community. Paul Menzer, for example, is suspicious of the 'language of creeping empiricism' in the work by Gurr, Kiernan and their associates, with its focus on 'experiments', 'tests', 'trials', 'discoveries', 'test-tubes' and so forth (2006: 224–5). Douglas Lanier argues that the use of such terms 'is designed to push the scholarly, educational mission of the Globe to the fore while keeping a safe distance from the suspect notion of actually recreating the past' (2002: 162). In this, Lanier takes a similar line to W. B. Worthen, who is sceptical of the Globe's 'desire to see performance releasing original Shakespearean meanings', and describes the notion that 'the stage echoes, repeats, or restores meanings that originate in the text' as a 'misunderstanding' of the way in which theatrical meaning is produced (2003: 28–9).

But I wonder whether these critiques underestimate what I suspect is the more widespread use of terms like 'experiment' by Globe practitioners. When this word used in the context of *avant-garde* theatre, it makes no pretence towards objectivity, but is usually meant to signify work that is daring, provocative and exploratory – work that deliberately runs the risk of failure. It was this sense of the word, I think, that was invoked in Rylance's description of the Globe as 'the most experimental space in British theatre' (*Guardian*, 2 August 2000). Indeed, Kiernan was interested in recovering original performance conditions only so that they could 'invigorate live theatre today', and she notes at the start of her book that actors and directors over the first two seasons used terms such as 'strange', 'exciting', 'dangerous', 'new' and '*avant-garde*' to describe the space (1999: xi, 3). When the programme for 1998's *As You Like It* informed spectators that the steps leading from the stage to the yard were 'not a known original feature of the Globe but part of an experiment in the use of the space', the concept of 'experiment' being invoked was quite patently at odds with Gurr's desire for a recreation of original conditions (Shakespeare's Globe 1998a).[2] Rather, it suggests an experiment which is open-ended and speculative, and which finds its legitimation in the contingencies of performance here and now rather than in its recuperation of history. Chapter 3 will examine some of the ways in which the strangeness of the Globe space invited its actors and its audiences to explore new models of direct address and spectatorship.

From 'authenticity' to 'original practices'

It is perhaps this divergence between the academic basis for the project and the inclinations of its practitioners that explains a gradual shift in the way in which the people involved in performance at the Globe discussed its relationship with historical practices. Andrew Gurr's notes from the Globe's 1995 'Within This Wooden O' conference suggest that initially, academics and theatre practitioners were agreed that the theatre was to be 'a machine to test the current ideas about the original staging of the plays' (Gurr 1995). Conference attendees took votes on which aspects of 'authenticity' they wished to see re-enacted, from trying out original pronunciation ('exclusively in favour') to casting boys in female roles ('a perfect if unexpected deadlock').[3] The attendees were 'three-to-one against' the introduction of intervals, almost entirely in favour of 'authentic' costuming, and unanimous, apparently, in decreeing that staging and interpretive decisions should be sought from the text itself 'as opposed to other forms of directorial control and authority' (ibid.). As Rob Conkie has noted, however, the following years saw 'a gradual displacement and marginalization of academic agendas at the Globe' (2006: 187); Chapter 2 will examine some of the ways in which directing practice developed at the Globe in actuality.

It was evident from before his artistic directorship had even started that Rylance himself was uneasy about the concept of 'authenticity'. In an interview conducted just prior to the 1995 Workshop season, he told Barry Day that authenticity was 'a purpose but not the *prime* purpose' of the Globe project:

Authenticity is nothing unless it's authenticity that reveals better methods of doing things, that helps the plays function and work in new and unexpected ways … It would be sad if it became a purist house. I am all for people trying what they want on that stage, as long as they realise that this is a new kind of stage. (1996: 279)

Rylance's intention was evidently to use historical practices as the stimulus for the development of new work, rather than seeking 'authenticity' for its own sake. He distanced himself even further from the term in a talk at the Shakespeare Institute in 1996, saying that it was a 'big misconception that we are to be the authentic Globe' – the theatre was, he argued, 'an ongoing tool for experiment' (Rylance 1996). He stressed something similar to the cast of *Julius Caesar* in 1999, informing them on the first day of rehearsals that their work was to be 'experimental' in nature and that 'authenticity' was not a goal (Bessell 2000b: 11).

When Rylance did use the word 'authentic' in relation to the Globe's work, he made subtle attempts to redefine its meaning. His essay for *Shakespeare's Globe Rebuilt* in 1997, for example, suggested that he was more comfortable with concepts of authenticity as they related to imaginative engagement on the part of both actor and spectator:

As an actor it is not enough to know how a character speaks. To be authentic one must also know *why*. ... I am certain that the space he [Shakespeare] chose, especially one with a name like the Globe, will help to reveal much meaning through the authentic relationship between plays and audiences. (1997a: 175)

Here, for Rylance, 'authentic' theatrical meaning does not lie in the text or in some sort of retrievable historical practice; it is something contingent and fluid that emerges in the creative choices of the actors and their unfolding relationship with an audience. His notes for the 1997 *Festival of Firsts* programme develop this idea, asserting that '[t]he only place "authentic" Shakespeare exists is somewhere between each individual's heart and head, in the intuitive marriage of their thoughts and desires and actions' (Shakespeare's Globe 1997). By 2002, this had become Rylance's standard line on 'authenticity'. He assured spectators in his introduction to the 2002 production programmes that the company's 'imaginative play' was 'authentic only in its desire': 'Like Shakespeare and his fellows we have reconstructed an urban amphitheatre to resonate with words and stories for our time' (Shakespeare's Globe 2002).

In fact, the Globe had never been designed primarily as a site for 'authentic' productions, at least not by its founding artistic figures. In the 1970s, Wanamaker intended for the theatre to present one 'authentic' production per season alongside several 'modern' productions (Prescott 2013: 191). A draft Artistic Policy of 1988 calls for 'at least one play each season' to be 'be presented as authentically as possible', but also for 'plays by other writers and of other periods' (Carson and Karim-Cooper 2008: 236). In 1997, Rylance said that while one production per season would be as 'authentic' as possible, the other three would be 'left a free hand' (later, the terms 'authentic' and 'free hand' would be replaced with 'original practices' and 'modern practices' respectively; Miller-Schütz 1997). For much of his artistic directorship, Rylance stuck to this formula, or something like it: while the Prologue Season of 1996 featured only a modern-dress *Two Gentlemen of Verona* and two visiting productions, the seasons of 1997, 1998, 1999, 2000 and 2002 all featured either one or two 'authentic' or 'original practices' productions per year alongside two or three 'free hand' ones. The 2001 season was unique in that it programmed three experimental modern productions with no 'original practices' at all; Rob Conkie has called this the 'season of anti-authenticity' (2006: 185). Rylance swung back in the other direction towards the end of his tenure, staging seven 'original practices' productions alongside only one 'modern practices' one over the 2003 and 2004 seasons.[4] His final season in 2005 was more experimental, combining one 'original practices' production with five modern ones, including a devised piece and a new play.[5] It might thus surprise readers who associate Rylance's Globe with 'original practices' to learn that only fifteen of the thirty-eight different in-house Rylance-era productions – in other words, less than half – were directed according to the 'authentic' or 'original practices' brief.

It became clear very early on, in fact, that the distinction between 'authentic' and non-authentic productions was not really sustainable. *Henry V* was the Opening Season's designated 'authentic' production, and Kiernan explains that its supposedly 'authentic' practices included an all-male cast, cuts to the text to speed up performance time, five interval-free performances, doubling, research into historical clothing and music, authentic weapons, ticket prices set at rough equivalents of Elizabethan playhouse prices, and the use of the stage trap, Lords' rooms, music room and cannon (1999: 95–8). She also notes some '[d]eliberately non-authentic aspects of the production', including the use of the yard by the actors and the playing of African drums; she quotes director Richard Olivier explaining that the desire was to 'allow a kind of breath of modern air [to] hopefully come in and reinvigorate those authentic methods' (1999: 99, 142). Her Research Bulletin for the following season's *The Merchant of Venice* lists a similar set of 'authentic' elements, but notes that the creative team had chosen not to employ an all-male cast (1998b: 4–5). As Company Manager Marian Spon observed in 1999, the Globe tended 'to ignore aspects of original staging that don't suit us' (Bessell 2000d: 8). All productions inevitably used a mixture of modern practices and historical ones.

It was for this reason that around 1999, Rylance quietly dropped the term 'authentic' in favour of 'original practices', and by 2003, 'authentic' was almost taboo. Rylance argued that the word was 'confusing and arrogant', while his Associate Director Tim Carroll called it

a claim that is begging to be shot down. Anybody with an opinion or a bit of knowledge you lack or have chosen to ignore is able to stand up and say, 'You're charlatans.' We know it would be madness to claim what we do is authentic in detail. (*Pittsburgh Post-Gazette*, 2 November 2003)

But the transition from 'authenticity' to 'original practices' was not seamless. A piece in the 2002 *Twelfth Night* programme by Zoë Gray, a member of the theatre's Communications Department, opened with the claim that the production was 'the most authentic that the Globe Theatre Company has staged to date', and this was widely repeated in the production's reviews (Shakespeare's Globe 2002).[6] When *Twelfth Night* was revived the following year, Gray's essay was reprinted in the new programme with a modified opening sentence, in which the production was described instead as 'the most thorough-going attempt to recreate 16th-century theatre practices that the Globe Theatre Company had attempted' (Shakespeare's Globe 2003c). Globe audiences were by now being warned away from notions of 'authenticity', being informed by Carroll in the programme for 2003's *Richard II*, for example, that the word was 'not a claim that we could live up to' (Shakespeare's Globe 2003a). While Conkie wryly suggests that Rylance and Carroll's preferred term 'original practices' was merely a 'euphemised version' of 'authenticity', I think it marks a significant shift in the theatre's understanding of its use of historical practices (2006: 200). Rylance explained in a letter to the cast of *Twelfth Night* in 2001 that he preferred 'original practices' to 'authentic' because 'we choose which known "original practices" may be helpful to the modern relationship between actor and audience and reject those we think will constrict that relationship' (Rylance 2001b). Where 'authenticity' conjures up a nostalgic image of a lost and better past, 'original practices' recognizes that Globe practitioners hand-pick what is useful from historical performance in order to transform modern theatre practice. This book is an attempt to illustrate some of the ways in which this was done.

1

Experiment and Reaction: The 1995–1998 Seasons

Shakespeare's Globe opened slowly. There was a two-year gap between the first public performances in the building and its official opening, during which time the parameters of the Globe experiment started to be defined more clearly. It was a process of conflict, negotiation and compromise. With so many competing agendas within the organization itself, and widespread reservations and misunderstandings about the project beyond it, the years 1995 to 1998 were an important period in defining precisely what it was that the Globe was trying to achieve. While the work undertaken by the theatre during this period showed that performance at the new Globe was exciting and full of possibilities, a number of problems also emerged. Throughout the period, Globe practitioners were invited to reflect upon their discoveries, and those reflections help to chart the project's challenges to theatrical orthodoxies. Commentators in the press and in academia found themselves especially preoccupied with the issue of audience response at the theatre, and their writings serve both as a useful record of that response and as a means of exploring the theoretical and ideological questions it raised; they also hint at the Globe's implicit challenges to some of the assumptions on which traditional theatre criticism rests. This chapter will examine some of the ways in which the Globe's first four seasons, and the critical reactions to them, helped to set the agenda for the rest of Rylance's Artistic Directorship.

The Workshop Season, 1995

Rylance's Artistic Directorship was officially announced at a press conference at the Globe site on 1 August 1995. He told the assembled reporters that the theatre would be offering a fusion of high art and popular culture, and that he anticipated 'a sensual theatre' that would 'mix the high classical Greek and Roman form with the very common and grounded form of a bear-baiting pit or a courtyard or a bordello or a circus or a carnival' (*The Times*, 2 August 1995). He welcomed the prospects of both a casual audience ('If you come and just want to actually enjoy the sunshine or the rain, then you can come and relax, no problem') and a participatory one ('I would be very happy for people to throw things and shout things'), but stressed that he hoped the theatre would provide a space for a deeply communal, highly embodied form of spectatorship, appealing equally to 'your head and your heart and your body and your soul' (*The Times*, 2 August 1995; *Reuters News*, 1 August 1995). He also emphasized that the project was no mere exercise in Bardolatry or English heritage, pointing out that the new Globe company would be staging a number of non-Shakespearean plays and assembling an international ensemble of actors.

The five-week Workshop Season opened a few days later on 9 August. This season should not be considered part of Rylance's artistic directorship, which did not begin officially until the following January: in fact Rylance was unable to attend many of the workshops because he was busy rehearsing his forthcoming production of *Macbeth* with Phoebus Cart. Nonetheless, as the first season of performances in the new Globe, the Workshop Season played an important role in laying the foundations for Rylance's directorship. Each of the forty-five workshops was presented before an audience in the as-yet-unfinished Globe building. The main structure of the auditorium was complete but undecorated, while a temporary stage and *frons scenae* had been constructed from steel scaffolding and plywood. The idea was to use the workshops to finalize the design of the stage; as the Globe's Chief Executive Michael Holden explained in a Globe newsletter, each workshop was 'intended to explore a physical aspect of the Globe stage' (Holden 1995). The varied programme included workshops by several leading directors, including Richard Cottrell, Stephen Unwin, William Gaskill, Barbara Gaines, Sean Holmes, Yvonne Brewster, Ian Judge, Helena Kaut-Howson, Philip Hedley and Sir Peter Hall, and international contributions from the Izumi Kyogen School, Mansai Nomura, the Shakespeare Globe Centre Australia, the Bremer Shakespeare Company, and a number of American companies and practitioners. There were two 'audience participation' workshops, and sessions on Elizabethan fighting techniques, oratory, storytelling and verse. A workshop by Rylance, titled '360 degrees in character playing in Shakespeare', explored 'how the actor works with the audience all around and above him' (Shakespeare's Globe 1995). While some of the workshops were interactive, others were more like scratch performances, rehearsed readings or recitals; there were performances by major British actors including Richard Griffiths, Julian Glover, Judi Dench, Prunella Scales and James Bolam, and even a one-man show about the nineteenth-century American actor Edwin Booth. Kiernan reports that some of the practitioners involved used their workshops 'more as a rehearsal period for a current production' than as a specific exploration of the Globe space, though she notes that others 'embraced the theatre as a radical space of theatrical experimentation' (1999: 65).

Kiernan's Research Bulletin on the workshops records some disjunction between the performance work and demands of the space. Almost all her findings, she reports, 'turned out to be related to the kind of expectations the participants brought with them into the theatre' (1995: 2). Both practitioners and spectators tended to project the codes and conventions they had learned in proscenium-arch theatres onto this less familiar space: Kiernan observes that groundlings tended automatically to sit down on the floor in the yard, while gallery spectators would choose seats in the booths facing the stage rather than at the sides, and workshop presenters were often reluctant to move them from these positions. Kiernan notes problems with 'the modern actor's training and experience of blocking', including what she calls 'Twentieth-century Parallel Acting' – presumably the tendency for actors playing a scene together to face each other in a line parallel to that of the front of the stage (1995: 1, 3). Some workshops eschewed the stage altogether and worked entirely in the yard; several actors apparently reported that they were 'more comfortable in the pit', perhaps in part because of the emptiness of the auditorium (the Workshop Season performances never played to more than a third of the Globe's capacity; 1995: 4). Kiernan's report nonetheless strikes a positive note, casting the theatre as an excitingly experimental space with a 'radically new dynamic' that offered 'radical possibilities for shared experience on the part of the audience' (1995: 4–5).

According to Kiernan's report, the new theatre's teething problems were almost entirely because actors and directors had not yet learned how to use the space. This was not how some of the practitioners involved saw it. In his essay for *Shakespeare's Globe Rebuilt*, architect Jon Greenfield points out that while the Workshop Season's international participants had 'varied and mixed' reactions to the space, the British classical actors involved 'spoke with convincing consistency' on what they perceived as a number of problems: the stage was the wrong size and shape, its cover was too large, its pillars 'were too far forward and too close to the edge of the stage', and the two side entrances from the tiring house 'were too close together' (1997: 94). Sir Peter Hall, one of the Globe trustees, used the last workshop of the season to make a public attack on the 'frightfully wrong' design of the stage (*The*

Times, 13 September 1995). His objections focused especially on the positioning of pillars, lamenting their impediments to sightlines and blocking – the strips of the stage outside of the pillars were apparently too small and remote to be theatrically useful. Hall wrote to Sir Michael Perry, Chairman of the Globe trustees, complaining that 'I personally would find it very difficult to stage a Shakespeare play on the space ... and in no sense would I find it a liberation' (Day 1996: 296). Naturally this reaction alarmed the Globe's administration, who had no desire to alienate the very artists they hoped to attract to work at the finished theatre, and they set about trying to negotiate a compromise between the imperatives of historical accuracy and artistic pragmatism.

Press coverage of the Workshop Season set the tone for much of what would follow over the next few years. Benedict Nightingale wrote a piece for *The Times* in which he speculated as to the difficulty of 'a boy actor creating a rich, subtle Cleopatra' in a context like that of the original Globe, and quoted Casca's disparaging description of a theatre audience in *Julius Caesar* as evidence that 'Shakespeare was not over-fond of the groundlings who milled about the Globe's well'. Rylance, he argued, would 'have to mix a football crowd with the clientele of a Soho nightclub' if he wanted to approximate this rough-and-ready popular audience, and in the context of his article it is not clear that Nightingale thought it would be a good idea for him to try (10 August 1995). By its end, the Workshop Season had convinced Nightingale that the Globe, while it was 'one of our era's more eccentric projects', might foster a playing style in which 'soliloquy became less private and dialogue more of a three-way process', and 'teach players to reach out more boldly and audiences to use their imaginations more fully' (*The Times*, 13 September 1995).

Much of the press attention was focused on the dispute between practitioners and academics over the theatre's architecture. The headlines say it all: 'Theatre Wars' (*Guardian*, 13 September 1995); 'Argument rages round the Globe' (*The Times*, 13 September 1995); 'Dramatic conflict' (*Sunday*

Times, 1 October 1995). Michael Billington characterized it as 'a fierce debate ... between authenticity-seeking academics and pragmatic theatrical practitioners', quoting both Hall's objections and Andrew Gurr's riposte that Hall was rejecting 'the consensus of 120 international Shakespeare scholars' (*Guardian*, 13 September 1995). In John Peter's account of the 'polite but ferocious row', none of the actors and directors present at the end-of-season discussion endorsed the current stage design, and the practitioners responded with 'an indignant outcry' when they were informed by the academic participants that 'the timber for the stage was already being cut' (*Sunday Times*, 1 October 1995). Gurr was quoted in the *Guardian* suggesting that architectural compromises based on the whims of modern practitioners would threaten the legitimacy of the whole project. The point, he argued, was that the theatre 'should not be a Disneyfied tourist-attraction but should be as close as humanly possible to the original' (13 September 1995).

The debate raised some crucial questions that remained unsettled as Rylance embarked upon his inaugural year as Artistic Director. What sort of performance work was the Globe to undertake? Was it to be practical research into historic practices, a kind of experimental archaeology? Or was it rather an open-ended exploration into the possibilities of open-air amphitheatre performance for modern practice? If both, then how would the demands of these competing agendas be negotiated in the theatre's year-by-year programming and staging decisions? Tensions between the project's academic and artistic participants had been in evidence even before the Workshop season, when Rylance had predicted that '[i]f the academic world is going to come in without an open mind, high handedly – as I feel some are – it won't be a happy marriage' (Day 1996: 279). The controversy over the pillars led some academic commentators to complain that the practitioners were guilty, in Alan C. Dessen's phrase, of 'theatrical essentialism': the assumption that, regardless of any evidence to the contrary, 'performance choices in Shakespeare's time would be identical or, at the least, comparable to 1990s choices' (1998: 195–6). For Stephen Orgel, the historical evidence 'overwhelmingly' supported the scholars' case for the positioning of the pillars: 'it is the actors,' he concluded, 'who are not authentic' (1998: 191). As we have seen, though, some of the artists involved had different ideas about what constituted 'authenticity', seeing their primary responsibility as being to the felt experience of the modern audience rather than to strict historical accuracy. As Christie Carson and Farah Karim-Cooper observe, 'the difficulties inherent in the somewhat naively anticipated, collaborative dialogue between actors and academics' were beginning to emerge (2008: 4).

The Prologue Season, 1996

The Globe did not offer a full season in 1996. The theatre's official opening was deferred until 1997, allowing the new Globe company to continue to explore the space with a short run of *The Two Gentlemen of Verona* from 21 August until 15 September. The production was directed by Jack Shepherd, and featured Rylance as Proteus. The theatre also played host to two visiting productions, Northern Broadsides' touring *A Midsummer Night's Dream* and an all-female production of Richard Edwardes's *Damon and Pythias*, each of which was performed for one night only in September. It is interesting that – perhaps provocatively in light of the 1995 academic conference's votes in favour of 'authentic' costuming and an absence of modern intervals – all three of these productions had 'an anachronistic interval of fifteen minutes half-way through the performance' and made 'no attempt at reconstructing period costume' (Kiernan 1996a: 5, 7). Following the previous year's argument, the stage had been redesigned in order to move the pillars further back and closer together. Rylance's Globe thus opened with a fairly clear assertion that it was prioritizing modern theatrical experiment over historical reconstruction.

Figure 1 *Mark Rylance as Proteus in* The Two Gentlemen of
Verona *(1996). Photograph by John Tramper. Shakespeare's Globe:
Archive.*

This priority extended to the choice of play. *The Two
Gentlemen of Verona* (Figure 1), one of Shakespeare's earliest
plays, was certainly not written for the original Globe, and
is not especially well known today. Rylance told Day that
he had chosen this play for the Prologue Season because
audiences were unlikely to arrive with preconceptions of
it, but it contained 'many seeds of later work in character,
theme and stagecraft, including use of the balcony, a forest
and rapid changes of location' (1996: 314). The aim of the
season, he said, was 'to establish the relationship between the
actors and the audience, no more' (ibid.). In order to make
the play feel contemporary, the production was staged in
twentieth-century costume, and the stage filled with modern
furniture. A multiracial, international cast reflected the mixed
demographics of the audience (several American accents could
be heard onstage). Shepherd and Rylance chose to revive the
historical practice of a post-show jig by commissioning a skit

on 'sleaze' in the John Major government; this jig featured modern music by Claire van Kampen and masks by Trestle Theatre, and made no attempt 'to reconstruct any of the original music and movement of the Elizabethan jig' (Kiernan 1996a: 7). The production was finding modern equivalents for historic practices rather than recreating them – controversially for Gurr, who apparently wrote to Rylance objecting to his decision to stage the play in modern dress (Conkie 2006: 190).

The Prologue season was attended by over 40,000 people, approximately 94 per cent of capacity (Day 1996: 316). It thus allowed the Globe company to experiment with what had been conspicuously lacking in the previous season – a full audience – and it became clear that much of this audience was keen to participate. Both Kiernan and Charles Spencer recall a spectator yelling out 'You can't start yet, we haven't found our seats!' as one performance began (Kiernan 1999: 18; *Daily Telegraph*, 23 August 1996); the audience, says Kiernan, 'seemed to be performing along with the actors' (1999: 23). As Stephanie Roth's Julia and Rylance's Proteus parted in 2.2 and Julia suggested that they seal their exchange of rings 'with a holy kiss' (2.2.7), one of the groundlings shouted 'Go on, give her a kiss!', prompting an audience cheer (Kiernan 1999: 30–1). Later in the act, as Proteus's duplicity became apparent, spectators started to boo him. By the time Julia was articulating her misplaced faith in Proteus in 2.7, playgoers were making their growing scorn for him so audible that Roth had 'to ignore the playgoers' responses to her words' and 'go on creating the fiction' (ibid.: 32–3):

His words are bonds, his oaths are oracles,
His love sincere, his thoughts immaculate,
His tears pure messengers sent from his heart,
His heart as far from fraud as heaven from earth. (2.7.75–8)

This boisterous response worried Shepherd, who came backstage during the opening performance to tell the cast to 'calm it down' (Kiernan 1999: 24). Rylance told him not to worry, observing that this was just the start of a process in which the actors would learn how to 'shape' audience response at the theatre (Day 1996: 317). Kiernan likewise found herself concerned about the effect of the audience's raucous participation on the play's darker moments, especially Proteus's attempted rape of Sylvia at the play's climax, but discovered that this 'sudden turn from comfortably light-hearted comedy to potential disturbing menace' tended to hush the audience and heighten the dramatic effect (1999: 31).

The Globe's artistic team learned many lessons from the season. *The Two Gentlemen of Verona*'s naturalistic modern setting created some difficulties, not least in its inter-mittent exclusion of the audience and its bulky furniture, which frequently caused problems with sightlines and even audibility (Kiernan 1999: 85). In an end-of-season interview, designer Jenny Tiramani reflected that the tokenistic use of furniture had not really worked, and that the production had made her 'readdress modern traditions about staging' (Kiernan 1996a: 18). Composer Claire van Kampen described her key challenge as 'de-conditioning' the Globe audience from the 'usual mechanism' of opening a show by dimming house lights, raising lights on the stage and playing music – her attempt at an overture had failed, she said, because audiences simply did not listen to it, and she eventually intro-duced a gong to signal the start of the show (ibid.: 20). The main lesson for Rylance was that at the Globe, the narrative of the play was no longer 'in the control of the players but shared between the audience and the actors' (Day 1996: 317). In his interview with Day, he gave an example from the end of the play:

When Valentine asked Julia to forgive me and take me back, the audience shouted out – 'Don't do it, Julia!' And I'm thinking – 'My God, if she doesn't have me back, this is what it feels like to have a mob around you who might take justice into their own hands!' So my pleading as a character was greatly motivated! And she took me back as she never had before, in defiance of their merciless justice. In that way *the audience is shaping the narrative*. (Day 1996: 318)

The shout of 'Don't do it, Julia!', of course, did not come from the whole audience but from a single spectator. The importance of this moment in shaping the meaning of this particular performance is evidenced by the fact that the same heckle is referred to by both Kiernan and the *Jewish Chronicle*'s theatre critic David Nathan – but interestingly, Nathan heard it as 'Go to it, Julia!' (Kiernan 1999: 33; *Jewish Chronicle*, 30 August 1996). The fact that this mishearing creates almost the opposite dramatic effect testifies even further to the contingency of theatrical meaning at the Globe.

The press response to the season was mixed. Rylance had done little to ease his troubled relationship with the newspaper critics: they were apparently 'surprised and offended' to receive a letter just before the season opened asking them to purchase their own tickets, and an article in the *Independent* quoted the objections of several major critics, including David Nathan, Nicholas de Jongh of the *Evening Standard*, and Michael Coveney of the *Observer*. Coveney interpreted Rylance's decision as 'revenge on the critics who didn't like his production of *Macbeth*', though for his part, Rylance attributed it to the theatre's precarious finances (2 August 1996). The reviews themselves were not entirely unkind, but they certainly demonstrated many of the assumptions that Paul Prescott has since identified as having underpinned the press responses to Shakespeare's Globe throughout its first few years: that Shakespearean audiences ought to be silent and reverent, that Shakespeare himself 'had a low opinion of the groundlings', that foreign audience members were often 'disruptive and incompetent readers of drama', and that Shakespearean performance should be 'uncontaminated by contact with popular cultural forms such as television, pantomime, or football' (2005: 373). As Prescott implies, the Globe's performance work has tended to rest on precisely the opposite set of assumptions.

The *Independent*'s John Walsh stated overtly what was implicit in most of the reviews: 'such is the nature of the evening that you spend your time reviewing the audience' (29 August 1996). The reviewers of the *Sunday Times*, the *Observer* and the *Financial Times* all likened the Globe audience to that of a Proms concert, noting its good humour and its willingness to participate (*Sunday Times*, 25 August 1996; *Observer*, 25 August 1996; *Financial Times*, 26 August 1996). Descriptions of off-putting audience members abounded, with noisy rainwear coming in for particular criticism from the reviewers of the *Guardian* and the *Financial Times*. The international composition of the audience in the yard was a feature for Nightingale, who drew attention to the 'Italian with the long ponytail' and 'the Japanese in the grey business suit' standing near him (*The Times*, 24 August 1996). Numerous reviewers were unimpressed by the participatory audience. Billington warned of 'the creeping danger of audience self-consciousness', complaining that the hissing and booing undermined the subtleties of Rylance's performance (*Guardian*, 26 August 1996). Coveney worried about 'raucous participation at the expense of intelligent engagement' (*Observer*, 25 August 1996); both de Jongh and Charles Spencer felt that spectators were responding as though they were 'at a pantomime', though Spencer valued this for the 'direct contact' it allowed between stage and audience, and noted that 'in the darker passages, attention was rapt' (*Evening Standard*, 22 August 1996; *Daily Telegraph*, 23 August 1996). Numerous reviews approvingly described the 'rapport' between the audience and the actors, and Rylance especially was noted for his abilities in this respect. Several critics were unconvinced by the decision to do the play in modern dress, de Jongh in particular complaining that it 'outraged sense' and Sheridan Morley thinking it 'wilful lunacy', but John Gross felt it helped 'to preserve the rapport between actors and spectators' (*Evening Standard*, 22 August 1996; *Spectator*, 31 August 1996; *Sunday Telegraph*, 1 September 1996).

The reviews tended to conclude that for all its faults, the

season signalled exciting work ahead. They were remarkably consistent in identifying that the Globe was steering a course between two equally undesirable fates. For Billington, the Globe was to be 'more than a scholar's toy or a Disneyfied tourist-trap'; Neil Smith characterized these twin dangers as, respectively, 'a resurrected wooden fossil, or an Elizabethan theme-park'; Paul Taylor saw the season as 'a welcome signal that this is not to be a theme park or hive of stuffy antiquarianism'; Spencer likewise saw it as 'proof that the Globe won't be allowed to degenerate into a dull museum piece or, worse still, an Elizabethan theme park' (*Guardian*, 26 August 1996; *What's On*, 28 August 1996; *Independent*, 24 August 1996; *Daily Telegraph*, 23 August 1996). Each of these reviewers seemed deeply suspicious of the Globe project's academic origins, anxious that the theatre should not be devoted solely to scholarly historical reconstruction; but they were equally concerned, like Gurr, that the opposite course risked a descent into the kitsch phoniness of a theme park.

Academic reactions to the season were, on the whole, more sceptical. Predictably, Gurr himself felt that the modern design and costuming was contrary to the spirit of the project, and concluded that 'we've learnt more about what shouldn't be done than what should' (*Independent*, 24 September 1996). Stanley Wells, then director of the Shakespeare Institute and a Globe Board member, lamented Rylance's decision to open with *The Two Gentlemen of Verona*, 'the slightest of Shakespeare's plays' (*Independent*, 24 September 1996); in a review for *Speech and Drama*, Gabriel Egan agreed that the choice was 'odd' (1997: 21). In his essay for *Shakespeare Survey*, Robert Smallwood described the production as 'a terrible disappointment', objecting that 'there was nothing here to make one think again about this play' (1997: 201, 203); Egan likewise complained in *The Times Literary Supplement* that the production had shed 'no new light' on the play (6 September 1996). Academic commentators almost uniformly deplored, in Smallwood's words, 'the audience's puerile eagerness to hiss and boo' (1997: 201). Wells found it 'impossible to believe that [Shakespeare's] plays were ever received in such a way', and unflattering comparisons with pantomime recurred with some frequency: Victoria McKee felt the response was too close to 'that of a pantomime'; Smallwood that some of the acting 'came straight from the world of pantomime and elicited identical audience reactions'; and Egan, noting that 'Proteus is hissed and booed like a pantomime villain', found himself suspicious that the theatre's management had installed plants in the audience 'to catalyze a supposedly authentic Elizabethan reaction' (they had not) (*Independent*, 23 August 96; Smallwood 1997: 201; *Independent*, 24 September 1996; *Times Literary Supplement*, 6 September 1996). Writing in the *Hudson Review*, Richard Hornby gave the production a rather warmer response, finding it 'actually impressive' and praising the decision to do 'a minor Shakespeare play at the outset, rather than leaping into the raging seas of *King Lear* or *Hamlet*' (1997: 651).

The Opening Season, 1997

The high-profile Opening Season saw the development of many of these trends in both the Globe's work and the reception of that work. Perhaps because of the substantial political and cultural changes underway in the country in 1997, the Season also tied the Globe project much more explicitly to myth-making about British national identity. The choice of play for the first official performance was instrumental in this: the 'authentic', all-male, historically costumed *Henry V*, directed by Laurence Olivier's son Richard, opened on Saturday 14 June. The older Olivier's film of the play had been a definitive piece of national propaganda during the Second World War, and his son's production was well positioned to tread a similar path. As the leading article for *The Times* noted in a tongue-in-cheek piece of cod-Shakespearean doggerel anticipating the Globe's official opening,

... Gower and Fluellen,
Macmorris and Jamy represent the unity
Of Britain under Henry, or new Labour,
(Forgetting that daft plan for devolution). (21 May 1997)

On the evening of 12 June, two days before the inaugural performance of *Henry V*, Queen Elizabeth II and Prince Phillip (the Patron of the Shakespeare's Globe Trust) travelled along the Thames on the Royal Barge for the theatre's official opening. When they arrived at the theatre, they joined an audience that included a number of foreign dignitaries to watch *Triumphes and Mirth*, 'a specially created performance to celebrate the completion of the Globe Theatre' (Shakespeare's Globe 1997: 4). This performance, mostly comprising excerpts from the Opening Season's productions of *Henry V* and *The Winter's Tale*, opened with Sam Wanamaker's daughter Zoë speaking the *Henry V* prologue, featured Jane Lapotaire entering the theatre on horseback in costume as Elizabeth I, and concluded with a fireworks display over the Thames and a champagne reception. It was an evening deep in patriotic sentiment. Lapotaire's appearance must surely have borne connotations of Elizabeth I's mythical Tilbury address and its scorn for any presumptuous foreigners who 'should dare invade the borders of my realm', while the *Henry V* excerpts included the victory at Agincourt and the moment at which Henry concludes that 'God fought for us' (4.8.121).

Like the previous season's *The Two Gentlemen of Verona*, the full production of *Henry V* was met with loud and hearty audience participation. The play itself invited this from its opening moments: as the Chorus (played for the first speech by Rylance) asked the audience, 'Can this cockpit hold / The vasty fields of France?' (Prologue 11–12), spectators throughout the play's run would shout out, 'Yes!' When Rylance's Henry emerged onstage at the start of 3.1 to deliver 'Once more unto the breach, dear friends, once more' (3.1.1), audiences tended to applaud, in the words of Yu Jin Ko, 'as though the first bars of a signature aria had been sung' (1999:

115). At the end of the speech, spectators could be relied upon to cry 'God for Harry! England and Saint George!' (3.1.34). In keeping with the production's wider cultural framing, audience members took the opportunity to engage in jingoistic role-play: the French characters were routinely booed, and McCrum reports that at the show he saw, the defeated governor of Harfleur was heckled with 'Jump, you frog!' (*Observer*, 1 June 1997). At one performance, apparently, a 'middle-aged lady ... bombarded the French army with baguettes' (Miller-Schütz 1997). At some performances, there were even cheers at the announcement of the number of French dead (4.8.77–82), though Rylance did his best to subdue such responses by modifying his delivery of the lines (Kiernan 1999: 20).

Although *Henry V* was the Globe's first official performance, both it and David Freeman's *The Winter's Tale* had been in previews for some time before this, and in fact the Opening Season's first press night was a performance of *The Winter's Tale* on 5 June. One of the season's 'free hand' productions, *The Winter's Tale* was not tied to any notions of authenticity, and Chantal Miller-Schütz's Research Bulletin reveals that it was set in 'a fantasy world inspired by Third World cultures' (1998: 4). Tom Phillips's design filled the Globe stage with sand and tractor-tyres, and Freeman's rehearsal process used physical exercises and improvisations to create as full a sense as possible of the play's imaginary worlds. Unlike *Henry V*, Freeman's production was 'mainly conceived as remote from the audience' and – aside from Nicholas Le Prevost's Autolycus, who interacted with the groundlings – its actors were instructed 'to be remote from the world around them and completely engrossed in the two worlds created on stage' (Miller-Schütz 1998: 18, 10).

For all their differences, both of the Opening Season's Shakespeare plays were participating in a similar process of ritualistic myth making. In the season programme, Freeman characterized *The Winter's Tale* as a 'myth of birth, death and rebirth, a winter/summer rite of passage', and observed that the 'connections between the rebirth of Shakespeare's Globe and this great religious drama of rebirth are powerful' (Shakespeare's Globe 1997). In his piece for the same programme, Olivier noted *Henry V*'s 'remarkable parallels to the reopening of the Globe':

> One man has a vision of reclaiming something lost; he unites a disparate group of diverse interests into a 'band of brothers' who together cross old boundaries and mortal obstacles in quest of this long lost, fertile territory.

His production was, he wrote, a 'ritual re-enactment' of this myth, and he referred to the spectator as an 'observer-participant' in it (Shakespeare's Globe 1997). In the production's Research Bulletin, Freeman likewise described *The Winter's Tale* as 'a mystery, not meant to be explained but to be experienced' (Miller-Schütz 1998: 4). Doubtless under the encouragement of Rylance, who hoped the Globe would provide an 'electric mixture of the Mythic and the real' (Shakespeare's Globe 1997), these directors were constructing the theatre as an almost temple-like space for the collective experience of ancient myths, and the creation of new ones.

The Opening Season's repertory also included in-house productions of Middleton's *A Chaste Maid in Cheapside* and Beaumont and Fletcher's *The Maid's Tragedy*, and a one-week visit from Welcome Msomi's South African production of *Umabatha: The Zulu Macbeth* (discussed in Chapter 4). The non-Shakespearean plays were rather more subversive in tone than their Shakespearean counterparts. Malcolm McKay's 'punk-Elizabethan' production of *A Chaste Maid in Cheapside* partially rewrote the play to include anachronistic topical allusions and local references (Miller-Schütz 2000: 20). Its actors were encouraged to ad-lib, and Moll's escape during the play's climax was staged as a mad chase through the yard, up the front one of the galleries, and down a rope that extended from the roof of the stage to the floor. Lucy Bailey's production of *The Maid's Tragedy*, meanwhile, was the Globe's first attempt at a tragedy. Bailey saw the play as one in which 'there is a lot that [is] to be handed over to the audience, because it is so bold, because it is not a private play' (ibid.: 4). The theatre was still to stage a Shakespearean tragedy, and in performance, *The Maid's Tragedy* confirmed some of the worries that had been expressed about the performance of tragedy at the Globe: the climactic scene in which Evadne kills the King, for example, was met with loud laughter, a reaction that 'came as a complete surprise' to the actors and director (ibid.: 7).

Kiernan and Miller-Schütz conducted interviews with the practitioners involved in the season, and these revealed a number of emerging discoveries. There was a great deal of discussion over how to use the pillars, possibly because of the 1995 controversy. It was widely accepted that the Globe was, in the words of William Russell, 'very much an actor's space' (Kiernan 1998a: 27), and a challenge for any directors or designers who tried to 'control' it: Ben Walden felt that 'a very strict directorial vision of how a play should look will get broken up here' (ibid.: 42), while Jenny Tiramani observed that 'the Globe requires designers to reduce their ego' (Miller-Schütz 2000: 24). Actors tended to be highly defensive about the oft-repeated charge in reviews that the theatre was encouraging a pantomime-like style of acting, and usually spoke about audience involvement in more positive terms; references to the theatre's 'energy' recurred in many, perhaps most, of the interviews. There was a sense, though, of the dangers of an over-responsive audience, and actors were aware of their own responsibilities in maintaining some level of control. There was some disappointment amongst the cast of *The Maid's Tragedy*, for example, that they had not been able to prevent audience laughter during the play's death scenes.

As in the previous two years, the theatre held a review conference at the end of the season. Once again, the participants were alert to the problems thrown up over the season by over-enthusiastic audiences, and, given the tendency for xenophobic responses in *Henry V* and the laughter at the deaths in *The Maid's Tragedy*, concerns were raised about the kinds of reactions likely to be released 'when we present plays like *Othello* and *The Merchant of Venice*' (Miller-Schütz 1997). The conference also allowed for an articulation of some of the season's lessons in stagecraft: the importance of playing to the sides, using diagonals, avoiding the 'valley of death' between the pillars (a dynamically weak area of the stage, especially bad for sightlines), and standing as far away from one's scene partner as possible. Rylance asked the participants to 'try to define a set of principles (not laws) on how to use the Globe space', an exercise that resulted in the following list:

- Flexible blocking
- Improvisatory skills
- Telling a story
- Concentrating on the music of the verse
- Training audiences to perceive all the information presented in the first 50 lines of an unfamiliar play
- Different ways of warming up the house (Miller-Schütz 1997)

As Chapters 2 and 3 will show, most of these principles remained priorities for the Globe throughout Rylance's artistic directorship.

The coverage of the season in the national press continued along familiar lines. With a few exceptions, the consensus was that Rylance and his team had successfully avoided 'all heritage and theme park expectations' (*Daily Mail*, 13 June 1997). Rylance's performance as Henry was widely praised, many reviewers noting their surprise at the level of nuance he was able to achieve in this big, shared-light space. *The Winter's Tale* tended to suffer by comparison with *Henry V*, and its blocking was repeatedly criticized, though several critics found its final scene moving; it was generally noted to have offered 'little scope for the actors to play to the audience' (*Mail on Sunday*, 15 June 1997), Nicholas Le Prevost's Autolycus being the main exception. The Globe audience continued to dominate the reviews, with several critics once again finding themselves distracted by their fellow spectators, and again, some reviewers chose to characterize these spectators as distinctly tourist-like: Billington complained of 'the audible chat of the squatting backpackers' in the yard (*Guardian*, 7 June 1997), Taylor of 'a young Japanese woman who kept a camera trained on the production throughout as though it were some extended alternative to the Changing of the Guard' (*Independent*, 9 June 1997). This year, for the first time, the Globe's ushers were also frequently cited as distractions. The strength of the audience's engagement was remarked upon repeatedly: Nightingale was impressed by the way in which the characters of *The Winter's Tale* were 'talking to you, asking you questions, involving you in their fears' (*The Times*, 6 June 1997), while at *Henry V*, John Peter found himself struck by an 'almost palpable silence of hundreds of attentive people close together, such as I have not experienced before' (*Sunday Times*, 15 June 1997).

But the audience's involvement was not always considered such a positive factor. The comparison with pantomime recurred this year with some force: whereas in 1996, Alastair Macaulay had felt that the Globe audience were 'as attentive and responsive as the best prommers' at the Albert Hall (*Financial Times*, 26 August 1996), in 1997 he rejected the comparison, noting that they were being encouraged 'to behave as if these plays were Christmas pantomimes' (*Financial Times*, 10 June 1997). Patrick Marmion agreed that *Henry V* had been played 'as broad pantomime complete with booing and hissing' (*Evening Standard*, 9 June 1997), while the crowd-pleasing comedy and audience participation of *A Chaste Maid in Cheapside* was compared with that of a pantomime by the critics of the *Evening Standard* (27 August 1997), the *Guardian* (27 August 1997), the *Telegraph* (29 August 1997) and the *Financial Times* (30 August 1997). Several reviewers noted the audience's laughter during the tragic scenes of *The Maid's Tragedy*, some complaining that Bailey was 'almost too keen to play for laughs' (*Evening Standard*, 27 August 1997), while others recognized that the laughter seemed to be in spite of the actors' efforts to the contrary (*The Times*, 28 August 1997). Most critics commented on the booing of the French in *Henry V*: Nightingale remarked upon the audience's 'dislike of French swank and sympathy with English Euro-bashing' (*The Times*, 7 June 1997); Coveney was 'not sure that the loud booing of the French will delight any stray visitors from the European Commission' (*Daily Mail*, 13 June 1997); Marmion found the crowd's response to the killing of the French prisoners 'depressing' (*Evening Standard*, 9 June 1997), while Taylor wondered whether the production had done 'enough to put such atavistic jingoism into perspective', and speculated – just as the attendees at the Globe's end-of-season conference would – as to how such an audience might respond to *The Merchant of Venice* (*Independent*, 9 June 1997).

Academic critiques of the season were not dissimilar. Dessen argued in *Shakespeare Quarterly* that the theatre's 'boisterous crowd' was in danger of becoming 'a monster needing feeding, a monster that can elicit the worst from some actors' (1998: 196), while in *Shakespeare Survey*, Robert Smallwood complained of the 'loathsomeness' of spectators' 'mindless booing' of *Henry V*'s French characters (1999: 244). Those members of the academic community looking for insights into historical performance practices continued to be disappointed: the strong directorial concept of Freeman's 'free hand' *The Winter's Tale* meant that the production was 'of little value' to the theatre historian, wrote Dessen (1998: 196), while Orgel agreed that the production did not 'make any sense at all in such a house' and questioned the theatre's 'commitment to authenticity' (1998: 193). Scholars of modern Shakespearean performance, however, were more sympathetic to the Globe's work, and Yu Jin Ko and Cynthia Marshall read the audience role-play in *Henry V* as having been potentially more progressive in nature.[1] Michael Cordner's article on the season for *Shakespeare Survey* recognized that the theatre's work was 'a radical move into uncharted territory' (1998: 206), and reflected on its impact on theoretical concerns about the relationship between actor, character and audience.

The Season of Justice and Mercy, 1998

Programming for the 1998 season followed a similar pattern to that of the previous year. Richard Olivier and many of the team behind *Henry V* returned for an 'authentic' production of *The Merchant of Venice*, with Rylance as Bassanio, although whereas *Henry V* had been all-male, this production had a mixed-gender cast. The season's 'free hand' Shakespeare was Lucy Bailey's *As You Like It*, a production that also featured the return of several actors from the 1996 and 1997 seasons, and that made deliberately non-authentic use of the yard by staging a number of scenes in it. The Shakespearean plays were once again joined in the repertory by productions of two plays by Shakespeare's contemporaries. Middleton's *A Mad World, My Masters* was directed by the Globe's movement coach Sue Lefton, and featured a design scheme by Kandis Cook that anachronistically blended Elizabethan styles with fabrics and colours of the 1970s. Both parts of Dekker and Middleton's *The Honest Whore*, meanwhile, had been adapted and conflated by Rylance and Jack Shepherd, and transplanted into a naturalistic 1950s setting. The season was rounded off by four hour-long performances of John Blow's seventeenth-century opera *Venus and Adonis*, and a second one-week residency by a foreign production, in this case the Cuban company Teatro Buendia's *Otra Tempestad* (*Another Tempest*, discussed in Chapter 4).

Both the Globe and its reviewers had speculated as to the potential problems of a production of *The Merchant of Venice* at the theatre, and perhaps predictably, Olivier's production brought these anxieties about over-responsive audiences to a head. Kiernan's Research Bulletin shows that the creative team were keen to avoid encouraging a rowdy response to the production, but also that audience reactions had not been at the forefront of their minds during rehearsals, when the focus had been more 'on creating a completely circumscribed fictional world that will be as strong as the audience's reality' (Kiernan 1998b: 18). Audience responses to the German actor Norbert Kentrup's Shylock varied 'greatly from performance to performance', according to his 'Adopt an Actor' blog:

> Sometimes Norbert has to fight against an openly racist reaction to the character of Shylock – as they hiss at him and cheer when he is defeated in the trial scene. Audience reactions in this scene can be quite extreme – Shylock is either booed or cheered. Sometimes these extreme reactions lead to debate between audience members. (Kentrup 1998: 10 June)

Kentrup felt that the play's Christians had been made to 'appear as very attractive characters', a conclusion supported by actor Andrew French's assertion that he had tried to make Gratiano 'a very attractive character as this then makes his racism even more difficult to deal with' (Kentrup 1998: 10 June; French 1998: 29 April). French's assumption is debatable. The video of the production in the Globe's archive records repeated audience laughter at Gratiano's baiting of Shylock during the trial scene, and at Antonio's demand that Shylock 'become a Christian' (4.1.383), but of course not all spectators were laughing at these moments, and as we shall see, several were horrified by the laughter of their fellow audience members (Shakespeare's Globe 1998c).

The production was also notable for its clown. Rylance had invited the co-founder of Théâtre de Complicité Marcello Magni to join the company, both as an actor and as director of mask work. A *commedia*-trained performer, Magni was tasked with bringing a flavour of Venetian carnival to the production, interacting with the audience as a masked *commedia dell'arte* clown during the intervals and applying the same chaotic energy to the role of Launcelot Gobbo in the play itself (Figure 2). An extended pre-show devised by Magni set the tone for much of what would follow: a group of black-clad choral singers on the stage competed for the audience's attention with a band of anarchic *commedia* performers in Venetian carnival masks, who were singing and drumming amidst the groundlings in the yard. Later, in the often-cut scene between Launcelot and his blind father, Magni ad-libbed around the text, extending his character's trickery of the old man by mimicking a dog, a cat and a horse, and climbing a pillar. During the longest of the performance's four intervals, he stayed onstage or in the yard, flirting with audience members, dragging them up onto the stage, posing for photographs and stealing their personal items. The Globe's 1998 show reports are almost a catalogue of his anarchic tendencies, recording a variety of incidents that seem to have upset the

Figure 2   *Marcello Magni with an audience member during an interval in* The Merchant of Venice *(1998). Photograph by John Tramper. Shakespeare's Globe: Archive.*

stage management: breaking a folding chair, throwing apples, even emptying water bottles over patrons' heads. The report from 15 August describes 'a long interval, and a lively one for Mr Magni, who concluded proceedings by putting an ice cream on the head on an audience member' (a different hand assures the reader that the unfortunate playgoer was a friend of Magni's, though of course the rest of the audience were not to know this). The archive video shows the extent to which Magni's clowning activities warmed the audience up, making them more inclined to laugh and make vocal contributions as the play continued (Shakespeare's Globe 1998c); Kiernan suggests that 'the role of the clown and his relationship to the audience' was one aspect of 'original staging practices' on which the production helped to shed light (1998b: 16).

As in previous years, an end-of-season conference and a number of practitioner interviews gave those who had worked on the season the opportunity to reflect upon its problems and discoveries. Once again, practitioners consolidated their findings about the dynamics of the Globe space: the necessity of playing to the sides and avoiding the 'valley of death', the degree of motion required to keep the stage visually interesting, and the value of overlapping entrances and exits so that incoming characters 'push the ones from the previous scene off' (Miller-Schütz 2000: 4). The inadequacy of rehearsals in preparing actors for the Globe space was a recurring concern – blocking had often been completely rethought when productions moved from the rehearsal room to the theatre, and the absence of an audience during rehearsals meant that actors would often be surprised or side-tracked by spectator responses during the first few performances.[2] The conference involved a great deal of discussion of the booing and cheering at *The Merchant of Venice*; Kentrup had apparently tried in vain to get audience members sympathetic to Shylock 'to express their anger' at his treatment, while Rylance reported that his hope, like Olivier's, had been that the anti-Semites in the audience 'would be seen and shamed'. The academic and director Ros King argued that in both this production and the previous year's *Henry V*, 'the booing was directly caused by the staging', and Rylance conceded that Salerio's quiet hissing of Shylock as he entered the trial scene had probably encouraged spectators to boo, since when actor Neil D'Souza dropped it, 'the booing immediately stopped' (Kiernan 1998d).

Debate over the propriety of the audience's responses dominated the reviews in the national press. Billington accused the Globe of 'dumbing down', 'ironing out Shakespeare's ambiguities and turning the plays into simple contests between heroes and villains' (*Guardian*, 1 June 1998). Bailey's *As You Like It* was widely characterized as going 'full throttle for groundling-pleasing excess' (*Evening Standard*, 5 June 1998), reducing the play to 'a one-dimensional good-natured romp' (*Herald*, 9 June 1998) or 'the summer equivalent of Christmas pantomime' (*Financial Times*, 1 June 1998), though John Peter defended it as 'one of the best pieces of popular theatre I have seen in years' (*Sunday Times*, 7 June 1998). Magni was praised for his ability to make *Merchant*'s Launcelot Gobbo scenes genuinely funny, but a few critics objected to his populist style. Reviewers were broadly appreciative of Rylance's continuing efforts to stage rarely performed plays by Shakespeare's contemporaries, though despite the creative team's desire 'to create a hard, bad world with a dangerous edge to it' (Miller-Schütz 2000: 18), *A Mad World, My Masters* was generally agreed to have smothered 'any darker dimensions the play may have' (*Financial Times*, 18 August 1998) in favour of 'pure farce' (*Sunday Telegraph*, 30 August 1998); Nathan read it as an attempt to appeal to 'the Globe's unerring sense of destination, the tabloid end of the theatrical spectrum' (*Jewish Chronicle*, 21 August 1998). Critics tended to recognize that *The Honest Whore* was more serious in tone than any of the other productions in the Globe's 1998 repertory, but while some found this 'more dramatically satisfying' (*Daily Telegraph*, 17 August 1998), others simply thought it 'tedious and unpleasing' (*The Times*, 17 August 1998). Several reviewers claimed that the Globe was providing 'an uncanny sense of what it must have been like to be part of an Elizabethan audience' (*Observer*, 31 May 1998) and could allow spectators to 'feel in touch with Shakespeare as no other theatre can' (*Sunday Telegraph*, 7 June 1998), but for at least one critic, this was not a recommendation: Ian Herbert found himself suspecting that 'the Globe may well have caught the true atmosphere of Shakespeare's times' with its 'two-dimensional acting' and 'boorish crowd behaviour' (*Theatre Record*, 21 May–3 June 1998).

The Merchant of Venice was a focal point in this discussion. 'When you come away from a production of *The Merchant* in which Gratiano has been cheered and Shylock hissed,' complained Billington, 'something disturbing has occurred' (*Guardian*, 1 June 1998). Carole Woddis felt the production confirmed that Shakespeare's play 'still uncomfortably reinforces racial, Jewish stereotypes' (*Herald*, 9 June 1998); Nathan likewise suggested that the audience laughter at Shylock's forced conversion rather debunked the notion that 'the play could be used as a lesson in anti-racism' (*Jewish Chronicle*, 5 June 1998). Writing in the *New Statesman*, Anthony Robert Julius found his experience of the Globe audience 'unselfconsciously celebrating Shylock's defeat' both 'troubling' and 'indecent' (5 June 1998). For Dominic Cavendish, however, the audience role-playing was an important part of the production's 'ambivalent' effect: the audience had 'to wrestle with its conscience not to hiss at Norbert Kentrup's facelessly placid usurer', and found itself 'directly implicated' as, almost imperceptibly, the game turned sour and the play's events started to 'get really unpleasant' (*Independent*, 1 June 1998).

The climax to this debate was played out in the pages of *The Times* over the first two weeks of August. Prompted by an anecdote about Magni's misjudged interactions with a terrified foreign student during a performance of *The Merchant of Venice*, Benedict Nightingale penned a 'friendly warning' to Rylance under the title 'Send out the clowns at the Globe'. Audience participation, he argued, was threatening the quality of the work at the venue. The boos for

Shylock in 1998 and for *Henry V*'s French characters the previous season, and the cheers at the killing of the French prisoners, at Shylock's forced conversion to Christianity, and for the 'grossly anti-Semitic' Gratiano, were, he argued, leading to the plays becoming 'more coarsened than a big, tall theatre open to the sky makes inevitable'. He cited Magni's clowning, and a moment from *As You Like It* in which John McEnery's Jaques threw an apple into the yard, as examples of 'self-indulgent silliness' (3 August 1998). Just over a week later, following a discussion with Nightingale on Radio 4's *Today* programme, Rylance published a reply in *The Times* in order to 'clear up a few misconceptions'. He pointed out that Globe spectators were not invited to respond as anything other than themselves, and that he encouraged his fellow actors to 'play and sometimes talk directly *with* the audience, rather than *to* or *at* them'. He denied that audiences had ever cheered the killing of the French prisoners, and though he admitted that he too was 'concerned' about hissing and booing, he noted that such responses tended to occur when spectators wanted to make it known that 'they are displeased with a character's actions'. McEnery's apple-throwing, which occurred as he started his 'All the world's a stage' speech, was 'a simple gesture beautifully illustrating the illusionary nature of the division between actor and audience', while Magni's clowning – which Rylance noted Nightingale had not actually seen – was 'doing exactly what the text suggests, which is to play tricks on his near-blind father' (14 August 1998).

It is striking, and perhaps indicative of a shift in academic assumptions about what it was that the Globe was doing, that the major academic write-ups of the 1998 season were much more sympathetic to the production. In his essay for *Shakespeare Survey*, Richard Proudfoot observed that all four 1998 productions had 'exerted a grip on audiences', and that 'the self-conscious over-reaction from the yard, and even the galleries, which was a marked feature of the 1997 season was happily absent' (1999: 217). *The Merchant of*

Venice, he argued, 'did little to massage audience sympathies', allowing those sympathies 'to grow and change as the play progressed' (1999: 221). In her piece for *Shakespeare Quarterly*, Lois Potter argued that the production 'problematized' its audience's laughter (1999: 75). She read its anarchic pre-show as a battle between Carnival and Lent that anticipated the debate between Gratiano and Antonio in the play's first scene, and saw the comic set piece in which Magni's Launcelot physically and emotionally mistreated his father as 'the epitome of carnivalesque behaviour' in its gleeful cruelty (1999: 75). Her review of the play concluded with the observation that the politics of performance lie more in reception than they do in design:

> [P]erformance criticism is based on spectator response, not directorial intention. Some people apparently felt hurt and alienated by the production, to the point of not wanting to discuss it at all; their feelings are real. But so are the feelings of those who were stimulated by it, of whom I was one. (1999: 75)

In her reflections on the season as a whole, she made the point that it was possible for a Globe production to make opposite meanings in different parts of the auditorium. 'Because the cheapest tickets are the closest to the stage and the best seats the farthest from it,' she argued, 'you can choose whether to be the type who stands for anything or the type who sits in judgment' (1999: 81). Her conclusions are useful in highlighting the Globe's key challenge to the making of theatrical meaning: in a theatre that foregrounds the reactions of its audience, meaning is contingent, negotiable, unstable and fragmented.

Continuing experiments, 1999–2005

The Globe continued to experiment throughout the Rylance era, and many of those experiments will be considered in later chapters. In 1999, the Globe staged its first new play, Peter Oswald's *Augustine's Oak*, and Oswald wrote a further two plays for the space in 2002 and 2005; the Globe would become home to a wider range of new writing under Rylance's successor Dominic Dromgoole. The theatre's experiments with cross-gender casting continued with further all-male productions in 1999, 2002, 2003 and 2005, all-female companies in 2003 and 2004, and cross-gender casting in a handful of mixed-gender productions. A desire to explore 'original pronunciation' had been expressed at the 'Within This Wooden O' conference in 1995, was re-articulated at 1997's end-of-season conference, and was eventually realized with the help of David Crystal in 2004 and 2005.[3] Some experiments continued only intermittently: the 'Globe to Globe' programme of visiting international productions lasted only until 2001 (though it was revived under Dromgoole), and regular productions of plays by Shakespeare's contemporaries ceased after 1998 (the only exceptions being productions of Brome's *The Antipodes* in 2000, and of Marlowe's *Dido, Queen of Carthage* and *Edward II* in 2003).[4]

When the Globe opened, several reviewers noted its need for, in the words of Jane Edwardes, 'a committed company of actors, directors and designers who are able to learn from previous mistakes' (*Time Out*, 11 June 1997). The concern was shared by members of the company. In 1998, Norbert Kentrup stressed the importance of assembling a permanent ensemble of actors at the Globe: it would, he suggested, allow for 'an honest and frank discussion about the results of the work' as well as building a company style and supporting the development of actors' skills (1998b: 33–4).[5] Actor Robert Woods agreed, arguing that Globe audiences 'deserve better than to suffer the experimentations of new actors every year'

(1998b: 30). Though there was never a permanent company at the Globe, an unofficial ensemble started to emerge more clearly after 1999, with some actors returning for up to five consecutive seasons. Some of their discoveries will be detailed in the next two chapters.

By the end of the 1998 season, the Globe was still untested as a venue for Shakespearean tragedy. This was deliberate: its Chief Executive Michael Holden had told *The Observer* in 1997 that the plan was 'to proceed with caution towards performances of the great tragedies, feeling the way towards an understanding of the way the new Globe works' (1 June 1997). Reviewers had been questioning throughout the first few seasons whether or not tragedy would work at the space, and Nightingale's 1998 provocation in *The Times* suggested he had serious reservations. Rylance's decision to stage two major Shakespearean tragedies in 1999 – *Julius Caesar* and *Antony and Cleopatra* – thus had what incoming Head of Globe Research Jaq Bessell described as 'an element of gauntlet-tossing about it' (2000a: 19). As the next two chapters will show, both productions showed that the Globe was able to exploit its capacity for audience involvement without undermining the plays' more serious moments.

The first few years of Rylance's Artistic Directorship saw a shift in the theatre's relationship with academia. If theatre historians had understood the Globe project as a reconstruction in which historical staging conventions and forgotten meanings could be rediscovered, by 1998, Rylance's sometimes tendentious programming decisions had made it clear that he and his artistic team saw the experiment in different terms. These competing agendas led, in the early years of the project, to some uncomfortable clashes. Robert Shaughnessy recalls a 'wilfully confrontational' practitioner-led workshop at the 1996 end-of-season conference as 'an artful exercise in goading [the] academic audience-participants into making fools of themselves', and remembers its main lesson as being that 'the actor and the scholar could not be further apart' (2011: 422). At the 1998 conference, Director of Globe Education Patrick Spottiswoode characterized the meeting between academics and artists as 'a *confrontation* of theory and practice', and Rylance saw the relationship in similarly antagonistic terms: it was important, he argued, 'that academics like Andrew Gurr should hold their hard line and have the artistic teams throw rotten eggs at him' (Kiernan 1998d). Gurr remained heavily involved in the theatre throughout Rylance's artistic directorship, but no further end-of-season conferences were held, and much of the scholarly community began to keep its distance. On the one hand, the Globe's deliberately anachronistic and defiantly non-conceptual performance work alienated and frustrated those who were looking for 'authenticity' or for insights into the texts as literary artefacts. On the other, as we shall see in Chapter 4, politicized critics often found themselves suspicious of the Globe's position as part of the heritage industry. For both camps, the Globe's claims to 'authenticity' were dubious, and the charge that the theatre had rather too much of the theme park about it began to take hold. (It is striking that both of these objections to the project, different as they are, rest upon the arguably erroneous assumption that the Globe was striving for 'authenticity' in the first place.) Potter found that 'a surprising number' of academics at the International Shakespeare Conference in Stratford-upon-Avon in 1998 'were ready to claim, on the basis of one visit, or indeed none, that the whole enterprise was irretrievably flawed' (1999: 74), and throughout Rylance's Artistic Directorship, reviews in academic journals would frequently dismiss the Globe's work as lightweight and simplistic.

The Globe's productions, like those of any theatre, were sometimes problematic. But it may be the case that some of the resistance to the theatre's work amongst the academic community was down to a misunderstanding about what it was that Rylance and his team were trying to achieve. They were not seeking some kind of ersatz historical 'authenticity', though this did not become explicit until Rylance started to openly reject the word later in his Artistic Directorship. Neither were they making any deliberate attempt to coarsen the plays; rather, in giving so much artistic and narrative control over to their audiences, they were changing the way in which theatrical meanings were produced. Critics of *Henry V* seemed to blame the production for the audience's booing of the French characters, but Kiernan's Research Bulletin suggests that the actors were not aiming for this reaction; the creative team behind *The Merchant of Venice* were likewise anxious to avoid audience cheers at Shylock's forced conversion, but were held accountable for it in the press all the same. If Miller-Schütz's Research Bulletin is anything to go by, the casts of *The Maid's Tragedy* and *A Mad World, My Masters* evidently thought they had produced much darker pieces of work than their audiences eventually allowed them to become (Miller-Schütz 2000). The Globe's practitioners certainly made mistakes, both in the opening seasons and subsequently, often failing to anticipate problematic audience reactions or to complicate temptingly simplistic ones: Gabriel Egan complained that the Prologue Season's audience restricted itself to 'binary responses' – hissing or cheering – leaving it 'in no state to make fine distinctions' (1997: 22). But the Globe project was a reflexive, evolving experiment, and such mistakes were part of its process of discovery. The fact that this process of trial and error was undertaken in public and rigorously documented is part of what makes the theatre a unique and important object of study for the scholar of modern Shakespearean performance.

The Globe's radically open way of working raised some crucial questions. What was the role of the director in this new mode of classical performance in which the generation of meaning was contingent and not fully controllable? Reviewers keen to identify a director's *interpretation* of a play would often be frustrated by the Globe's work, dependent as it was on the audience's response and the actor's invention for its meanings, which could vary wildly from performance to performance and even from spectator to spectator. The oft-repeated desire on the part of several newspaper critics to see 'the foremost Shakespearian directors' work at the Globe (*Sunday Times*, 7 June 1998) was thus perhaps misguided, since 'director's theatre' was precisely what the Globe was not doing, and its work required not *auteurs* but directors who saw themselves as part of a team of artistic collaborators. The next chapter will consider the way in which the Globe's work rethought contemporary directing practice.

But if the first few seasons had shown that audience response was not entirely predictable, they had also proved that actors could exert considerable influence on the sorts of reactions spectators were likely to contribute. Actors and directors were beginning to discover the ways in which they could steer audience response while at the same time allowing space for that response to influence the performance. To what extent *should* actors attempt to control the audience? To what extent should the Globe's work allow audiences to find their own way into the debates and conflicts raised by a performance, even if their responses were troubling for the artists involved? Could audiences be trusted to learn alongside the actors, developing conventions of spectatorship that moved beyond binary responses and allowed for greater nuance? How might Globe performance facilitate and encourage this? The theatre's attempts to answer these questions will be explored in Chapter 3.

2

Masters of Play:
Directing at the Globe

Despite the wealth of documentation provided in the theatre's online archives, relatively little academic attention has been paid to the practice of directing at Shakespeare's Globe. This may be because of the extent to which performance at the Globe has foregrounded the roles of actor and audience in making meaning in the space, at the expense of the director; as Bridget Escolme has put it, Rylance's artistic directorship at the Globe challenged 'the very notion of a Shakespeare waiting to be released by one man or woman's creative vision' (2008: 407). It may also be because the Globe has made little attempt to replicate the rehearsal conditions of early modern English drama, a handful of experiments with 'cue scripts' notwithstanding. The notion of 'directing' is itself a modern one derived from the late nineteenth century, and so any study of the work of directors at the Globe is self-evidently an account of modern, rather than 'original', practices. In this chapter and the next, I want to argue that the Globe under Rylance's directorship pioneered a form of directing which was also beginning to emerge elsewhere in the theatre of the 1990s: unmistakeably modern in its appropriation of various forms of psychological realism, and yet simultaneously non-naturalistic and deeply responsive to the presence of the audience. Directing, I will argue, became a radically collaborative process under Rylance's leadership at the Globe, displacing directors from their role as the author of a production's concept and positioning them instead as the guide, or coach, of an ensemble.

Rylance was evidently dissatisfied with the dominant trends in modern directing before his artistic directorship had begun. In the 1980s, he had formed the London Theatre of Imagination, the 'parent company' of Phoebus' Cart, in order to 'explore working without a director' (Rylance 1997a: 169), and in an interview with Barry Day conducted just before the 1995 Workshop Season, he voiced his frustration with the way in which modern actors had become separated from the intellectual work of theatre-making: 'they go to work for a company on an idea that a particular director is going to teach them, which is quite different from working on a play' (1996: 273). He continued:

> Actors have abdicated responsibility for the planning stage that takes place before rehearsal. They must take more responsibility for the whole, working *with* not merely *for* the director. Unless they do so, unless they take on board that they're part of a live event and that you can't present the same thing time after time, they'll end up not talking to anyone but to an *image* of someone. (1996: 273)

Rylance's essay for *Shakespeare's Globe Rebuilt* in 1997 makes it clear that he saw the displacement of the director as a response to the Globe space, since the shared light and visible presence of the audience would make it 'very difficult to "present" a play there, to present a "solution" to a play'. Comparing the responsive 'playing' required at the Globe with the fixed 'presentation' of cinema and television, he concluded that '[t]o create a space like the Globe, where playing is all, will I hope benefit and refresh theatre performance generally' (1997a: 171). As this last sentence suggests, Rylance's desire to find a more collaborative role for the director was just as rooted in the context of late twentieth-century theatrical culture as it was in the architecture of the reconstructed playhouse. Until recently, he argued, directors had been 'expected to be fathers, teachers, therapists, patrons, gurus', but in the 1990s there had been a general 'swing in the conception of the director's role' towards allowing a greater 'freedom of communication between actors and audience' (1997a: 170). His essay does not refer to any companies by name, but his description is evocative of such ensembles as Shared Experience, Théâtre du Soleil and Complicite (then called Théâtre de Complicité).

By the end of the 1997 season, it had become clear that the Globe was challenging directors in many of the ways Rylance had hoped. The directors of the earliest productions had found themselves abandoning much of their blocking during the last week of rehearsals, when they moved from the rehearsal room to the stage; during the runs themselves, actors tended either to depart from set blocking, or to feel frustrated and constrained by the director's instructions. Kiernan notes that the experiences of the 1996 and 1997 companies showed that 'some processes which we normally associate with the term "rehearsals" continue well into the play's run' (1999: 29); indeed, the fact that Globe productions were evidently not 'finished' by Press Night may have contributed to the often-hostile press responses outlined in Chapter 1. In the 1997 company interviews, actor Michael Gould observed that Globe directors were 'going to have to trust actors far more than they do elsewhere', while his fellow company member Patrick Godfrey argued that the space was more receptive to 'story-telling' than it was to any 'directorial concept'; both actors remarked that this lesson had been better understood by Lucy Bailey (director of *The Maid's Tragedy*) than it had by David Freeman (*The Winter's Tale*) (Miller-Schütz 1998: 40, 42). Several attendees of the 1997 Opening Season review conference suggested that 'studio rehearsals should be devoted to character study, verse work and relationship between characters' and that directors should be 'freer' in their work with actors; it was apparently 'generally felt that blocking should not be too inflexible, that directors should be encouraged to loosen it' (Miller-Schütz 1997).

Rylance was aware from the 1997 Opening Season that there was 'a genuine risk of the Globe being perceived as anti-director' (Miller-Schütz 1997). Certainly he found it difficult to recruit well-known directors to the Globe throughout his tenure. In his interview with me, he listed some of the directors whom he had been unable to convince, among them Sam Mendes, Deborah Warner, Matthew Warchus, Simon McBurney, Robert Lepage and Janet Suzman. The problem, he said, was that directors tended to be put off by what they considered to be the 'constraining rigour' of Original Practices (OP):

> The difficulty for modern directors is that most of them have had big success because they wrangle lighting and sets very well, and they go into anonymous spaces, black boxes – or if they go into the West End, they usually mask up and don't leave the lights on in the auditorium. (Rylance 2016a)

Rylance told Lyn Gardner in 2000 that some of the directors he had approached seemed to 'be reluctant to surrender control over the audience'; Declan Donnellan and Deborah Warner, he suggested, may have turned him down because they 'have a puritan aesthetic, and the Globe is a busy aesthetic' (*Guardian*, 2 August 2000). Directors who worked repeatedly at the Globe during the Rylance era, however, seem to have been enthused by the challenges of working in the space: Tim Carroll wrote in 2008, for example, that 'for me the most exciting thing about the Globe has been the fact that I *could not* control everything' (Carroll 2008: 39). Barry Kyle noted in 2001 that though the director's role in other theatres is often to 'create a whole visual and conceptual life for the play', at the Globe, 'that layer is gone'; Kyle hoped that 'a brave, brazen honesty' would take the place of the technical elements he would usually rely upon, and precisely what he might have meant by this will be explored below (Bessell

2002d: 4). Actor Paul Chahidi argued in a 2008 interview that the Globe was 'definitely more an actor's theatre than a director's theatre' – a phrase repeated across countless Globe interviews – but he went on to note that this meant 'that the director's craft in that space is not acknowledged enough by critics' (Rylance et al. 2008: 205). This chapter is an attempt to redress this deficiency.

A total of nineteen directors worked on the in-house productions during Rylance's artistic directorship. Some of them, including Kathryn Hunter, Richard Olivier and Jack Shepherd, were members of the Globe's Artistic Directorate: four (Rylance, Shepherd, Hunter and Timothy Walker) were also actors at the theatre. Ten directed only one production each, though it should be noted that many of these one-off directors worked on other productions in other capacities: Sue Lefton (*A Mad World, My Masters*, 1998) as a movement coach and choreographer, Timothy Walker (*Edward II*, 2003) as an actor, Tamara Harvey (*Much Ado About Nothing*, 2004) as assistant director, and Rylance himself (*Julius Caesar*, 1999), of course, in numerous roles. Six directors (Olivier, Hunter, Kyle, Lucy Bailey, Mike Alfreds and John Dove) did two productions each, and two directed three (Jack Shepherd and Giles Block). With ten productions to his name during the Rylance era, Tim Carroll was by far the most prolific director of the period.

General trends

With such a wide range of directors and productions, it is impossible to generalize about directing at the Globe, and no two productions shared exactly the same process. It is possible, however, to pick out some recurring tendencies. Most productions followed a six-week rehearsal process, moving from the studio to the stage in the last week; following this, a relatively large number of preview performances was typical, presumably in order to allow the actors room to adapt to, and anticipate, likely audience responses. As is common in late twentieth- and early twenty-first-century Shakespearean rehearsals, many rehearsals at the Globe appear to have concentrated on character analysis – though as we shall see, some directors, notably Tim Carroll, had rather different priorities.

There was no standard procedure regarding blocking at the Globe, but a higher than usual proportion of productions allowed actors to move freely without reference to a set pattern of blocking. Early productions seem to have fixed blocking during rehearsals only to realize the necessity of changing it as the production took to the stage. In 1997, the cast of *Henry V* were evidently given a certain amount of freedom: actor David Fielder noted that blocking for the production ended up not so much as a fixed pattern of movements as a set of *strategies*, 'a question of hot spots and cool spots' (Kiernan 1999: 135). Members of *The Winter's Tale*'s company, on the other hand, reported feeling uncomfortable with the inflexibility of that production's direction: Joy Richardson, for example, reported that she had 'never been happy' with the blocking of her first scene as Paulina since its upstage left positioning made her 'feel more cut off than I want to be', but 'had to remain there because of the way entrances and exits work' (Miller-Schütz 1998: 34). (Indeed, some reviews criticized the staging of this scene.) The Research Bulletin for *As You Like It* (1998) shows that while its director Lucy Bailey paid detailed attention to blocking in some scenes – Bailey felt that 5.1, for example, 'needed to be choreographed very carefully' – other scenes allowed actors 'a great deal of freedom' and were 'not blocked except for some key moments' (Miller-Schütz 1999a: 28, 24, 22). In directing the latter, Bailey appears to have concentrated on guidelines for movement rather than specific choreography. Rehearsing 3.2, for example,

> [t]he actors were simply asked to keep it in movement, running after each other across the entire stage and around

the pillars in a mood of total playfulness and physical closeness ... The scene remained mostly improvisatory during the whole run, the main instruction to the actors being to always use the depth of the stage and avoid ending up on the pillar-to-pillar line. (Miller-Schütz 1999a: 22)

Members of the same season's *Merchant of Venice* company evidently felt they might have been better equipped for such freedom had they been allowed more time to rehearse on the stage itself: Sonia Ritter argued that 'three weeks are needed at the beginning of the preparation period to be wholly *au fait* with the space', while Norbert Kentrup found the lack of rehearsal time on the stage itself 'absolutely absurd' (Kiernan 1998b: 24, 31). Similar worries surface in actor interviews throughout the Rylance era; it seems likely that logistical considerations made it impossible for companies to have much more than a week of rehearsals on the stage, though in later seasons, actors were given movement and voice classes on the Globe stage much earlier in their rehearsal processes. As time went on, directors – especially Tim Carroll and Mike Alfreds – seem to have become more comfortable in trusting that their actors understood the space well enough to be able to determine their own movements around it. Carroll's later productions for the Globe tended to be entirely un-blocked, aside from entrances, exits, fights, crowd scenes and dances.

A recurring feature in the fifteen 'Original Practices' productions of the Rylance era is the involvement in an advisory capacity of members of the Tudor Group, an 'historical interpretation society' who research, reconstruct and re-enact elements of everyday life in Tudor England. Members of the Group were involved in the rehearsal processes of most OP productions, usually for a single session: they would provide guidance on Elizabethan etiquette and customs, and although their input varied from production to production, they seem to have focused largely on social hierarchies, bowing, and handling swords and hats.[1] Actors vary in their opinions of the usefulness of such sessions. Some describe the ways in which the Group's input directly influenced their playing of particular scenes,[2] while others express reservations: Liam Brennan felt that the *Twelfth Night* session 'was helpful to a certain extent' but that the production 'would have been in danger of becoming a bit gimmicky if we had spent more than an afternoon with them' (Ryan 2002b: 15), while Rachel Sanders noted that 'at the end of the day the audience haven't come to see people take swords out of sheaths – they've come to see a story acted well' (2004: 18 April). It is for its story-telling utility that the Tudor Group's knowledge seems to have been most prized; 'I just want to create a realistic person,' Brennan argued in 2003, 'and then all of the other original practices information will just feed itself in' (2003: 11 April). Tim Carroll points out in the *Twelfth Night* programme that '[s]ince I was trying to create a believable set of Elizabethans, accurate research was a simple necessity' (Shakespeare's Globe 2002), and he appears to have followed up the Tudor Group sessions with his own explorations of rank and status in rehearsals for both *Twelfth Night* (Ryan 2002a: 9–10) and *Romeo and Juliet* (Kirimi 2004: 9 April).

The desire to create a set of realistic characters in a believable fictional world underlies another of the Rylance-era Globe's recurring rehearsal techniques: the immersive residency. Just as the Tudor Group decamps en masse to a secluded location in order to live as fully as possible in an imaginatively recreated historical world, so did several Globe companies. The casts of Richard Olivier's productions of *Henry V* (1997) and *The Merchant of Venice* (1998) each spent several days in a disused military camp in Dorset, improvising scenes about 'death and survival' for the former and creating 'Portia's Belmont, Antonio's Venice, and Shylock's Ghetto' for the latter, improvising their way through the events of each play (Kiernan 1999: 99; Kiernan 1998b: 10). The aim, according to Olivier, was to give the actors 'a physical memory of the whole structure of the play' (Kiernan 1998b: 10). Lucy Bailey's cast for *As You Like It* (1998) undertook a similar two-day residency at Otley Hall, a large Tudor house in rural Suffolk, improvising the play's events in both the house and the surrounding countryside 'in order to experience the reality of the forest of Arden' (Miller-Schütz 1999a: 11). The companies of *Julius Caesar* and *Hamlet* returned to Otley Hall in 1999 and 2000 respectively, once again improvising the events of each narrative in real time in order 'to try to "live through" the play as fully as possible, giving everyone powerful memories of the play's events to feed upon for performances' (Bessell 2001b: 10). In both cases, the companies were required to live communally and to stay in character for long stretches of time, improvising some scenes at night. Bessell's bulletins for both productions note numerous occasions when actors found their Otley Hall improvisations helpful during subsequent rehearsals in filling out the detail of the imaginary world: the *Julius Caesar* actors, for example, were able to share memories of events which are narrated but not seen in the play, such as Casca's description of the rabble's behaviour at the end of 1.2, or the executions reported in 4.1, while the *Hamlet* cast used the memories of their nocturnal improvisations in order to more convincingly play the 'darkness' of the first scene (Bessell 2000b: 15, 25; Bessell 2001b: 12). The cast of 2000's *The Tempest* also visited Otley Hall, though their activities there are not documented in the production's Research Bulletin; in 2003, the *Richard II* company spent several days at Gaunt's House in Dorset (a house built on the same plot of land as John of Gaunt's fourteenth-century home). Once again, the residency involved 'a huge group improvisation' of the play's back story, 'from Richard's coronation to the death of the Duke of Gloucester', though this time the events of several years were condensed into a few hours (Shorey 2003: 11 April). In interviews, Globe actors almost always speak about these residencies with great enthusiasm, emphasizing not only the usefulness of shared physical memories in creating an imaginative world when they returned to the rehearsal room, but also their role in creating a sense of fellow-feeling amongst the company.

Even when companies stayed in the rehearsal room, improvisation seems to have been a key tool. Jack Shepherd encouraged the casts of *The Two Gentlemen of Verona* and *The Honest Whore* to improvise scenes in order to establish character relationships (Kiernan 1996: 10–11; 1998d), while Giles Block used improvisations during *Antony and Cleopatra* rehearsals in order to help his actors generate 'an imagined picture of the lives of the characters prior to the events of the play' (Bessell 2000a: 4). Similar processes are recounted in actor interviews for *Twelfth Night* (Dyer 2002: 15 April), *Richard III* (Harris 2003: 5 May, Ogbomo 2003: 5 May) and *Romeo and Juliet* (Burke 2004: 23 April, Kirimi 2004: 23 April), among others. This Method-like insistence on lived memory as raw material for Shakespearean performance may give scholars pause; indeed, at the 1998 season review conference, Ros King questioned the Globe's reliance upon improvisation (and presumably its attendant modes of psychological realism).[3] When some of the actors present responded that 'such work is meaningful because the emotions in Shakespeare's plays still ring true', I suspect King's scepticism might not have been allayed: the assertion elides both historical difference (how can a modern actor, with modern habits and impulses, improvise accurately as a sixteenth-century person?) and Shakespearean form (these are poetic dramas, often in verse, not naturalistic plays). The actors' next assertion, though, points towards one of the key reasons why I suspect the Globe has found improvisation so useful: 'because actors need to know in their guts the reasons why they say the words they say' (Kiernan 1998d). Bessell explains in her *Julius Caesar* bulletin that for Rylance, 'improvisation is simply a hunt for the need to speak, or act'; as Rylance himself puts it,

> [w]hat we must continue to hunt for is the *need to speak*. We come into the scenes with a *need*, and afterwards we *refine* that into the words we speak. (Bessell 2000b: 4, 5)

Though this understanding of acting is grounded in many ideas that are arguably anachronistic to Shakespeare's theatre, it was central to practice at the Rylance-era Globe, in which the principles of Stanislavskian realism were adapted to the performance of non-naturalistic drama.

Stanislavskian Shakespeare

'What is interesting about Shakespeare's Globe,' wrote *The Financial Times*'s Alastair Macaulay in 2003,

> is that its productions have scrubbed off all the Romantic barnacles from Shakespeare. Whether in period or modern dress there is seldom any Stanislavskian attention to detail of characterisation. (16 May 2003)

Indeed, from an outside perspective, the Globe's Shakespeare performances seem some of the *least* Stanislavskian in modern theatre. Actors and spectators alike cannot fail to be aware of the presence of the audience, and the best performances at the Globe have tended to use that presence almost constantly – whereas for Stanislavski, 'an actor must have a point of attention, and this point of attention must not be in the auditorium' (1989: 75). Nonetheless, several interviews with Globe actors reveal a broadly Stanislavskian approach. Many seem to have begun their preparations for a role by making a series of lists, in Mariah Gale's words, of 'what my character says about other characters, what other characters say about me, [and] what I say about myself' (2004: 18 April). Bessell calls this a 'context-gathering exercise common to many post-Stanislavski approaches to characterisation' (2012: 94), and indeed some actors may have utilized it not because they were asked to do so by Globe directors (though Mark Rylance and Mike Alfreds certainly encouraged its use) but because it is widely taught in modern actor training. Juliet Rylance, for example, traced the exercise to her training at RADA, noting that she used it in preparation for 2005's *The Winter's Tale*:

I did quite a lot of Stanislavski work on Perdita, using all the clues in the text to build up a picture of the world she grew up in, what her childhood might have been like, what sort of relationships she has with other people. (2005: 6 May)

Following Stanislavski, actors frequently use information and conjecture of this sort in order to determine a 'super objective' and 'main line of action' for their characters (Bessell 2002b: 6). Such analysis during the *Cymbeline* rehearsals resulted, for example, in actor Fergus O'Donnell deciding that Pisanio's super objective was 'to serve loyally' and main line of action 'to look after Imogen for Posthumus' sake', while Guiderius's super objective was 'to fulfil what he sees as his potential' and main line of action 'to look after Fidele and to fight Cloten' (2002b: 7, 8). Different actors, of course, would arrive at different conclusions.

It might be objected that such analysis is not fully applicable to Shakespeare. Tom Cornford, who assistant-directed at the Globe in 2004 before embarking on his academic career, has summarized 'the pitfalls of grafting a predominantly Freudian conception of the human subject onto an early modern play-text':

Rather than presenting a plausible psychological through-line, Shakespeare's plays often unfold through a series of discontinuities, with characters playing different roles in different scenes. In order to portray that, actors must be capable of treating characters as a series of images to be embodied, rather than a single psychological narrative. (2012: 487)

It may be worth remarking here that actors can pick and choose from Stanislavski's techniques without investing fully in the notion of character as a self-contained psychological subject. Indeed, actor Michael Gould, arguing in 2001 that 'on certain levels Stanislavski and Shakespeare are entirely compatible', observed that Shakespeare's texts 'are really clear in terms of external action, for instance – how you seek to affect another character – but perhaps less so on the introspective side' (Bessell 2002d: 21). What is striking in Globe practitioners' uses of Stanislavskian techniques is the frequency with which the former comes up.

It is almost a truism in Globe actor interviews that, in the words of Penny Layden, 'playing the truth of your intentions within the bigger picture of the story is the most important thing' (Bessell 2001c: 40). While some actors articulate their focus on character objectives as a personal choice, others indicate the importance of the director in determining them. 'What we're actually doing in rehearsal,' said Mariah Gale of Tamara Harvey's *Much Ado About Nothing* in 2004,

> is pairing the huge range of possibilities down to a core that consists of what is going on. Actually, the core is pretty simple: what does your character want? What do they do to get it? (2004: 18 April)

According to Ann Ogbomo, such analysis facilitates the kind of free blocking described above. Establishing her character's objectives, she says,

> doesn't mean that the way I play scenes will stay the same every time we do them, but I have to make sure that my character's intentions, the platform [from] which I can start to experiment with my scenes, is secure. (2003: 19 May)

Globe actors and directors regularly employed the technique known as 'actioning' in order to facilitate this kind of specificity. Penelope Beaumont describes learning the technique from a fellow actor in 2005:

> You take each thought and give it an action – what you want the thought to do to the person you're talking to. So you might want the thought in one line 'to reassure' or

'to soothe' or 'to comfort'. That helps to clarify why your character is speaking. (2005: 12 May)

Numerous actors appear to have found the exercise helpful in unlocking the dramatic potential of otherwise neutral or opaque lines. Amanda Harris, for example, noted that Buckingham's terms of address for his fellow characters in *Richard III* might change depending on whether he was 'trying to flatter them, to insult them, [or] to threaten them' (2003: 15 May), while Melanie Jessop found it useful to action even her silences as Lady Capulet: 'I always try to answer the question: "Why am I not speaking?" ... We are in trouble if we mistake silence for passivity' (2004: 16 April). When Tim Carroll asked the *Romeo and Juliet* cast to try an exercise in which they pointed at whichever character (on or offstage) they were currently trying to affect with their lines, Bette Bourne – the actor playing the Nurse – found it 'very strenuous', but helpful when he discovered that he was pointing a lot at himself (Bourne 2004: 23 April). It might be noted that 'actioning' of this sort is not, in fact, incompatible with the discontinuity of early modern dramatic characters described by Cornford, since the focus is always on what the stage figure wants at each *particular* moment, not necessarily on any psychological through-line. When Rylance wrote in 1997 that it was important for his actors to know *why* their characters are speaking, he asked, 'Is the desire at any particular moment to stir, soothe, illumine, ridicule?' (1997a: 175).[4] It is striking here that each of these verbs – *stir, soothe, illumine, ridicule* – is an action that an actor might attempt upon an *audience* just as much as it is one that a character might play upon another. The next chapter will discuss this observation in more detail.

Rylance described this kind of acting as a form of 'authenticity' (1997a: 175), and the word that crops up most frequently in actor interviews in relation to it is 'truthful'. 'You have to be totally truthful,' said *Twelfth Night*'s Peter Hamilton Dyer in 2002, 'both in the way you address your lines to others, and in the way you respond when they address you' (2002: 15 April); 'good acting,' argued his fellow company member Liam Brennan, is about 'trying to be as honest and truthful as you possibly can' (Ryan 2002b: 17). Again, this sounds like the kind of essentialism that sets academic alarm-bells ringing, as if the speaker were claiming to have discovered the fixed and unalterable 'truth' of a line, but in the context of the discussion above it is clear, I think, that this is not usually what is meant. Rather, 'truthfulness' at the Globe seems to be about spontaneity and responsiveness, a willingness on the part of the actors to play their actions *live* rather than rehearsing and 'pre-programming' them – and a willingness on the part of directors to let them (Kiernan 1999: 69).

There are inevitably problems here. Serving the 'truth' of a character's objective can risk excluding the audience, and the next chapter will explore some of the ways in which Globe actors and directors have sought to adapt objective-driven performance techniques to the Globe's visible audience. Perhaps more importantly, this 'actor-centred' approach to staging Shakespeare risks disavowing the role of the director in shaping the interpretation of the play. As Norbert Kentrup complained in 1998,

> it is absolutely not enough to say we want to stage plays authentically, that we will not interpret, but only play with the story. Each blocking, each casting, each cut is an inter-pretation. ... If I have a German Shylock between an Indian and Chinese Solanio and Salerio, this is an interpretation. (Kiernan 1998b: 32)

Kentrup implied that Olivier's reluctance 'to decide the focus and who gets the sympathy' in *The Merchant of Venice* may have been to blame for some of the problems with the production's reception outlined in Chapter 1 (Kiernan 1998b: 32). Kentrup's *Adopt an Actor* notes observed that his own Bremer Shakespeare Company 'takes a very different approach to productions', beginning 'with a concept of what they would like to tell or communicate with their production of a play' (Kentrup 1998: 29 April).

Early directors, 1996–1998

The first three seasons at the Globe were strongly rooted in the post-Stanislavskian tradition described above, though over that period the directors seem to have gradually moved away from the creation of a self-contained fictional world and more towards one that directly incorporated the presence of the audience. Rylance's appointment of a fellow actor, Jack Shepherd, to direct the Prologue Season's *The Two Gentlemen of Verona* was a surprise to some: Robert Smallwood seemed rather taken aback in his *Shakespeare Survey* review that Rylance had not chosen to direct it himself (1997: 201), while *Time Out*'s Jane Edwardes considered it 'an odd decision to choose an inexperienced Shakespearean director' (28 August 1996). But Rylance's choice of Shepherd was provoked by his expectation that the Globe would require a new kind of directing: 'I wanted someone who put the needs of the players first, not some great conceptual director,' he explained to the *Guardian* (16 August 1996). Indeed, Alastair Macaulay's review in *The Financial Times* observed that Shepherd's production 'in no way ever feels like director's theatre', noting that the actors 'played with the freedom of those who feel their only responsibility is to the play and the audience' (26 August 1996).

Shepherd, an alumnus of the Royal Court Theatre and the National Theatre's Cottesloe Company under Bill Bryden, brought his pedigree in 'kitchen sink' realism to the Globe. His productions of *Two Gentlemen of Verona* and *The Honest Whore* relocated both plays to modern settings and filled the stage with realistic furniture; the Research Bulletin for the latter notes that 'the scenes which take place in the home of the now-married Bellafront and Matheo were to be deliberately domestic in atmosphere, with a dining table and chairs, a pile of washing,' and even 'an imagined "kitchen sink" in the discovery space' (Kiernan 1998c: 5). Shepherd engaged both casts in numerous improvisations, each time instructing his actors to think of the relationship between thought and language as a 'pressure-cooker': 'to suppress the thought, build it up, and allow it to come out eventually as language' (Kiernan 1998c: 5). He encouraged his actors to remain entirely within the fictional world of the play for the duration of each performance. In one scene in *The Two Gentlemen of Verona*, for example, Mark Rylance (playing Proteus) began to move around the café tables of the set 'in order to create more visual inroads for the audience': Shepherd apparently objected to this on the grounds that Rylance's movements 'were motivated by concern for the audience and not by the reality of the scene or the needs of [the] character' (Rylance 1997a: 173). At the time, Rylance agreed that 'a commitment to the reality of the scene has to take precedence over any attempt to provide to the audience with a pleasing or significant visual rendering of location', though I wonder whether as time went on Rylance began to revise this priority (Rylance 1997a: 173). Certainly some commentators did not appreciate Shepherd's commitment to realism at the expense of clear storytelling; Lois Potter, for example, complained that the chairs and tables onstage in *The Honest Whore* 'pinned the actors to just that part of the stage where they were least visible to audiences at the side' (1999: 8).[5]

Richard Olivier joined the Globe's roster of directors in 1997 for *Henry V*, and returned for *The Merchant of Venice* the following year. Like Shepherd, Olivier was committed to a fully realized dramatic world exclusive of the audience. Kiernan's account of rehearsals for *The Merchant of Venice* notes that he encouraged his actors 'to stop thinking about how things will work in the theatre to a full house, and concentrate instead on creating a completely circumscribed fictional world' (Kiernan 1998b: 18). As we have already seen,

Olivier's major contribution to this way of working at the Globe was his introduction of the residential retreats, which he continued to work on even after his directing stint at the Globe came to an end; it is worth noting that alongside the naturalistic improvisations of these retreats, Olivier also introduced elements of ritual and mythology. During the *Hamlet* residency at Otley Hall, for example, he suggested 'an Earth Ritual, a Shamanistic kind of meditation, with people buried up to their necks in muddy graves in order to get in touch with the earth' (Bessell 2001b: 11). Olivier seems to have developed the ritualistic elements of his work at the Globe into a programme of personal development and leadership training called 'Mythodrama', which he now runs for 'global corporations, government and public sector groups, education, the not-for-profit sector, [and] consultancies and leading business schools' (Olivier 2015). According to his website, he remained 'Master of Mythodrama' at the Globe until 2003.

David Freeman's directorial approach to *The Winter's Tale* (1997) seems on the surface to have been rather similar to Olivier's. Seeing the play as a 'myth of birth, death and rebirth', Freeman also spent a great deal of rehearsal time on ritual, in this case encouraging his actors to build 'shrines' from clay and pray to them (Shakespeare's Globe 1997; Miller-Schütz 1998: 6). He likewise instructed the actors that they were 'to be remote from the world around them and completely engrossed in the two worlds [Sicilia and Bohemia] created on stage': this was 'a production mainly conceived as remote from the audience' (Miller-Schütz 1998: 10, 18). Unlike Shepherd and Olivier, however, Freeman soon found himself at odds with his cast. About halfway into rehearsals, the actors began to voice their concerns that they were spending too much rehearsal time on improvisations and not enough on the text. Freeman apparently 'insisted that the improvisation work had proved extraordinarily beneficial and rewarding, but agreed that it was now time to concentrate on more text and character work' (ibid.: 7). By the time the production was into its run, another rift had opened up, since many of the actors 'felt constrained by directorial decisions based on the "closed world" conception that had been made at the time of rehearsals' (ibid.: 23). The root of both problems, according to some of the actors quoted in Miller-Schütz's Research Bulletin, was the same: it is necessary at the Globe 'to start from the text rather than a director's concept', and 'anything conceptual gets into the way of the story and breaks the rapport between actor and audience' (ibid.: 7, 23).

Lucy Bailey had the advantage of being able to learn from Freeman's mistakes, working on *The Maid's Tragedy* with the cast of *The Winter's Tale* after the latter had opened. When Bailey asked them for feedback on their first day of rehearsals with her, they warned her (among other things) that her predecessor had been too worried 'about handing over control to the audience' (Miller-Schütz 2000: 4). The reports of Bailey's rehearsal processes for *The Maid's Tragedy* and her subsequent *As You Like It* indicate that she took the Globe space and audience into account much more frequently than had Freeman, Olivier or Shepherd, and had a strong awareness of which lines might usefully be delivered direct to spectators. In *As You Like It* especially she devised various strategies in order to foster a kind of playful liveness, feeling that while *The Maid's Tragedy* 'required a clean clear formality', *As You Like It* needed to be 'much more loose and organic' (Miller-Schütz 1999b: 3). She made the actors rehearse the scene of Ganymede and Orlando's first meeting 'with a ball or a coin that they threw to each other', while the mock wedding ceremony of 4.1 evolved from a rehearsal game into a 'favourite moment for extemporisation' in the production itself (Miller-Schütz 1999a: 23, 26). Most controversially, she chose to stage several scenes in the yard. Bailey did not return to direct a third production at the Globe during the Rylance era, but she did build upon these early discoveries during Dominic Dromgoole's artistic directorship: her productions of *Titus Andronicus* (2006), *Timon of Athens* (2008) and *Macbeth* (2010) each made innovative use of the presence of the audience.

The Masters system

The shifting role of the director over these first few seasons was reflected in 1999 by Rylance's introduction of the 'Masters' system. Directors became known as 'Masters of Play', musical directors 'Masters of Music', and designers 'Masters of Costume and Properties'. Voice, movement and verse coaches were titled Masters of each of those disciplines, and other Masters were appointed as necessary by production (such positions included 'Master of Fights', 'Master of Dance' and 'Master of Comedic Play'). Rylance explained the rationale for the system in his book *Play*:

> So much theatre of today is born from a rehearsal of ideas rather than the actual craft of acting. I liked the way sports teams had many coaches for the different skills required, under the leadership of one manager. I liked the way ballet companies gave their dancers classes each morning quite separate from rehearsal. I liked the way opera companies had a producer responsible for the story and a conductor responsible for the singers' relationship to the score. We changed our own government to a circle of 'masters' in verse, voice, movement, dance, music, clothing, led by the Master of Play, and all serving the actors and the audience. (2003: 88)

Rylance reassured the cast of *Twelfth Night* in a 2001 letter that the term 'Master' was not meant to imply a position of unassailable authority, merely that such practitioners had 'a mastery of their particular craft'; he advised the actors to consider themselves likewise 'masters of acting' (Rylance 2001b). In a 2003 interview, Tim Carroll explained that the title was 'really a matter of emphasis', designed by Rylance to distance practice at the Globe from the kind of theatre hierarchy where 'the director is at the apex, a combination of philosopher, tyrant, guru, father figure and

Svengali' (*Pittsburgh Post-Gazette*, 2 November 2003). At the Globe, the director was to be just one expert amongst many, albeit still the 'captain of the ship' (Rylance 2016a). The title 'Master of Play' also exploited the ambiguity of the word 'play' itself, suggesting not only that the director is responsible for the presentation of the play, but that he or she should direct it *playfully*.

The introduction of the Masters system made it clear that Rylance wished the Globe to be understood as a deeply collaborative institution. In 1999, musician Tom Lees observed that he considered himself 'lucky to work in an environment that allows us to have a say in what we do', noting that Master of Music Claire van Kampen was 'very open to our suggestions about instruments and the ways we can move with the instruments and things that we do on stage' (Bessell 2000d: 20). Several actors have made similar observations about the way in which Master of Costume and Properties Jenny Tiramani would solicit and respond to their input on costume design. It became traditional on the first day of rehearsals for each of the Masters to give a speech, introducing themselves and their work to the company, and to conclude the day with a 'ritual dedication for the season' that brought the actors into the theatre and 'set out [their] hopes for the production' (Gould 2001: 7 April; Gale 2004: 11 April). The Globe is repeatedly described in actor interviews as a friendly and supportive environment, and the Masters system seems to have been instrumental in developing actors' skills. By 2003, actors were training three times a week with the Masters of Voice, Movement and Verse; Rylance never appointed a 'Master of Space', but it seems clear that in later seasons, various practitioners (including Rylance himself) led regular training sessions on the particular spatial dynamics of the Globe stage.

The Masters system was not without its disadvantages. When a rehearsal for *Macbeth* in 2001 included notes from the Masters of Play, Dance, Words, Voice and Movement and the Assistant to the Master of Play, actor Chu Omambala described the experience as 'a bit mind-boggling', because 'so many notes from so many different people' were difficult to process in a single sitting (2001: 21 May). The American director Gerald Freedman, who served as Master of Play for *The Antipodes* in 2000, published excerpts from his journal in *American Theatre* magazine the following year, revealing that though his experience at the Globe had been largely positive, he had had repeated anxieties about his level of control over the production. Though there was 'a great spirit of collaboration' at the Globe, he wrote, it 'often muddies the creative waters'; he recorded his frustration with the 'lack of artistic communication' from the central artistic team, who would sometimes make production decisions between themselves without consulting him. Admitting that he was accustomed to having 'a central, controlling vision', Freedman evidently found the proliferation of Masters unsettling: the amount of time afforded to discussion and debate meant that key artistic decisions were not taken until much later in the production process than he was used to, though he did note that van Kampen's input especially, while frequently critical, often led to 'creative thinking, re-thinking and solutions'. Rylance was also in the cast of *The Antipodes*, and his contributions during rehearsals led Freedman to 'worry that with little nibbles there will be an indiscernible erosion of what I can do'. Later, Freedman observed that Rylance had 'a disconcerting predilection to address the company, as an actor, making suggestions about playing that I think are more appropriately the director's province' (Freedman 2001).

The Masters system saw the introduction of the 'Master of Verse'. The first three seasons at the Globe had indicated that modern actor training is frequently deficient in this area, with some actors unable to tell the difference between verse and prose (Miller-Schütz 1999b: 40). Both reviews and company interviews indicate a general consensus that the introduction of these verse specialists (Giles Block and Tim Carroll) for the 1999 season greatly improved the company's verse speaking. Initially, the role was interpreted by many as being something like a co-director: actor Mark Lewis Jones used the word 'separation' to describe the distinction between the roles of Master of Verse and Master of Play in *Julius Caesar*, as if he would normally expect the two to be done by the same person (Bessell 2000d: 19), while reviewers in the press tended to see the production as 'the combined efforts of Mark Rylance and Giles Block as Masters of Play and Verse respectively' (Sam Marlowe, *What's On*, 2 June 1999). Certainly the Globe's Masters of Verse were also directors: Block and Carroll were Masters of both Verse and Play on different productions in 1999. Directing in 2001, Barry Kyle found 'the notion of someone else other than the director doing the verse ... initially odd', but went on to note that his work with Block had been 'collaborative rather than divisive' (Bessell 2002d: 5). In fact, Block seems to have been scrupulous in not treading on directors' toes, often working with actors on text from another play entirely so as not to dictate specific choices or line readings. Actors tend to describe their sessions with Block as open-ended rather than prescriptive, observing, for example, that he 'helps you to discover things for yourself' (Ryan 2002b: 25) and 'never ever tells you how to say something' (Beaumont 2005: 5 May).

There were only ever two Masters of Verse at the Globe, and from 2001 onwards only Block was credited as such in Globe programmes. From 2002, he became 'Master of the Words', presumably to more accurately reflect his work on prose as well as verse. Block's methods are detailed in his book *Speaking the Speech* (2013), so I will not set them down at length here. It may be useful, though, to detail some of his most influential ideas as reported by Globe actors. Though he tended to reassure actors that 'there are no rules at all' (Beaumont 2005: 5 May), Block clearly has a set of theories and preferred techniques that in some way represent the Globe's house style; Alex Hassell observed in 2004 that 'it's fair to say that Giles represents the way that verse is spoken at the Globe, so it's good to try and get on the same page' (Hassell 2004: 20 April). Block's key idea is the importance of actors 'thinking and speaking at the same time', as he explained to Jaq Bessell in 2000:

What we're aiming for is the line which is the response to some spontaneous need you have to express, which sounds like the only *possible* thing you could say, that fully defines the need of the moment and of the emotion of the moment. (Bessell 2001c: 13)

One can see direct links here between Block's practice, Shepherd's 'pressure cooker' metaphor, and Rylance's 'need to speak'. Block argues that a line of iambic pentameter is roughly the same length as a human breath; a pause for breath at the end of each line can give the actor/character a moment to think about what he or she is going to say next. As Roger McKern explains it, Block encourages actors to 'keep pushing through to the end of the line, and if you take a pause, you pause at the end of the line, rather than at punctuation marks mid-line' (Bessell 2002d: 35). Block's technique thus lays particular emphasis on the words at the end of each line, suggesting that each may be a prompt for the line that follows. James Garnon illustrates Block's work on this with three lines of Mercutio's 'Queen Mab' speech:

Sometime she driveth o'er a soldier's neck,
And then dreams he of cutting foreign throats,
Of breaches, ambuscados, Spanish blades, ... (*Romeo and Juliet*, 1.4.82–4)

'Neck', explains Garnon, prompts 'foreign throats':

[B]lades cut throats so 'throats' leads to 'blades'. One of the most helpful things I realised during the session was that speaking verse is all about having enough courage to ignore the fact that you know exactly what's coming next, and find each thought as it was written. (2004: 29 April)

Several actors describe working with Block in this fashion to sustain a single complex thought-unit over multiple lines. Sometimes this work involves an examination of the punctuation in the first Folio, which can result in dubious interpretations: Patricia Kerrigan, for example, suggests that '[i]f a line does not end with punctuation', it means 'that the person was unsure how to end the sentence', little recognizing that Folio punctuation can be erratic and is by no means authorial (2001: 14 April). On the other hand, the Folio's proliferation of commas and semi-colons can be 'quite freeing', in the words of Quill Roberts, for actors who might otherwise be inclined to start a new thought at every full-stop (Bessell 2000d: 24).

As a director, Block's methods were entirely consistent with the Globe's emerging house style. Asked about his directorial method in the programme for 2005's *Troilus and Cressida*, he replied that he did not really have one:

> [S]ome directors work with an overt method, but I think my approach is more pragmatic. I have found that the greatest challenge in directing Shakespeare is to find a way in which thoughts can resonate. When you are speaking, more emphasis goes on how you shape a thought, rather than the actual words that you use. (Shakespeare's Globe 2005b)

Like his fellow Masters of Play, Block's process seems to have involved numerous improvisations, but the rehearsals detailed in the Research Bulletins for his productions of *Antony and Cleopatra* (1999) and *Hamlet* (2000) suggest that read-throughs, discussions, and (naturally) sessions of verse analysis were rather more prevalent than they had been in the rehearsal processes of other directors at the Globe. There was a general consensus amongst 1999's Red Company that having had Block as Master of Verse on *Julius Caesar* allowed for a shared shorthand when he became Master of Play for the same company on *Antony and Cleopatra*.

Mike Alfreds and Mark Rylance

Although Mike Alfreds did not direct at the Globe until 2001's *Cymbeline*, his influence upon practice there was clear much earlier. Alfreds had directed Rylance in his 1987 productions of *The Wandering Jew* and *Countrymania* at the National Theatre (a season for which Rylance apparently turned down a role in Steven Spielberg's *Empire of the Sun*), and at the beginning of his artistic directorship at the Globe, Rylance was citing Alfreds as a major influence on his own work (Rylance 1997a: 171). Rylance has said that he wanted Alfreds to work at the Globe from the moment he became its Artistic Director, and when Alfreds finally became available in 2001, Rylance invited him to choose for himself which play he wished to direct (2001a: 23 June). When Alfreds's book *Different Every Night* was published in 2007, its back cover quoted a glowing endorsement from Rylance:

> If I was allowed to train again as an actor, but I was only allowed one teacher, it would have to be Mike Alfreds. To me he is a genius when it comes to acting and storytelling. I will spend my life trying to be true to what he perceives possible in the theatre.

Certainly an analysis of Rylance's own directing practice reveals numerous exercises borrowed from Alfreds, and Alfreds's rehearsal work exemplifies much of what Rylance sought to encourage.

Alfreds's approach to directing, as the title of *Different Every Night* suggests, is underpinned by his preference for theatre's 'element of uncertainty, of possibility, of the unexpected' (2007: 23). When he directs, Alfreds wants each performance to be a 'disciplined improvisation' in which actors play their actions and objectives with relative consistency, but attempt to achieve them by employing different tactics each time; this is not 'change for the sake of change', he insists, 'but for the sake of being alive and true to each moment as it occurs' (2007: 25). Actors are forced to be creative as they respond, live, to the stimulation of their improvising scene partners, and the audience share in the possibility of 'experiencing those thrilling moments that seem mostly to happen during rehearsal' (2007: 25). This sort of work requires actors to know the text very well, and to develop great confidence not only in their own improvisational abilities but also in those of their fellow cast members. For this reason, Alfreds was granted a rehearsal period of ten weeks, rather than the usual six, for both of his Globe productions.

His rehearsal processes for *Cymbeline* and the following year's *A Midsummer Night's Dream* appear to have been similar. Prior to the start of rehearsals, Alfreds asked both casts to prepare a set of lists similar to those described above. According to the *Cymbeline* Research Bulletin, these lists comprised:

1 the 'facts' about your character, e.g. Imogen has two brothers,
2 what your character says about others in the play,
3 what other characters say about your character in the play,
4 what your 'super objective' might be,
5 what your 'main line of action' might be. (Bessell 2002b: 6)

Actors also seem to have been asked to compile lists of what their characters say about *themselves* (Alfreds 2007: 206; Rylance 2001a: 9 June), and in his book, Alfreds notes that for actors working on Shakespeare 'or any writer who uses heightened language', there can be an 'optional' further list detailing the imagery associated with each character (2007: 206–7). The early stages of rehearsal would then be devoted to a detailed analysis of each character in turn, undertaken by the whole company in discussion. With reference to the same set of lists, each member of the company might take turns at playing the same character. Alfreds would lead physical exercises in order to establish the quality of each character's movement, or where their 'physical centre' might lie (Bessell 2002b: 6). He frequently used Rudolf Laban's system of 'Efforts' in order to determine whether a character's movement was Light or Strong, Direct or Flexible, Sustained or Broken (Bessell 2002b: 4; Alfreds 2007: 229–40): Rylance's Posthumus, for example, was 'strong, sustained and direct' (Rylance 2001a: 9 June). Alfreds was adamant, though, that such movement must not be made for its own sake, as he explained to actor Simon Trinder in 2002: 'there must be a reason behind every movement or gesture' (Trinder 2002: 22 July).

As we have seen, Alfreds's analysis tended to focus on objectives and actions (as Alfreds explains it, 'what characters do to try to achieve their objectives' [2007: 65]). Each scene was given a title to describe its central piece of action – 1.1–2 of *Cymbeline*, for example, becoming 'Cymbeline banishes Posthumus' – and was then broken down into its component 'units of action', each of which was also given a sub-title (for example, 'The Queen assures Imogen and Posthumus she is on their side' [Bessell 2002b: 12]). The actors were asked to articulate an objective for each unit of action, so that, for example, during the unit 'Imogen and Posthumus declare a vow of love and faithfulness to each other' Imogen's objective was 'to assure Posthumus she will be able to handle her father in his absence', while Posthumus's was 'to prevent her from breaking down, or making him break down' (Bessell 2002b: 12–13). The actors would play each unit multiple times without changing their objectives, but altering the tactics used to achieve them; Alfreds would encourage them to approach their performances with similar flexibility.

Alfreds employed an exercise called 'points of concentration' in order to foster this flexibility.[6] At each run-through, he would ask his actors to play their actions whilst simultaneously focusing on a new aspect of the scene: this could be a matter of form, such as line-endings, of character ('the boys have heard this story from Belarius many, many times before'), or of setting ('the fact that it is dawn' [Bessell 2002b: 34]). Philippa Stanton gives an example in her account of rehearsing Hermia in *A Midsummer Night's Dream*:

> For example, having worked on a scene in detail, Mike might tell me to try it again using my love for Lysander as a point of concentration; this means that everything I say and do in that scene is affected, even if only a little, by my love for Lysander. ... Each point of concentration is relevant in some way to the scene, and you mustn't use each point of concentration more than a few times because your ideas would get stale.

Stanton notes that some of these ideas returned during her performances, while others did not, but that the exercise in general encouraged her to have confidence in exploring new ideas in performance (2002: 29 July).

Preparation of this sort allowed Alfreds's actors to go into performances without having anything blocked. The performance-within-a-performance of *Pyramus and Thisbe*, for example, was never directed by Alfreds, but rehearsed in character by the actors playing the mechanicals. As actor John Ramm (Bottom) explained it,

> [e]very night, our 'play' is different, and occasionally even topical; Paul Trussell [Peter Quince] brought on a set of red and yellow cards one afternoon when England were playing in the World Cup. (2002: 5 August)

Alfreds would work with his actors on keeping pragmatic issues like sightlines in mind, but otherwise left the staging to them. The 2002 actor interviews testify to a general enthusiasm for this approach, though one or two sound a note of caution. Keith Dunphy (Demetrius) noted that when actors are tired or not 'firing on all cylinders', 'things can go slightly wrong because you don't have any blocking to fall back on'; Patrick Lennox (Snout), meanwhile, observed that 'some performances threw up choices that were quite clearly wrong, but once you've committed to something you must go with it despite that knowledge' (Ryan 2002b: 12, 18). This is, of course, the price one pays for spontaneity: as Lennox concludes, '[t]he next time you perform you just don't choose it' (Ryan 2002b: 18).

Both of Alfreds's Globe productions were self-advertisingly theatrical in form. *Cymbeline* was performed by a cast of just six, alongside two onstage musicians. The actors wore plain white costumes and each played multiple roles, distinguishing one character from another through voice and movement alone (Figure 3). The only props used in the show were percussion instruments, meaning that all fictional objects – books, candles, bottles – were represented by non-literal equivalents. *Dream* had a much larger cast of fourteen, but the mortals still doubled with the fairies, and like *Cymbeline* it was performed with non-realistic costumes and props: in

Figure 3 *Mark Rylance and company in* Cymbeline *(2001). Photograph by John Tramper. Shakespeare's Globe: Archive.*

this case, everyone was clothed in blue pyjamas, and all the props were objects associated with bedrooms and bathrooms (Bottom's ears, for example, were a pair of 'mule' slippers). As Alfreds explained in the programme for *Cymbeline*, the aim was to invite the audience to 'collaborate in an act of shared imagination by which we suggest what's there and the audience sees what isn't there at all' (Shakespeare's Globe 2001).

Mark Rylance directed only one production during his time at the Globe – 1999's *Julius Caesar* – but the Research Bulletin and actor interviews make his debt to Alfreds clear. Rylance's rehearsal process for this production made use of several now-familiar exercises: using lists to create character biographies and determine super-objectives, extended improvisations, and points of concentration. This chapter has already documented Rylance's concern with finding the 'need to speak', and he developed an Alfreds exercise in order to work on this in detail. Alfreds advocates a process he calls 'feeding-in', in which the actors rehearse a scene without scripts and have a fellow actor 'feed them their lines, beat by beat' (2007: 178). Bessell explains the exercise as Rylance presented it to the cast of *Julius Caesar*:

> The 'feeders' stayed close to their assigned actor and fed them lines without projection or emphasis. The challenge for the 'feeders' was to closely shadow their actor, without impeding them in any way. MR advised the 'feeders' to feed thoughts, and not necessarily complete lines to the actors. (2000b: 4)

This exercise meant that actors were able to treat the text from the start of rehearsals as spoken *thought*. As Bessell explains in her account of it during rehearsals for *Cymbeline*, it 'meant that actors could not focus on what was *going* to be said; instead they were able to focus entirely on what was *being* said in the moment' (2002b: 19).

Rylance chose not to serve as Master of Play a second time, finding that leading from within the ensemble was a 'much more comfortable' role for him (Rylance et al. 2008: 194). In an interview conducted shortly after the 1999 season, he was frank about the difficulties he had as a director in finding ways to encourage actors towards spontaneous playing:

> As a Master of Play I have been able to see that this is a frightening prospect for actors. I haven't yet been able to find the right way to encourage this freedom, without sacrificing the necessary structure to prevent everything becoming muddled. (Bessell 2000d: 4)

Nonetheless, Rylance continued to play a director-like role in numerous subsequent productions. When Tim Carroll was absent for a short period during rehearsals for *Macbeth* in 2001, Rylance led the cast in the 'feeding' exercise and in a long improvisation session; the following year, he led the cast of Carroll's *Twelfth Night* in Alfreds-style characterization exercises, using lists, discussions, improvisations and physical exercises (Ryan 2002a: 12–15). He served as Master of Voice for *Romeo and Juliet* in 2004, and led voice sessions with other members of the 2004 company. He also led movement sessions on the Globe stage in order to help actors discover how to use the space without having to rely on set blocking.

Tim Carroll

Tim Carroll was the director of just over a quarter of the total number of Rylance-era Globe productions. He first worked for the theatre in 1999, having been appointed on the recommendation of the playwright Peter Oswald (with whom he was then working on an eventually unrealized draft play for the Globe). Oswald and Carroll had collaborated on a production of Racine's *Phaedra* at the Battersea Arts Centre in 1998, the same year that Oswald was appointed the Globe's first writer-in-residence; Rylance, impressed by the elegant simplicity of Carroll's direction and the rigour of his work on verse, invited him to the Globe to direct Oswald's play *Augustine's Oak* and to work as Master of Verse on Kathryn Hunter's *The Comedy of Errors*. Carroll would go on to direct all of Oswald's subsequent work for the Globe, namely *The Golden Ass* in 2002 and *The Storm* in 2005, as well as six plays by Shakespeare and one by Marlowe (*Dido, Queen of Carthage* in 2003).

Carroll characterizes his approach to directing verse drama as one that encourages 'maximum spontaneity within maximum attention to the form' (Carroll 2016). He is keen to enforce close attention to the rules of scansion; in 2000, for example, when he served as Master of Verse on *The Tempest*, he worked with the actors on recognizing lines in which the modern actor might be inclined to stress the word 'not', or a personal pronoun, but in which the metre suggests these words should be spoken in unstressed positions (Bessell 2001a: 8). He often asks actors to engage in some sort of rhythmic movement while speaking lines of verse during rehearsal, such as throwing a tennis ball on the last stressed syllable of each line and catching it again on the first stressed syllable of the next. Eve Best gives an example:

Glamis thou art, and Cawdor, and shalt *be* – chuck the ball – What *thou* – catch the ball – art promised. (*Macbeth*, 1.5.15–16)

Best found the exercise difficult but helpful in her preparations for Lady Macbeth, noting that 'if you throw the ball, you're carrying on the thought, so you're not stopping dead at the end of the line' (2001: 14 May); in this respect, Carroll's practice elaborates on one of the central tenets of Block's. Actors wedded to a naturalistic conception of theatrical speech have not always found Carroll's insistence on metrical precision so rewarding: Chu Omambala, for example, the same production's Malcolm, complained that his priority was 'to make the lines sound natural and believable', and that if a strict adherence to iambic pentameter 'doesn't sound right, then I won't say the line that way' (2001: 30 April). On the other hand, some of Carroll's more frequent collaborators have identified his strictness with the verse as paradoxically liberating. 'By restricting yourself in one way,' explained James Garnon, 'you are more creative in other ways and discover things that you might have otherwise overlooked' (2004: 1 April). As we shall see, the notion that formal constraints can provoke creativity is central to Carroll's practice.

Like many of the directors discussed in this chapter, Carroll prefers relatively un-blocked, objective-driven performances. Some of his rehearsal techniques are similar to those of Mike Alfreds, though Carroll notes that he was not familiar with Alfreds's practices before they worked together at the Globe (Carroll 2016). The account of his process for 2000's *Two Noble Kinsmen* gives perhaps the fullest illustration of this aspect of his work: during one rehearsal, for example, actors were asked to play the same scene multiple times, 'each time using slightly different tactics', while at another, actors were encouraged to freeze the action at any point and 'give voice to what we might otherwise refer to as the "intentions" or "subtext" of the scene' (Bessell 2001d: 9, 13). Two years later, Carroll would describe *Twelfth Night* to his cast as 'one of Shakespeare's most Chekhovian plays, concentrated around the pursuit of agendas and speaking at cross-purposes' (Ryan 2002a: 33).

Carroll's rehearsal games are often designed to combine close attention to verbal detail with responsiveness to the stimulation of one's co-performer. A perennial exercise is 'trigger words', in which actors identify a single word in the cue spoken by their fellow actor as a 'trigger' for their own line, and repeat it before they speak. The example given in the *Macbeth* bulletin is as follows:

Macbeth Duncan comes here tonight.
Lady Macbeth DUNCAN? And when goes hence?
Macbeth HENCE? Tomorrow, as he purposes. (*Macbeth*, 1.5.59–60; Bessell 2002c: 12)

Rehearsing *Macbeth*'s 1.7 in this manner, Eve Best apparently noted that 'the constant triggers helped the speaker to make their argument clear and forceful, and to deal with their partner's questions or objections' (Bessell 2002c: 14); for Liam Brennan, the exercise 'really just tunes up your attentiveness, your listening skills' (2001: 11 April). The *Macbeth* bulletin details numerous instances in which this game unearthed unexpected meanings: when Jasper Britton's Macbeth took the word *leave* in his wife's line 'You must leave this' as the cue for 'O, full of scorpions is my mind, dear wife' (3.2.36–7), for example, it highlighted the extent to which 'the scorpions in his mind are inescapable' (Bessell 2002c: 16). The actors observed that as the Macbeths 'begin to talk at cross-purposes', the trigger word exercise became harder to do (ibid.: 17).

As Bessell points out, in this conception of dramatic speech, 'the motivation to speak is *entirely* because the other person spoke' (ibid.: 14). Much of Carroll's rehearsal work fosters this understanding of the live, rapidly shifting interdependency of theatrical dialogue. Another favourite exercise is to run through a scene with the instruction that each speaker should start their line before the previous speaker has finished, thus forcing the actors to 'fight for the right to speak' (ibid.: 15). During rehearsals for *Romeo and Juliet*, Carroll provided his cast with 'cue scripts' that gave them only their own lines and a brief cue; actors noted that the exercise made them 'really listen to what other people were saying' (Burke 2004: 2 April) and 'react more spontaneously' (Kirimi 2004: 2 April).

Tom Burke explains that the overlapping speech exercise 'stops you consciously "acting" or trying to convey certain emotions or moods' (2004: 16 April). This is another central aim in Carroll's process. As Macduff, Liam Brennan was asked to play his reaction to the news of the murder of his entire family 'as if I was unaffected'; such an approach, says Brennan, 'allows the audience's imagination to work' and refrains from 'forcing something' upon them (2001: 16 April). Carroll made frequent reference during rehearsals to David

Mamet's book *True and False*, in which the author argues against the necessity of 'character-work' in the rehearsal room:

> The actor does not need to 'become' the character. The phrase, in fact, has no meaning. There *is* no character. There are only lines upon a page. They are lines of dialogue meant to be said by the actor. When he or she says them simply, in an attempt to achieve an object more or less like that suggested by the author, the audience sees an *illusion* of a character upon the stage. (1998: 9)

The practice advocated by Mamet is a radically simplified version of that discussed earlier in this chapter, in which the identification of a plausible objective and the playing of actions in order to achieve that objective are all that is required of the actor. 'Moment to moment and night to night the play will change,' explains Mamet, 'as you and your adversaries onstage change, as your conflicting actions butt up against each other. *That* play, *that* interchange, is drama' (1998: 62). References to *True and False* recur in several interviews with members of the Globe company.[7] Carroll told me that he enjoys 'setting Mamet against Stanislavski', noting that while his focus on objectives and actions is broadly Stanislavskian, 'a lot of my most fruitful approaches are somehow mischievously set against Stanislavski ... I really do, to the extent I can, outlaw talk about character' (Carroll 2016). During rehearsals, he tends to refer to actors by their own names rather than those of their characters (Bourne 2004: 23 April), and trusts that the illusion of character will be created in the imaginative engagement of the audience rather than in the minds of the actors (Brennan 2003: 11 April). Having said this, many of the actors working with Carroll have a great deal to say about their characters in their interviews, and the cast of *Twelfth Night* even had 'character' sessions with Rylance in Carroll's absence (Ryan 2002a: 12–15).

One of Carroll's key tools is the 'obstruction'. This is similar in some respects to Mike Alfreds's notion of the 'point of concentration', though it is also more explicitly non-naturalistic and game-like. Once his actors have identified their objectives for a scene, Carroll will give them an unrelated and often arbitrary task to complete alongside the pursuit of their objectives. During a run-through of *Two Noble Kinsmen*'s 2.1, for example, each actor was given a 'secret action' to perform (such as 'to lie down at some point in the scene') which would provoke the actors into pursuing their objectives in unexpected ways (Bessell 2001d: 13–14). Other examples included an improvised performance of *Macbeth* in which 'each cast member had to appear in every scene' (Britton 2001: 30 April), a run-through of *Twelfth Night*'s Act 5 in which actors were instructed to pick one other character 'who would be their focus, or even obsession' throughout (Ryan 2002a: 33), and a version of *Richard II*'s 2.3 in which the actors were prohibited from looking at the person to whom they were speaking (Shorey 2003: 18 April). It is primarily an exercise in the pluralization of meaning: each obstruction forces the actor into making choices that might not otherwise have occurred to them. These choices are provisional rather than conscious acts of interpretation: after a run-though of 1.2 of *Romeo and Juliet* in which he had been instructed to take his shoes off, turn the lights out and threaten his fellow actor with a fire extinguisher, Tom Burke observed that 'it's almost like you've just let the scene happen by itself whilst your concentration is immediately occupied elsewhere' (2004: 16 April).

Carroll began to use the term 'obstruction' for this exercise after seeing Lars von Trier's 2003 film *The Five Obstructions*, in which von Trier challenges his mentor and fellow filmmaker Jørgen Leth to remake his 1967 film *The Perfect Human* five times, each time with a different set of arbitrary constraints. As Carroll explains,

it's a really moving film, because what you see is that Lars von Trier is really humbled by watching his attempts to mess up his hero fail, gloriously, as his hero makes five astonishingly beautiful films. (Carroll 2016)

Following his departure from the Globe in 2005, Carroll developed this exercise into a form in its own right, directing the theatre company The Factory (many of whom were themselves Globe alumni) in a series of semi-improvised performances of *Hamlet* and *The Seagull* where each show was performed by a different line-up of actors from its ensemble of players, without blocking, in a different space and with a different set of 'obstructions'. The moment-by-moment decisions made by actors under these conditions do not always work, but they often make sense of a line in surprising and sometimes thrilling new ways.

Carroll's directing process, then, like Alfreds's, is all about keeping actors responsive to new stimuli so that the meanings of their performances remain contingent rather than fixed. He explained in an interview in 2003 that rather than attempting to control a production, his directing practice aims instead 'at creating situations which are fruitful and allow interesting things to happen' (*Pittsburgh Post-Gazette*, 2 November 2003). In performance, Carroll's actors must resist the temptation to repeat previous discoveries, as James Garnon articulates:

> The first time, whatever happened was the result of focus: you had the focus and you did something with it. The second time, you have to get the same focus to repeat what you did, which slows you down. That's why it never works the second time. (2004: 1 April)

Playing Macbeth in 2001, Jasper Britton said that if he were 'good enough', he would 'probably perform all of it differently every day' (Bessell 2002d: 15).

Carroll seems to have become bolder in this aspect of his work over his time at the Globe. Though he was already 'getting more and more interested in leaving things to chance', he told me, when he came to the Globe in 1999 he was 'really only 20% there' (Carroll 2016); indeed, though his interview for the 1999 Research Bulletin makes it clear that he preferred to 'keep everything very fluid', it also shows that he felt he 'had to do more "left a bit, right a bit" directing' than he might have liked (Bessell 2000c: 7). As time went on – perhaps because the actors he was working with began to develop a more instinctive understanding of the Globe space – Carroll started to trust them more and more. 'I was lucky enough to work with really playful, crazy actors,' he told me, naming Geraldine Alexander, Jasper Britton, Paul Chahidi, Will Keen and Yolanda Vazquez as examples of ensemble members who 'weren't afraid of trying something different' (Carroll 2016). Rylance notes that by 2002, a 'real ensemble of experienced actors' was emerging at the Globe (2008: 196), and it is striking that many of the names he gives are also actors who worked with Carroll over the period between 1999 and 2002 – including Terry McGinity and Jules Melvin (who joined the company alongside Chahidi and Vazquez in 1999), and Liam Brennan, Patrick Brennan and Colin Hurley (who joined in 2001). While the Research Bulletin for Carroll's 2002 production of *The Golden Ass* documents quite a lot of set blocking – perhaps because of its large cast, short rehearsal period and frequent set pieces – the same year's *Twelfth Night* evidently allowed actors 'a fair amount of freedom with the blocking within each scene, changing it slightly each time a scene was run' (Howey-Nunn 2002; Ryan 2002a: 34).

Macbeth (2001) was in some ways the apotheosis of Carroll's work at the Globe. Since the Globe space made impossible the design aesthetic common to most indoor productions of the play – candlelight, shadows, dry ice and sound effects – Carroll decided instead to create a world of 'rough metaphor' (Bessell 2002c: 2). As in Alfreds's concurrent production of *Cymbeline*, nothing in Carroll's *Macbeth* was represented literally: the actors were costumed in modern evening dress, the only scenery was a row of chairs, and each of the characters carried a pebble which would be dropped into a bucket to signify their death. The production did feature sequences of choreographed group movement, but aside from this, Carroll was keen 'to not set anything particularly for the actual performances, literally not to "block" the scenes' (Best 2001: 21 May). Carroll's directing strategy, then, was to set up a series of formal constraints in which actions could be played live and relatively unplanned. In some cases, these took the form of party games: Banquo's murder, for example, was a version of Piggy-in-the-Middle in which Banquo was blind-folded while his murderers playfully and maliciously threw his pebble between them, while the climactic fight between Macbeth and Macduff saw the characters engage in increas-ingly frantic attempts to rip the pebble from their opponent's shirt pocket.

The production was largely dismissed as a failure by reviewers. John Peter called it 'one of the most witless and pretentious productions of this play, indeed of any Shakespeare play, I've ever seen' (*Sunday Times*, 10 June 2001); Alastair Macaulay likewise found it 'boring, unstylish, pretentious', and characteristic of everything wrong with the Globe (*Financial Times*, 7 June 2001). Ironically for a production that had been designed to allow its actors an unusual degree of freedom, a key source of complaint was that it was 'self-indulgent "director's theatre" at its worst' (Charles Spencer, *Daily Telegraph*, 7 June 2001) and let down by 'phenomenally silly directorial concepts' (Kate Bassett, *Independent on Sunday*, 10 June 2001). Indeed, several reviewers took a distinctly angry tone, as if they suspected that Carroll had staged a deliberately impenetrable concept ('pretentious' was a repeated criticism) in order to make them feel stupid: the 'crazy, mixed-up production' hit Nicholas de Jongh, for example, 'with all the force of an insult' (*Evening Standard*, 6 June 2001). I suspect the trouble was that these reviewers, used to interpreting all stage action as an aspect of the director's thesis on the play, found it difficult to under-stand that *Macbeth*'s design aesthetic was not expressive of a *concept*, but rather a *form*. Like Alfreds's work, the form required an imaginative willingness on the part of its spectators to play the game of signification along with the actors (and in this case, the game was not at all hard to understand – even the most hostile reviewers understood, for example, what the pebbles represented). In this respect, Carroll's work was not unlike the sort of challenge to representational realism being made around the same time by avant-garde playwrights like Tim Crouch, whose plays *My Arm* (2002) and *An Oak Tree* (2005) ask their audiences to do similar imaginative work. For his part, Carroll defends *Macbeth* as 'the best thing I've ever done' (*Independent*, 29 June 2003) and as the Globe show of which he is proudest (Carroll 2016); it is certainly the closest of his Globe productions to the work he subsequently developed with The Factory.

Physical theatre

Physical and movement-based theatre was an important part of the Globe's work from the start. Sue Lefton, a graduate of the famous École Internationale de Théâtre Jacques Lecoq in Paris, was the Movement Coach for all of the Opening Season productions, and was appointed as the director of Middleton's *A Mad World, My Masters* the following year. This production allowed her to develop further the physical work she had begun during the opening season, when she had learned that the Globe audience 'responds to strong definition' (Kiernan 1999: 145). During rehearsals for *Mad World*, Lefton paid particular attention to the stories told by her actors' bodies, working 'from the outside in' rather than starting with questions of psychological motivation: 'all the characters were defined by their silhouette and the shape of their spines' (Miller-Schütz 2000: 29). As Inesse and Possibility, Guy Moore and Paul Hilton 'worked out a double act where there were constantly trying to get in front of each other, moving in curves and twists, and echoing each other's faces' (ibid.: 28). When Lefton played improvisation games with her cast, they were different from the immersive improvisations devised by her contemporaries Shepherd and

Olivier: these games were not so much attempts to realize the imaginative world of the play as they were explorations of the comic potential inherent in master-servant relationships.

Work of this sort is indebted to the Lecoq tradition, and Rylance was evidently keen to encourage the influence. In 1998 he invited two members of the Lecoq-based company Théâtre de Complicité, Marcello Magni and Lilo Baur, to join the casts of *The Merchant of Venice* and *The Honest Whore*; the following year saw Magni return to play the Dromios in a production of *The Comedy of Errors* directed by the frequent Complicité collaborator and member of the Globe Artistic Directorate Kathryn Hunter. Hunter returned to the Globe as an actor in 2003, and to direct *Pericles* in 2005; Magni returned during the same seasons as 'Trainer in Comedic Play' for *The Taming of the Shrew* (2003), as both an actor and 'Master of Physical Play' for *Pericles* (2005), and as an actor and 'Master of Mask' for *Man Falling Down* (2005). Papers in the Globe archive show that Rylance also approached Complicité co-founders Simon McBurney and Annabel Arden to work at the Globe, though this came to nothing. Rylance articulated the influence of Lecoq and Complicité on his work in a 2004 interview with the *Irish Times*, explaining that in recent years, London's theatre culture had 'moved much more into the physical senses' and there was 'much more delight now in the physical trickery, in the manifestation of theatrical form' (12 March 2004). In an interview with Magni and Baur in 1998, Alan Wade suggested that the Globe and Complicité shared an interest in 'physical exploration of the text through game playing', though Magni replied that he felt the Globe was more interested in improvisation games as 'psychological exercises' than as theatrical activities in their own rights (Wade 2000: 70–1).

Kathryn Hunter's rehearsal processes for *The Comedy of Errors* and *Pericles* seem to have fused Lecoq-style physical work with the emerging Globe aesthetics more successfully. Her work tended to focus on the visual: she had illustrations, photographs, costume items and props strewn around the rehearsal room so that actors could pick things up and play with them in order to create the appropriate stage images, and she seems to have devoted large amounts of rehearsal time to physical characterization, looking, for example, at characters' 'physical centres' and encouraging actors to move around as animal versions of their characters. She was keen for her casts to develop their productions as ensembles, asking them not to make any interpretive decisions before they began rehearsals. Some of her ensemble work was reminiscent of the 'back story' improvisations utilized by other Globe directors: in one rehearsal for *The Comedy of Errors*, for example, the company was split into small groups and asked to recreate three scenes from Adriana and Luciana's past together, 'with the entire cast brainstorming together on character' (Chahidi 1999: 3 May), while a rehearsal for *Pericles* saw the whole company improvising Marina's tenth birthday party (Rees 2005: 22 April). Other exercises were not psychological at all. The cast of *Pericles*, for example, used their bodies to 'become the sea', moving slowly forwards and backwards as a group (Gostelow 2005: 15 April); Magni explained in the programme that the aim was to portray the sea 'as an agent that manipulates the story' (Shakespeare's Globe 2005a). In the eventual performance, a couple of actors would hold two bamboo poles together to form the prow of Pericles' ship, while aerialist performers climbed ropes around the Globe's galleries as if they were sailors on the rigging, and the company moved as one to create the illusion of 'Neptune's billow' (3.0.45).

Like many of her Globe contemporaries, Hunter saw the clarification of character objectives as key to clear storytelling and spontaneous performance. As Adriana, Yolanda Vazquez was keen 'to be flexible and not to fix the way a moment is played', but recognized that 'this is only possible if the actors are clear about their character's motivation and relationship to the other characters in the scene' (1999: 24 May). Magni likewise felt that Globe actors should focus 'on what we are *doing*, and what we *want*', and reports that during a run of

The Comedy of Errors, Hunter issued the instruction, 'Let it come out, do not remember how you said it before' (Bessell 2000c: 15). But this approach owes just as much to Jacques Lecoq as it does to Stanislavski, as Magni explained to me:

> There must be always, in the relationship of a play, a certain *tactic*. In life we are like that: we charm, we entice. I see it in a playful way, like a game. So then I have to put it physically on stage. I have to find the dynamic of that play. Either it's attraction – pulling – or it's pushing, it's rejection. And then there are many different variations on doing that – searching, hunting. They're all physical expressions. (Magni 2010)

Thus, for the sequence in *The Comedy of Errors* in which Antipholus and Dromio of Syracuse share a quickfire exchange of puns about baldness (2.2.71–107), Magni and his fellow actor Vincenzo Nicoli found a physical expression for the 'game' of the scene by literally playing it as a tennis match, developing it from Antipholus's initial attempt to swipe Dromio with a metallic tray into a full-blown Wimbledon parody, complete with back massages, water swigging, and actual point-scoring (at one moment, Dromio announced the score as '40–30'). In this kind of performance, the standard Globe practice of changing tactics in order to achieve an objective becomes wild, mischievous, playful and clown-like.

Later directors, 2001–2005

The directors who came to the Globe during the second half of the Rylance era seem largely to have adopted what had by this point become the theatre's dominant style, though of course they continued to add their own touches. Barry Kyle, an Associate Director of the Royal Shakespeare Company, directed *King Lear* in 2001 and *Richard III* in 2003 (he also started to direct *The Taming of the Shrew* in 2003, more of which in Chapter 4). Like most of his Globe colleagues, his main priority was 'clarity and intensity of objectives', though the *King Lear* Research Bulletin shows that he felt it important that actors should 'strike a balance between playing a motive, and communicating to the audience' (Bessell 2002a: 67, 12). Kyle's process involved a great deal of discussion and attention to the language of the plays, as well as improvisation and ensemble-building exercises. When Kathryn Hunter played the title role in Kyle's *Richard III*, the two seem to have found common ground in their shared interest in game-like dramaturgy: Amanda Harris, who played Buckingham, reports that she and Hunter played out a 40-minute improvisation exploring 'how far Buckingham would go in supporting Richard' using only the word 'OK', and the various tactics employed by Hunter's Richard during this game made the actors realize that Richard and Buckingham 'have great fun together' (2003: 5 May). One of the most striking aspects of Kyle's technique is the way he involved his actors in the process of research: the cast of *Richard III* were asked to look up the biographies of their own characters and the history of the Wars of the Roses, while the *King Lear* actors were each assigned a historical topic to research, such as punishment, law, or household management (Bessell 2002a: 15–16).

Tamara Harvey directed only one Globe production during the Rylance era (2004's *Much Ado About Nothing*), but can nonetheless be considered one of its central figures due to her regular work as Tim Carroll's assistant director on *Macbeth* (2001), *Twelfth Night* (2002, 2003), *The Golden Ass* (2002) and *Richard II* (2003). Mariah Gale notes that Harvey's process 'helps you discover the intentions at the core of your character without forcing anything on anyone' (2004: 18 April), and in many respects one can see her work as a direct continuation of Carroll's: once again, there was no set blocking for the production, and the *Much Ado About Nothing* 'Adopt an Actor' interviews detail such borrowings as the tennis ball exercise, 'trigger words', the interrupting exercise, the improvisation of offstage scenes, and the exercise in which actors point to the person they think their character is trying to affect (Ogbomo 2004: 18 April, 25 April; Sanders 2004: 18 April; Vazquez 2004: 2 May). Harvey also developed new exercises in a similar vein, such as one in which Ann Ogbomo (playing Claudio) was asked to stand on one of several chairs on the second and fifth beat of each line; Ogbomo reports that the exercise 'helped give direction to what I said and it also helped to place things', so that the concept of 'love', for example, was located on one chair, and 'war' on another (2004: 9 May). This exercise evidently continued the Globe tradition of linking verse analysis with specific acting choices. Harvey returned to the Globe only briefly during the Droomgoole era, to direct a short run of Laura Wade's *Kreutzer vs. Kreutzer* at the Sam Wanamaker Playhouse in 2015; she continued to work with Carroll and various Globe alumni on projects with The Factory.

The Rylance-era director who provided the strongest seam of continuity into Dromgoole's artistic directorship was John Dove. Dove directed *Measure for Measure* for Rylance in 2004 and 2005, and *The Winter's Tale* in 2005, but his specialism before his arrival at the Globe was as a director of new writing; it was in the latter capacity that he was primarily employed under Dromgoole, directing the new plays *In Extremis* (2006) *Anne Boleyn* (2010, 2011, 2012), *Blue Stockings* (2013), *Doctor Scroggy's War* (2014), *Farinelli and the King* (2015), and *The Heresy of Love* (2015), alongside only one Shakespeare (*All's Well That Ends Well*, 2011). In rehearsals for *Measure for Measure* and *The Winter's Tale*, Dove encouraged the actors to think of the plays almost as if they were new writing, stressing the contingency of the plays' events and asking the actors to think as if at any moment something different might happen, as Peter Forbes (Polixenes in *The Winter's Tale*) explains:

As we rehearse, John constantly asks 'Now what if this happens? What if that happens?' That gets us to think about the situation rather than trying to follow the character's psychology through the scene. Everything has to be led by events rather than psychology: as John says 'If you are being led by the event, you are playing Shakespeare, if you're led by the psychology, you're playing Chekov.' (2005: 28 April)

Dove is frequently characterized by his actors as asking lots of questions: 'Why is the character there? What do they want? What are they expecting to happen? What do they need to happen?' (Rylance 2004a: 11 May). Once again, a focus on character objectives rather than emotions is understood as enabling an emphasis on 'story' over psychology, and for Rylance, 'uncovers a sense of unpredictability and spontaneity in the playing' (ibid.: 11 May).

A different model of directing

As this survey of Globe directing practice indicates, while no two directors shared exactly the same approach, certain tendencies were firmly established by the end of Rylance's artistic directorship. Blocking tended to be loose and flexible; clear storytelling was paramount; actors were asked to identify and play actions in order to achieve clearly defined character objectives, and encouraged to focus on those tasks in order to tell the story rather than express emotion for its own sake. Performance thus became a game of sorts (sometimes literally, as in Carroll's *Macbeth* and Hunter's *Comedy of Errors*), played live and relatively unplanned. While the notion of character objectives is derived from Stanislavski, directors became bolder over the period in departing from naturalistic form, finding ways in which audiences themselves could be co-opted into the imaginative game being played. The next chapter will explore this in further detail.

It is worth remarking that questions of 'Original Practice' rarely entered into the rehearsal process itself at the Globe. When elements of OP were used by directors, it was primarily to further the goal of spontaneous, objective-driven playing: Carroll's use of 'cue scripts' during *Romeo and Juliet* rehearsals, for example, was entirely in keeping with his other, non-OP exercises in keeping the actors alert to the stimulation of their fellow cast members, and he employed historical research and re-enactment in order to a create 'believable set of Elizabethans' governed by a coherent set of conventions. Some productions departed from OP quite explicitly – Rob Conkie has called the 2001 season of *Macbeth*, *Cymbeline* and *King Lear* the 'season of anti-authenticity', and argues that the hostile reception of *Macbeth* in particular may have been due to the production's implicit challenge to hegemonic ideas about 'the character's interiority' and 'Shakespeare's universalism' (2006: 185, 212, 215).

The Globe also fundamentally challenged dominant ideas about directing itself. As the ensemble developed, the actor became an increasingly central figure in the making of meaning, responsible for making moment-by-moment inter-pretive choices rather than following a director's plan. Carroll explained in the programme for *Twelfth Night* that he did not see it as his job 'to make the moods of the play cohere': 'I am quite happy if I can make each scene sound as though real people are talking to each other; for the rest, I assume that the author knew what he was doing' (Shakespeare's Globe 2002). It might be objected that this is an attempt to shrug off the intellectual work of directing, devolving responsibility for the production of meaning to actors, audience, and mere chance; there is no space in this model of directing for conceptual work of the kind associated with the early RSC, in which a director would explore a political or social thesis through the prism of a Shakespearean play. On the other hand, one could argue that the absence of a directorial thesis is far from apolitical, and that in entrusting its audience with the responsibility to make meaning, the Globe took an attitude towards them like that advocated by Jacques Rancière in 'The Emancipated Spectator': its work called for 'spectators who are active interpreters, who render their own translation, who appropriate the story for themselves, and who ultimately make their own story out of it' (Rancière 2007: 280). The director's role thus becomes a facilitator of 'fruitful' situations, to use Carroll's description – a figure whose primary responsibility is to usefully pluralize a play's meaning rather than to pin it down. This brings with it new challenges for the theatre critic, for whom the identification and evaluation of a directorial concept has often been the default mode of writing about a production. That reviewers have often been unwilling to depart from this form of theatre analysis has, perhaps, been one of the main reasons for the shaky critical reception of the Rylance-era Globe.

3

Shared Experiences: The Actor/Audience Relationship

Shakespeare's Globe is often claimed to have inaugurated a new kind of relationship between actors and audience. On one level, such claims must be treated with some caution, since the Globe's playing conditions were nothing new to British theatre in the 1990s: shared-light spaces and thrust stages had been widely used since the mid-twentieth century; open-air performances of Shakespeare were a staple of the summer months across the country; theatres like the Swan in Stratford and Manchester's Royal Exchange had already demonstrated the potential of the polygonal, galleried playhouse with the stage at its centre. But the particular configuration of these elements at the Globe, alongside the theatre's standing audiences and popular myths about Globe spectatorship in general, combined in such a way that performance at the theatre produced a highly participatory mode of audience response.

It was evident from the earliest seasons at the Globe that the theatre invited a mode of spectatorship very different from the quiet concentration conventional in most theatres. During the Prologue Season, *Two Gentlemen* director Jack Shepherd noted that the 'sharing of the play' between actors and audience was 'more intense than is usual' and called the phenomenon a 'shared experience' (Kiernan 1999: 154). The latter term was used again the following year when Belinda Davison remarked upon the active attention she had observed amongst the Globe audience, both as an actor and as a spectator: 'you get a wonderful feeling that the audience is also in the play with you … It's a shared experience, being in a play and watching a play' (Miller-Schütz 1998: 29). The phrase resurfaced again in actor Chris Tranchell's description of his experiences as a Globe spectator: when performers like John McEnery or Mark Rylance 'identified with the audience as players like themselves', Tranchell suggested, it engendered a 'shared experience that moves the heart' (Bessell 2001c: 62). It is perhaps no coincidence, given his influence upon practice at the Globe, that Shared Experience is the name of the theatre company founded by Mike Alfreds in 1975 devoted to 'the actors' and audience's shared act of imagination' (Alfreds 2007: 22). This chapter will analyse some of the ways in which performance practice at the Globe exploited and developed this sense of 'shared experience', frequently building on the responsive, objective-driven performance style detailed in Chapter 2.

Audience response, architecture and culture

This aspect of Globe spectatorship was, in part, a response to the architecture of the theatre itself. The Globe positions its spectators in the same light as its actors, in relatively close proximity to one another, in a circular formation, so that most of them can see the faces of about three quarters of the rest of the audience. As the Swedish director and designer Per Edström has pointed out, an open stage surrounded by spectators distinguishes itself from the 'monologue' form of the picture-frame stage by suggesting that 'the theatre performance can be a form of debate, containing giving and taking' (1990: 17). There is general agreement in Globe actor interviews that the most enjoyable part of the stage for the actor is the front, downstage of the pillars – especially the two corners – since these positions locate the actor at the centre of the playhouse in the midst of the groundlings, and enable direct address to specific spectators. Actors often contrast these interactive downstage positions with the more remote 'hotspot' or 'King's spot' directly in front of the *frons scenae* and underneath the Heavens trap, a spot 'generally accepted to be the "power position" on the Globe stage,' explains Miller-Schütz, 'because all the audience sightlines converge there and the pillars cause the least amount of hindrance' (1998: 10). Polly Pritchett noted in 1997 that while this spot was 'a very strong position' for the actor, 'you're actually quite removed from people, there's quite a long distance' (ibid.: 32). In 2004, Alex Hassell agreed that while it was 'the most powerful place to stand', 'it would be quite difficult to stay there because the position feels so far away from everyone'. The stage perimeter, argued Hassell, was 'a more vulnerable position' and thus allowed the actor a more 'intimate' relationship with the audience (2004: 11 May).

These spots had been theorized before the opening of the theatre using terms borrowed from Robert Weimann's *Shakespeare and the Popular Tradition in the Theater* (1978). In his concluding lecture at 1995's *Within this Wooden 'O'* conference, Andrew Gurr called the 'authority position' the *locus*, and the front of the stage the *platea*, or 'subversive position' (Gurr 1995). His Afterword to Kiernan's Research Bulletin on the Prologue season (co-authored by Mark Rylance) speculated as to the meanings that might be produced by a Richard III who occupied the *platea* position during 'the first two-thirds of the play', entertaining the audience in a clown-like fashion and winning their complicity, before moving to 'the authority position at the *locus*' when he became King, forfeiting the audience's sympathy (Kiernan 1996: 24–5). While Gurr's predictions were partially borne out by both of the Globe's productions of *Richard III* (starring Kathryn Hunter in 2003 and Rylance himself in 2012), their accuracy turned out to lie in their description of the arc of the character's relationship with the audience rather than of any particular use of stage space. Gurr's classification of the stage space may in fact be something of a simplification of Weimann's theory, which suggests that Elizabethan drama staged 'a flexible relationship between the play world and the real world' rather than any 'confrontation' or 'serious opposition' between them, and that it developed 'certain conventions of speech and movement that roughly correspond to *locus* and *platea*' rather than employing particular parts of the stage for contrasting effects (1978: 83). As time went on, practice at the Globe started to complicate this neat categorization of space: the *Merchant of Venice* Research Bulletin, for example, notes that Marcello Magni used the *locus* or 'authority position' during his irreverent performance as the clown Launcelot Gobbo in order to better 'include the playgoers at the sides of the stage on three levels' (Kiernan 1998b: 15). Perhaps the position is better understood not as one that necessarily grants its *characters* authority, but rather as the spot at which the performer can most easily command the whole space; a position on the perimeter, on the other hand, encourages actors to make appeals to specific sections of the audience, or even individual spectators, to the exclusion of others.

Groundlings and seated spectators were often addressed in different ways by the actors, and some Globe practitioners report a difference between the sorts of reactions that tended to predominate amongst the two groups. A recurring theme in Globe interviews is a worry that actors tend to focus too much on the groundlings at the expense of the other spectators: the groundlings are, after all, the closest to the performers, part of the stage picture in a way that seated spectators are not, and the act of standing up itself probably encourages a more participatory response than sitting down (audiences generally stand at festivals, pop concerts and carnivals; they tend to sit in front of screen media or at events that require their silence). *A Chaste Maid in Cheapside* director Malcolm McKay noted that the vocal participation of the groundlings made it 'tempting to play to them mostly', and easy to forget that their response was 'not necessarily the response of the audience as a whole' (Kiernan 1999: 21). It was a simple fact that the audience members standing in the yard had paid less for their tickets than those seated in the galleries, and this was sometimes exploited for comic effect. Magni's Launcelot Gobbo, for example, put his conundrum about whether or not he should stay in Shylock's employment to a show of hands from the audience: in the performance recorded on video for the Globe archive, he observes that while the yard seems to be in favour of his leaving a miserly employer, 'nobody in the galleries' has put their hands up. 'That's because you're all rich, you are!' he concludes, and when several gallery spectators raise their hands in favour of his staying, he encourages a bout of playful booing from the yard (Shakespeare's Globe 1998c). In 2002's *Twelfth Night*, on the other hand, Timothy Walker's Malvolio wanted nothing to do with the groundlings, sneering at or recoiling from their laughter and trying desperately to impress 'the most important people in the theatre, those who pay the most money and sit in the Lords Rooms' (Walker 2002: 22 April). His disdain added a further layer of comic conflict to the play.

The architecture of the auditorium began to be loosely theorized by members of the Globe company as their work developed. Around the 2000 and 2001 seasons, actors began to talk about the upper gallery, the lower and middle galleries and the yard as, respectively, the 'head', 'heart' and 'guts' of the theatre (the idea is ascribed in different interviews to both Giles Block and Mark Rylance). Terry McGinity explained in 2000 that addressing each section 'has a different quality', and warned that despite the temptation to play exclusively to the 'belly', actors needed to 'pay heed to the "heart", the middle tier and the "intellect", the top tier' (Bessell 2001c: 50). Jasper Britton pointed out that whereas he had tended to speak to the 'guts' of the audience as Caliban in 2000, when he returned

Figure 4   *Jasper Britton as Macbeth (2001). Photograph by Donald Cooper. Shakespeare's Globe: Archive.*

to play Macbeth the following year he was more comfortable addressing the character's 'high' thoughts at the beginning of the play to the upper gallery, working his way downwards 'as Macbeth's thoughts do' (Britton 2001: 11 June) (Figure 4). Speaking over the groundlings' heads, he found, paradoxically drew them in even more (Bessell 2002d: 16). This spatial symbolism may owe something to the ideas of Michael Chekhov, for whom, as Tom Cornford explains, the head corresponds to thought, the arms and chest to feelings, and the hips, legs and feet to will (2012: 498; Chekhov 2002: 78–82); Tim Carroll likewise suggests that for Rylance, the yard was 'the source of the appetite', while the people in the lower and middle galleries were the heart, 'intent on the emotions of the piece', and those in the upper gallery, the mind, 'appreciating the wit of the play' (2008: 41). Any suggestion that spectators in the yard would be incapable of an intellectual reaction, or that those in the upper gallery would be uninterested in an instinctive one, is of course highly questionable: in an interview with me, James Garnon said he resisted the idea that the 'high-minded' lines should be directed upwards and coarse ones to the yard, and noted that Rylance himself was particularly adept at subverting this tendency (Garnon 2006). Nonetheless, the frequency with which the discourse of the theatre's 'head', 'heart' and 'guts' recurs in Globe interviews indicates that certain kinds of responses may indeed have predominated in particular parts of the theatre, and the auditorium may well have been codified by the ways in which actors chose to address it.

Globe audiences do not arrive at the space without preconceptions, and the theatre's early seasons especially demonstrated the extent to which audience response can be conditioned by those expectations. The media coverage of Rylance's inaugural press conference in 1995 made a great deal of his throwaway comment that he 'would be very happy for people to throw things and shout things' (*Reuters News*, 1 August 1995); two years later, he complained that a small number of spectators might be arriving at the theatre 'completely misled by inaccurate press material telling them that it is a requirement for them to boo and hiss' (*The Times*, 14 August 1998). Certainly some spectators arrived at the Prologue and Opening Season performances ready to heckle. Reviewing *The Two Gentlemen of Verona* in 1996, Michael Billington warned against 'the creeping danger of audience self-consciousness', arguing that the audience's insistent booing of Proteus 'went against the grain of Rylance's performance, which subtly highlighted Proteus's tormented self-hatred' (*Guardian*, 26 August 1996); Victoria McKee's overview of the season likewise complained that audience response at the theatre was not yet distinct enough from that of pantomime, and she concluded that '[t]hings have been too self-conscious at the Globe so far' (*Independent*, 24 September 1996). The following year, some company members worried that the audience participation was 'contrived' (Kiernan 1999:

112, 144). Anna-Livia Ryan noted that disruptive interjections during *The Winter's Tale* in 1997 had been more common at the beginning of the season than they were at the end, suggesting that this was 'because of all the articles that had been written' (Miller-Schütz 1998: 37), though Anastasia Hille noticed the same pattern during the following season's runs of *The Merchant of Venice* and *As You Like It*, and put it down to 'the actors drawing cartoon characters at first and gradually making them more three-dimensional' (Miller-Schütz 1999b: 12). Perhaps the two conclusions are not mutually exclusive.

The Globe's position within wider cultural frameworks also has a role to play in conditioning audience response at the theatre. W. B. Worthen has argued that the Globe 'occupies a performative horizon shared at one end by theme parks and at the other by a range of living-history restorations', and that spectators' modes of behaviour at the theatre – what he terms 'Globe performativity' – will be shaped 'by expectations, modes of attention, and habits of participation learned at these venues of popular performance' (2003: 86). By this argument, for example, spectatorship at the Globe might be characterized by what Robert Shaughnessy has called 'the kind of Disneyland double consciousness simultaneously composed of amused engagement and sceptical distance' (2000: 3). Indeed, Worthen felt that Rylance, in his performance as Hamlet, played the Globe audience 'in ways that capitalize on the expectation of "ye olde" merriment as a crucial part of Globe performance' (2003: 106) – though we will consider other ways of thinking about this performance and audience reactions to it later in the chapter. Spectatorship in Elizabethan playhouses has been the subject of numerous fictional representations in the mass media, most notably in Laurence Olivier's 1944 film *Henry V* (in which the first Globe is presented, as Douglas Lanier puts it, 'as the site of an idealized, democratic popular culture' [2002: 144]) and John Madden's 1998 film *Shakespeare in Love* (in which the audience of a fictional performance of *Romeo and Juliet* is depicted cheering and applauding freely, and gasping, laughing and groaning in unison as they become caught up in the story on stage). Certainly numerous reviews of the Globe's 1999 season referred to Madden's film, one of them pointing out 'a whopping ad for the video release' in the *Julius Caesar* programme (*What's On*, 2 June 1999) and another suggesting that '[n]ow that everyone has seen *Shakespeare in Love*, the box office is booming for this, the thatched theatre the man worked in' (*Express*, 27 May 1999). It may not be a stretch to suggest that spectators might have come to the theatre ready to enact, self-consciously or otherwise, the modes of participation they had learned from popular culture.

As time went on, the factors conditioning audience response at the Globe began to shift. Spectators became more likely to have had prior experiences of watching performance at the theatre, and members of the Globe company became both more alert to the pitfalls of an over-responsive audience and more adept at provoking the sorts of reactions they wanted to encourage. By 1999, reviewers were characterizing the Globe audience as 'resolutely docile and attentive' (*Evening Standard*, 4 June 1999) and its participation as 'mercifully now much less panto-ish than it was' (*Daily Telegraph*, 9 June 1999). The booing and hissing so common during the first few seasons slowly became almost unheard of. A change was noticed by the actors, too: Steven Alvey noted that whereas the 1997 season had been met with 'amorphous' and 'blanket' audience responses – booing, for example, whenever characters perceived as 'baddies' came on – by 2000, audiences seemed 'to have grown up a bit with the Globe', reacting more subtly to the nuances of the actors' performances (Bessell 2001c: 8). John McEnery reported an usher's observation that in contrast to the early seasons, audiences in the galleries in 1999 'just sit down and are very quiet'. McEnery found the idea 'a bit sad', and hoped that it was not true (Bessell 2000d: 22).

Talking to the audience

The audience's visibility meant that performance at the Globe became much more of a conversation between actor and spectator than had generally been the case in classical theatre. Like any audience, the Globe's provided actors with instant feedback on their performances through the presence or absence of laughter, silence, applause, coughing and fidgeting, but the Globe's shared light meant these reactions were more evident to actors and fellow spectators alike. Jasper Britton suggested that the Globe audience 'teach me where I'm right and where I'm wrong' (Bessell 2001c: 16), while Liam Brennan described them almost as a director, able to 'give you crucial notes on your performance if you are sensitive enough to pick up on them' (2003: 1 May). But often the conversation between actor and audience at the theatre extended much further than this. In the Prologue Season's *The Two Gentlemen of Verona*, Mark Rylance found ways of both provoking and responding to audience reactions in his soliloquies as Proteus: Paul Taylor observed that Rylance 'works the crowd brilliantly in such sequences as, fundamentally unconvinced himself, he tries to persuade us of his casuistical justifications for betraying friend and lover' (*Independent*, 24 August 1996); as Alvey explains, 'audiences would react in a shocked way, and Proteus' next lines seemed to respond to their response perfectly' (Bessell 2001c: 8). The Shakespearean text's ability to anticipate and accommodate audience response was one of the key discoveries of the Rylance-era Globe, in that actors often found themselves able to answer an audience interjection with the lines more-or-less as written. Jem Wall gives an amusing example of a performance of 2002's *A Midsummer Night's Dream* in which Paul Higgins, as Oberon, came on stage and said 'I wonder if Titania be awak'd' (3.2.1), to which an audience member replied 'She is, she is awake!'; when Higgins continued with his speech as if in dialogue with this response ('...Then, what it was that next came in her eye, / Which she must dote on in extremity' [3.2.2–3]), the audience member duly replied 'An ass!', to which Higgins replied (off-text) with a shocked 'No!'. Wall reports that when Puck subsequently entered to report that 'Titania wak'd, and straightway lov'd an ass', Higgins 'looked at the audience member and the theatre was in uproar' (Ryan 2002b: 8).

At the Globe, Shakespeare's rhetorical questions were no longer merely rhetorical. In 2004's *Romeo and Juliet*, as Kananu Kirimi's Juliet prepared to take the Friar's potion, she asked the groundlings, 'What if this mixture do not work at all? / Shall I be married then tomorrow morning?' (4.3.21–2). According to David Crystal, when one of them replied 'Yes', Kirimi answered with the next word of the text: 'No!' (4.3.23; 2005: 154). Sometimes these questions were more searching. In 2000, Rylance's Hamlet came downstage to ask 'Am I a coward? / Who calls me villain?' (2.2.506–7), pausing – and sometimes even repeating the question – until he had got an answer. As Bridget Escolme puts it, Rylance's Hamlet seemed to be demanding at this moment 'that the audience condemn him for being an inadequate revenge hero' (2005: 71). Four years later in *Measure for Measure*, Liam Brennan's Angelo, perplexed by his attraction to Isabella, turned to the audience to ask a series of questions:

What's this? What's this? Is this her fault, or mine? The tempter, or the tempted, who sins most, ha? (2.2.163–4)

Brennan, aware that 'there will be times when someone in the audience actually gives the character an answer', noted that the next lines in the script could be used as a response to any answer that spectators might give: 'Not she; nor doth she tempt; but it is I ...' (2.2.165; 2004: 4 May). Brennan found it 'really interesting' that Shakespeare gave this morally reprehensible character so much direct address, seeing it as an indication that Angelo should not 'be such a monster that you can't relate to him at all' (2004: 27 April).

Some roles facilitate this sort of interaction more than others. Performing in *Richard II* in 2003, Brennan noticed that the text was built in such a way that whereas Richard (Mark Rylance) was 'often seeking help from the audience', his own role, Bolingbroke, was not: 'he never has a soliloquy or private conversation that lets us know what he's thinking' (2003: 15 May). Some of the roles one might expect to facilitate direct address were discovered to be surprisingly lacking in such opportunities: in 2002's *Twelfth Night*, for example, Peter Hamilton Dyer found that 'Feste doesn't have that many opportunities' for audience interaction (2002: 22 April), while in *Much Ado About Nothing* in 2004, Sarah Woodward likewise felt that her character Dogberry had very few moments of 'direct communication' with the audience (2004: 23 May). But perhaps such opportunities are not fixed in the texts of the plays so much as they are determined by the choices of the actor. In *The Winter's Tale* (2005), Peter Forbes, noting that 'Polixenes doesn't have any soliloquies to the audience', decided during rehearsals that he was going 'to try to allow the audience in on the scenes without "playing out" to them'; just two weeks later, however, a few days into Previews, Forbes reported that the cast were 'sharing [their] thoughts with the audience more frequently' and exploring opportunities for this sort of interaction outside of soliloquies and asides (2005: 26 May, 9 June).

Globe productions sometimes cast their audiences in specific fictional roles. In *Henry V*, for example, spectators were addressed as if they were the English army; in *Richard III*, they became the citizens of London during the scene at Baynard's Castle. The most extensive casting of the audience in a fictional role was perhaps 1999's *Julius Caesar*, in which spectators were invited to step in and out of the role of Rome's plebeian population throughout the performance. The staging of 1.2's Feast of Lupercal was aimed at generating a 'widespread and far-reaching sense of riotous carnival', encouraging spectators to cheer the actors as if they really were the 'plebeian masses' (Bessell 2000b: 13). But as Escolme points out, almost as soon as this fictional role had been established, it was problematized: having been cast as a 'mob of Caesar-worshippers', the audience then heard themselves disparaged, as Casca complained of the 'tag-rag people' who unthinkingly applauded Caesar 'as they use to do the players in the theatre' (1.2.257–9). This repositioning of the audience, says Escolme, 'made for a wryly self-conscious crowd of playgoers, aware of the parts they were being asked to play in the fiction' (2008: 413–14). For his funeral oration in 3.2, Mark Lewis Jones as Antony cast the audience as the plebeians once again by addressing them directly, moving down into the yard to show them Caesar's bloodstained mantle, while the actors playing plebeians encouraged their audience counterparts to cry out 'The will!' (3.2.140). The following scene troubled this alignment of the spectators with the addressees of Antony's rhetoric even further, as a group of actors-as-plebeians, whipped up into a murderous frenzy by Antony's words, jumped up onto the stage and killed Cinna the Poet by dousing him in petrol. While most of the characters in the play wore Elizabethan costume, these plebeians wore modern dress – the jeans, baseball caps and trainers that might have been worn by actual members of the 1999 Globe audience. The implication of this anachronism, as Rylance explained it during rehearsals, was that the assault on Cinna was 'coming directly from *our* world'; the murderers, he said, should respond to the gaze of the spectators in such a way as 'to *challenge* the audience to *do something about it*' (Bessell 2000b: 35, 24).

But the imposition of this play-acting role upon the audience was not without its problems. The murder of Cinna the Poet was not always taken seriously by spectators: John Peter complained that the scene's 'phoney audience involvement' led audience members to 'smirk uneasily, watch how others react, giggle like schoolboys – everything except feel that the "citizen" is one of them and that they are taking part in the action' (*Sunday Times*, 30 May 1999). Noting that there had been too much laughter over the first few previews, Rylance warned the actors that they had

to work extra hard to stay *within the story* ... to cling to
their belief in the reality and integrity of what they were
doing, and to never allow themselves to anticipate and play
to those laughs. (Bessell 2000b: 34)

Actor Liam Hourican observed that as the run progressed, the
cast 'got more control over the scene', and he characterized the
early performances as a process of 'wrestling with the audience
... to see who had control of the play' (Bessell 2000d: 18). It
may be that the production's attempt to implicate the audience
had fallen victim to the irony that the role-playing imposed:
it required spectators to move in and out of their roles as
gullible dupes, encouraging a sort of cynical detachment at
the same time as demanding their participation. As Madeleine
North put it, 'Antony's rousing, manipulative speech to the
masses ... could not incite rebellion in this audience, who
spotted a spin-doctored speech from the first heavily-loaded
compliment' (*Time Out*, 2 June 1999).

Soliloquies, of course, provided Globe actors with a more
straightforward mode of direct address to spectators. It is
generally recognized that the kind of acting implied in the
word 'soliloquy' (literally 'talking to oneself') became impossible at the Globe: actors could not stare vaguely into the
middle of the auditorium and 'think aloud', since that space
was filled not with the darkness of the proscenium arch
theatre, but with the visible faces of spectators. Rather, in
the words of Paul Chahidi, it became 'obvious' that at the
Globe, a soliloquy generally had to be 'a conversation with
the audience' (Rylance et al. 2008: 204). Rylance tended to
describe this conversation as a form of audience role-play in
which spectators were addressed as if they were part of the
character's psyche: whereas on film, he suggested, the actor
'might *turn in* to speak to himself, in the Globe he might *turn
out* to speak to himself' (1997a: 172). Rylance has consistently described playing his own soliloquies as if the audience
were his character's 'soul' or 'conscience', 'that part of you
that is so silent and very rarely speaks back, that you long for

some guidance from' (Day 1996: 317; Rylance 1997a: 172; 2008: 107).

Tim Carroll understood the audience's role in soliloquies in a similar way, imagining their presence as a tacit agreement to 'think, and even (in your imagination) say, anything that you need us to', or to 'hold any misconception or prejudice that will give you a reason to speak'. He gives two useful examples in his essay for *Shakespeare's Globe: A Theatrical Experiment*:

> So the audience can silently say to Viola, 'You know about that ring, don't you?' To which she can respond, '[No!] I left no ring with her' (*Twelfth Night* 2.2.17). When Richard II is in prison, the audience may be thinking, 'Well, of course, a spoiled brat like you – you must be banging your head against the wall, wailing and complaining to the gods.' And he says, '[No, actually,] I have been studying how I may compare / This prison where I live unto the world' (*Richard II* 5.5.1–2). (2008: 41)

In the Afterword to the same collection, Gordon McMullan objects that Carroll writes here 'as if he were directing everyone in the theatre, not just those on the stage' (2008: 232). This is, I think, a misunderstanding of Carroll's position. Of course Carroll cannot *control* the audience's responses to the soliloquizing actor, but this is not what he is suggesting. The actor makes an *offer* to the audience, casting them as a body to be persuaded, appealed to, negotiated with, or rejected. In an interview with me, Carroll explained that he would usually encourage actors to think about their characters' objectives towards the audience in one of two ways:

> It would either be, 'Your objective is to persuade the audience of something, and therefore you have to cast them' – and that casting, of course, can change from moment to moment – or it was, 'Your objective is to work out a problem, and you need the audience's help'. (Carroll 2016)

Audiences are under no obligation to *be* persuaded, or to help in actuality – in fact the interaction is probably more dramatic, as Carroll's examples from *Twelfth Night* and *Richard II* suggest, if the actor/character imagines the audience to be resistant to his or her objective. All that is required of the audience in such exchanges is a willingness to respond as if the actor/character's desires were real. In his interview with me, Carroll noted that actors would sometimes alter the ways in which they played their objectives in response to the audience's reactions. At one performance of *Two Noble Kinsmen*, for example, when Kate Fleetwood as the Jailer's Daughter asked the audience, 'What should I do to make him know I love him?' (2.4.29), a spectator shouted out 'Send him a rose!' According to Carroll, Fleetwood paused for a moment to consider the suggestion, before wrinkling her nose at it, effectively 'saying "yes" to the offer by really saying "no" to it' (Carroll 2016).

As one might expect, Globe actors paid a great deal of thought to the appropriateness or otherwise of direct address at particular moments. Sometimes it was considered potentially muddling. Geraldine Alexander, for example, found herself resisting direct address during her first appearance as Ariel in *The Tempest*, noting that when she had tried looking directly at the audience during this scene, it confused the storytelling: it was 'an inappropriate moment' for direct contact with the audience, she felt, because at that point in the story, 'Ariel's seeing the sea and the world of the island out there' (Bessell 2001c: 6). Some soliloquies were, in fact, considered best played in the style associated with proscenium arch theatres: in a 1999 interview, John McEnery noted that while he felt direct address 'generally works much better' than 'sort of [throwing] the lines up to the sky', in some instances the latter was preferable. He felt that Enobarbus's death speech in *Antony and Cleopatra* (4.9.6–26), for example, was

> not the kind of soliloquy that you can really address to an audience. It's a man on his own in a desperate state, and

you don't need to make contact with anybody. I just look at the thatched roof for that one. (Bessell 2000d: 24)

McEnery does not mention the good textual reason for this choice: namely, that Enobarbus's death speech is entirely apostrophized, first to the night and the moon, and then to the absent Antony, leaving no space for audience address without confusing the identity of the addressee. The same Research Bulletin shows actor Paul Shelley mulling over the question of whether or not Antony's 'All is lost' speech (4.12.9–30, also partly apostrophized) should be directed at the audience, weighing the advantages of Antony getting caught up in his emotional crisis against those of the character explaining his feelings to the audience (Bessell 2000d: 29–31). Several actors distinguish between two competing strategies in such instances: as Harry Gostelow puts it, the actor can either 'draw the audience in' or 'go out to them' (Bessell 2001c: 9). Paul Brennen, playing Edgar in 2001's *King Lear*, argued that particular sorts of soliloquies facilitated each: 'magnetic' soliloquies, he said, 'draw people in to what you are saying', while 'electric' soliloquies 'go straight out to the audience'.[1] He felt that Edgar's soliloquies start off as 'magnetic' and 'become more electric' as the play goes on, while Edmund's follow the opposite trajectory – the implication being that as Edgar begins to develop a complicity with the audience (culminating perhaps in the Dover cliff scene), Edmund starts to lose his (Brennen 2001: 2 June). It is possible to see a much more nuanced understanding of *locus* and *platea* emerging in these descriptions of Shakespeare's dramaturgy, in which the interplay between a fictional play-world and the real world of the playhouse becomes not so much a facet of theatrical space as it is a dynamic use – and withholding – of direct address.

This flexibility seems to have been theorized at the Globe using the metaphor of the 'fourth wall'. In naturalistic theatre, of course, this term is used to symbolize the imaginary boundary that separates the world of the fiction from that of the audience. The 2000 season actor interviews reveal some interesting contradictions as to whether or not such a concept is applicable to performance at the Globe. For Kate Fleetwood, '[t]here is no fourth wall here and everybody knows that so there's no point in pretending there is' (Bessell 2001c: 23); Karen Tomlin, by contrast, reported that she 'had to build a fourth wall for both *Hamlet* and *The Antipodes*' (ibid.: 60). For Terry McGinity, the 'fourth wall' at the Globe was one that the actor was 'able to penetrate or push out':

> You can sort of extend it outwards or bring it back at various times, according to how intimate you want to be or how open towards the audience you want to be, so the feeling of a fourth wall is quite flexible. (ibid.: 50)

His fellow cast member Will Keen seems to have agreed, noting that it was 'possible to be incredibly naturalistic' and at the same time 'treat the audience as your mind, so you can sort of find your thoughts in the audience' (ibid.: 36). By 2005, Rylance was apparently advising his actors that if there was a fourth wall at the Globe, it was one 'full of windows and doors': 'You can open those and play out, or you can close them and turn the scene back in to focus completely on the characters' (Forbes 2005: 26 May).

Direct address makes it necessary for the actor to negotiate two separate realities at once – the world of the play, and the world of the audience. For some actors, this appears to have been a binary choice in which the actor/character inhabits either one reality or the other – Joanna McCallum, for example, described her single moment of direct address as Gertrude as the breaking of a 'little seal', following which the character 'disappears back behind that thin veil again into what is happening on stage within her time' (Bessell 2001c: 46). For others, though – including Rylance – it was possible to inhabit both at once. Rylance explained that at the Globe he had found that he could be both 'in the story and in the audience making fun of myself in the story at the same time', and 'flip between these two seemingly contrary realities as if they were one' (2008: 109). Jasper Britton likewise found himself able to stay 'inside of the character but [step] out of the play' (Bessell 2001c: 17). For Paul Shelley, the fact that the audience was visible to the actors at the Globe meant they had to be visible to the characters too; he observed, 'I don't particularly feel I have to distinguish between actor and character on this point' (Bessell 2000d: 29). The reader will have noticed that this chapter's discussion of direct address has had to rely several times on the clumsy construction 'actor/character' to describe the stage figure who speaks to the audience during moments of direct address; this is because direct address often collapses actor and character into a single speaker who is simultaneously both inside and outside the fiction.

It may be helpful to theorize this seemingly self-contradictory doubleness with reference the concept of *bisociation*, a term coined by the philosopher Arthur Koestler to describe 'the perceiving of a situation or idea... in two self-consistent but habitually incompatible frames of reference' (1976: 35). The theatre phenomenologist Bert O. States illustrates it with reference to performances of *The Two Gentlemen of Verona*:

> Launce's dog Crab usually steals the show by simply being itself. Anything the dog does – ignoring Launce, yawning, wagging its tail, forgetting its 'lines' – becomes hilarious or cute because it is doglike. The effect here is comic because it is based on a *bisociation*, in Arthur Koestler's term. (1985: 33)

The dog is inescapably a real dog, not consciously 'acting', and yet everything it does on stage must be read simultaneously as the behaviour of both the real dog *and* the fictional one. This 'intersection of two independent and self-contained phenomenal chains', States continues, produces a 'flash' which is 'equivalent to the punch line of a joke' (ibid.). Indeed, States's explanation of theatrical bisociation may be more applicable to Globe performance than Koestler's own is.

Koestler argues that in the theatre, bisociation depends upon the spectator's 'perceiving the hero as Laurence Olivier and Prince Hamlet of Denmark at one and the same time; on the lightning oscillations of attention from one to the other, like sparks between charged electrodes' (1976: 306). Koestler, accustomed to the conventions of the proscenium arch frame and the darkened auditorium, sees the fictional there-and-then as existing simultaneously but separately from the here-and-now of the actor and the audience. At the Globe, however, I would argue that bisociation works much more along the lines that Koestler characterizes as underpinning humour and joking: 'universes of discourse collide, and frames get entangled' (ibid.: 40). Indeed, bisociation at the Globe frequently produces a particular kind of delighted laughter.

This phenomenon is best illustrated with reference to the way in which real-life birds or aircraft frequently intrude upon – and are incorporated by – the fictional realities of the theatre's imaginary worlds. Globe performances are often punctuated by the hum of helicopters flying overhead, and the Rylance-era actors tended to see this not merely as a distraction to deal with, but an 'offer'. In 2002's *A Midsummer Night's Dream*, for example, the actors playing the mechanicals would frequently break and look up whenever a helicopter passed by, treating it (in Patrick Lennox's words) as 'just another weird demon that's responsible for Bottom's transformation' (Ryan 2002b: 19). In a performance of *The Tempest* I saw in 2005, Mark Rylance's Stephano and Edward Hogg's Trinculo dropped what they were doing in order to wave at a passing helicopter for 'rescue'. The presence of pigeons and other birds was generally dealt with in a similar way. David Phelan noted in 2000 that he had often seen Rylance 'quite openly just watch a bird as it flies past, as though that is happening in the "real life" of the play' (Bessell 2001c: 56). The following year, Jasper Britton recounted the story of an occasion on which Eve Best was able to refer to a noisy seagull on her lines 'The raven himself is hoarse / That croaks the fatal entrance of Duncan / Under my battlements' (*Macbeth*

1.5.38–40; 2001: 11 June). Audiences tend to respond to such moments with laughter, enjoying the quick-wittedness of the improvising actors at the same time as recognizing the way in which the intrusion has been accommodated into the fictional world. Tim Carroll remembers a moment in which Britton's Macbeth responded to a pigeon that had landed on the stage: Britton looked at the bird 'as though its landing merely summed up the undignified absurdity of life' and then went on to refer to it as if it were the 'poor player, / That struts and frets his hour upon the stage' (5.5.23–4; Carroll 2008: 39). The audience laughter prompted by this moment of invention was not, says Carroll, 'a dismissive or empty response', but rather indicative of 'a moment of beautiful revelation' (2008: 39–40). He explained to me that he found himself able to distinguish those actors he wanted to work with from those he did not by their reactions to such intrusions: 'I noticed that the actors I didn't want to work with were the actors who pretended that it hadn't happened' (Carroll 2016).

Negotiating with the audience

Reviewing the Opening Season for *Shakespeare Survey*, Michael Cordner observed that the audience at the Globe had been 'empowered in a wholly unfamiliar, exhilarating, unpredictable, and sometimes perilous way', and noted that 'these new performer/spectator dynamics' would require actors who could 'relish' and 'exploit' this fact while simultaneously 'sustaining the credibility and intensity of their characters' involvement in the unfolding narrative' (1998: 206). Members of the Globe company had in fact already begun to grapple with this challenge. Despite their instruction from director David Freeman 'to be remote from the world around them and completely engrossed in the two worlds [Sicily and Bohemia] created on stage', cast members of *The Winter's Tale* had started to think about ways in which direct address to the audience could help them to achieve their characters' objectives (Miller-Schütz 1998: 10). Belinda Davison, for example, reports that as Hermione, she tended to look to the audience for 'someone I can appeal to', treating them as impartial witnesses by whom the character feels increasingly betrayed (ibid.: 29). Michael Gould's Polixenes used the audience similarly in his scene with Florizel (4.4), attempting to 'get them on my side, on the side of a father' (ibid.: 41).

Actors continued to explore these sorts of objective-driven interactions with the audience in subsequent seasons. In 1999, Danny Sapani described Brutus's soliloquies in *Julius Caesar* as speeches in which the character 'throws out thoughts and ideas that are not yet concluded or even justified in his own mind, and he waits for a response of some kind'; Sapani noted that sometimes 'the response may be so strong that he needs to change his mind, or reconsider something' (Bessell 2000d: 27). Philippa Stanton found herself including spectators more and more in her performance as Hermia in 2002's *A Midsummer Night's Dream*, playing her line 'Lysander riddles very prettily' (2.2.52) to the audience, for example, as an attempt 'to explain her momentary consideration' of his offer to share a bed, while her line 'Now I perceive that she hath made compare / Between our statures' (3.2.290–1) became an 'appeal to the audience for judgement' during her argument with Helena (2002: 31 August). Stanton's decisions in this respect are especially interesting because earlier in rehearsals she had considered Hermia 'such a contained and focused character that she doesn't speak to [the audience] that much' (2002: 29 July). Like Peter Forbes in *The Winter's Tale*, Stanton seems to have adapted her understanding of Shakespeare's dramaturgy as she gained practical experience of playing at the Globe.

A picture is starting to emerge here of a dramaturgy in which stage figures, who are indeterminately both actor and character at once, desire and seek things – affirmation, support, understanding, advice, judgment – from the audience. As Escolme observes, whereas in the naturalistic theatre it is impossible for any character to desire or have an interest in anything outside the fiction, Shakespeare's stage figures have another set of desires and interests, inseparable from those of the actor. They want the audience to listen to them, notice them, approve their performance, ignore others on stage for their sake. (2005: 16)

Escolme uses the deliberately post-Stanislavskian term 'performance objectives' to describe theatrical desires of this sort. It is a natural extension of the kind of objective-driven acting style detailed in Chapter 2 that practitioners at the Globe started to think about the actor's relationship with the audience in similar terms. Geraldine Alexander, for example, felt it necessary to be 'as precise in your relationship with [the audience] as you are with your objectives in the scene' (Bessell 2001c: 6). Mike Alfreds, though he condemns actors who 'invite the audience to watch them trying to move, amuse, disturb, enlighten and delight them', does ask the actors reading *Different Every Night* to consider 'the characters'/actors' objectives towards the audience' and the role – 'confidant, sympathiser, judge, evaluator, someone to be challenged' – with which the audience is being endowed at moments of direct address (2007: 65, 256). Indeed, Alfreds seems to have asked Fergus O'Donnell to play Pisanio's speech at the end of 3.5 in *Cymbeline* as a moment in which the character feels 'he has behaved so badly that he desperately needs to justify himself to the audience' (Bessell 2002b: 65).

The act of *actually* asking for something from an audience (rather than merely pretending to) opens an actor's performance up to all kinds of contingencies. Practitioners and critics alike have often spoken of the 'spontaneity' and even the 'risk' or 'danger' of performance at the Globe, and while this is sometimes in danger of being overstated – the spoken lines of the play, after all, will remain largely the same from performance to performance – the audience's power to alter the meanings of those lines in the moment of performance is especially pronounced at the theatre. Michael Gould gave a useful explanation of this in his account of playing Edmund in 2001's *King Lear*, when he directed many of the character's questions squarely at the audience. As Edmund mulled over his precarious relationships with both Goneril and Regan, Gould/Edmund asked the audience, 'Which of them shall I take?' (5.1.58). Gould found that whatever the reply from the yard, the next lines of the text would accommodate both an interaction with the audience's answer ('Both? One? Or neither?') and Edmund's chilling conclusion ('Neither can be enjoyed / If both remain alive' [5.1.58–60]). He enjoyed 'the fact that the audience feel engaged with the problem, and then also have to face the consequence of their solution' (2001: 19 May).[2] However, as he explained in a later blog post, playing with the audience in this way is 'one of the most dangerous things you can do' as an actor, since 'you don't know how they're going to react' (2001: 2 June). He found himself in agreement with the criticism of the *Independent*'s Paul Taylor, for example, that the crowd's enthusiastic response to Edmund during early performances was in danger of turning the character 'into an undisquietingly likeable rogue' (25 May 2001). But he noted a caveat:

> If I was in total control, then I would be responsible for fostering that reaction in the audience. However, I am not in total control. There is a relationship with the audience. Edmund needs them to acknowledge his ambitions for the play to progress. I do not see this review as a negative criticism, but as a positive one. It defines and acknowledges the actor's relationship with the audience. (Gould 2001: 2 June)

In his earlier blog post, Gould had suggested that it was possible for the audience to respond 'a little too positively to Edmund', and recognized his own complicity in allowing this to happen ('After the first preview, I was totally seduced by the audience') (2001: 19 May). Nonetheless, the point remains that the vocal participation of the audience can have a major bearing on the way in which Shakespeare's stage figures make meaning.

Gould's account opens up a perennial question: the extent to which Globe performers should attempt to regulate the ways in which audiences participate at the theatre. Shortly after the Prologue Season, Rylance described his 'ideal' performance as one that entirely relinquished any sense of control over the audience:

> The ideal is for the performance to grow and for things to be discovered, something new every night. We have to let go of the idea of controlling the reaction. The audience should be free to react in different ways. (Day 1996: 318)

By the Opening Season, however, the problems of this openness had started to emerge. Spectators were booing the French characters in *Henry V*, and in some cases even cheering the announcement of the numbers of French dead (4.8.77–82). Kiernan reports a debate between cast members after the first and second preview performances: while one actor suggested that actors needed 'to learn to control' audience response, another argued that spectators had 'the right to respond any way they want' (1999: 113). Rylance himself tended to deal with any audience reactions he found distasteful by responding to them in character as Henry, turning his back on those spectators who had cheered the number of French casualties, for example, as if the offending group were the king's 'unruly soldiers, whom he despised at that moment' (Miller-Schütz 1997).

Similar problems emerged in 2004's *Measure for Measure*. During his confrontation with Sophie Thompson's Isabella in 2.4, Liam Brennan's Angelo suddenly seized her groin as if he were attempting to rape her. In more than one performance, the moment was met with laughter. Understandably, this was deplored in several critical accounts of the production: Alastair Macaulay cited it as an example of

the way in which 'the Globe audience clutches at anything
it can find to laugh at' (*Financial Times*, 7 July 2004),
while Sam Marlowe lamented the audience's failure 'to
register the shift in tone', concluding that despite this being
'a play in which women are humiliated, tormented and
coerced', 'here none of it means a thing' (*The Times*, 2 July
2004). In his book on the Globe, Rob Conkie objects that
Brennan's pursuit of audience laughter at this 'unwarranted'
moment invited spectators to regard Isabella's plight 'as
little more than laughable' and 'eschewed wrestling with
the play's more troubling aspects' (2006: 244, 245, 246).
In a post-show talk, however, some of Brennan's fellow cast
members revealed that far from seeking audience laughter
in this scene, Brennan was in fact frustrated by its presence
(*Talking Theatre*, 21 August 2004); Sophie Thompson
likewise reported herself as having been 'surprised' by the
laughter, and put it down to a nervous reaction on the
part of the audience (2004: 6 July). The phenomenon was
objectionable, but it is hard to identify precisely where
the blame for it lay: perhaps the problem was not that the
production endorsed misogynistic attitudes, but rather that
it allowed room for the members of the *audience* to do so.
As Conkie suggests in relation to the Globe's *Henry V*, at
least a distasteful audience reaction 'exposes ideological
"faultlines" in a way that rarely happens at, for example,
the Royal Shakespeare Theatre' (2006: 75).

   Concerns that vociferous audience responses might
unbalance a performance resurface throughout the Globe
company interviews. Carroll observed in 2000 that there
was a danger that actors could become 'intoxicated' by the
audience's laughter, seeking it as an end in itself rather than
because it helped to tell the story. In one instance, he said, this
had resulted in a performance of *The Two Noble Kinsmen* in
which 'the groundlings decided it was an out-and-out comedy,
and they were not going to allow anything to be contemplative
or quiet', and the actors 'felt that they had shot themselves
in the foot' (Bessell 2001c: 20). Actors tend to recognize

the primacy of clear storytelling as the key rule governing audience interaction: Patricia Kerrigan, for example, argued in 2001 that '[y]ou can't change the story that you're telling' and that at the Globe, there was 'a danger that the audience won't give back the focus you give to them' (Bessell 2002d: 24). Paul Chahidi felt that the Globe actor needed 'to try to bridle and control' audience laughter, because otherwise 'it can hijack the whole story' (Rylance et al. 2008: 205). Metaphors of 'wrestling' with the audience over control of the play recur in several interviews.

The gaze of the actor seems to have been a key tool in this power tussle. Kerrigan, feeling that the serious tone of the play was in jeopardy when somebody in the audience hissed her entrance as Goneril in *King Lear*, silenced the offending spectator by giving him 'a very hard look' (2001: 16 June). Amanda Harris found a way of controlling two over-enthusiastic audience members during the Baynard's Castle scene in *Richard III* by speaking Buckingham's line 'No, so God help me, they spake not a word' (3.7.24) as a 'direct command' to them (2003: 4 June). In a *Measure for Measure* post-show talk, Alex Hassell reported that he would often employ the tactic of directing Claudio's speech beginning 'Ay, but to die' (3.1.117) entirely at any audience members who laughed at its first four words, in an attempt to subdue their laughter (*Talking Theatre*, 21 August 2004). Ultimately, though, Globe actors seem to have recognized that the theatre called for a balance between delimiting audience reactions within a certain margin of acceptability, but responding openly to them within that – as Eve Best put it, 'making sure that you're communicating with them properly, so that it's neither them controlling you nor you controlling them' (2001: 28 May). Rylance argued in 2000 that actors at the Globe should feel confident to 'pause for a moment and wait for the drama that is happening amongst the audience to play itself out, before picking up and carrying on with the drama on the stage' (Bessell 2000d: 5). Anticipating Chahidi's metaphor of 'bridling' the audience, he suggested that actors might learn 'from people who raise and train horses' and 'ride the audience' without worrying 'if at times they want to stop and drink, or buck, or jump over something' (ibid.: 5).

Playing games

One of the most widely used metaphors for performance at the Globe is that of competitive sport. The comparison was encouraged by the Globe, in fact, before the building was finished. Globe Education collaborated with Arsenal and Millwall Football Clubs in 1992 and 1993 respectively to encourage local schoolchildren to draw a link, in Patrick Spottiswoode's words, between 'games and plays, players and actors and crowds and audiences' (Shakespeare's Globe 1993b).[3] As the building neared completion, Ronnie Mulryne and Margaret Shewring made the same analogy in their introductory chapter to *Shakespeare's Globe Rebuilt*, noting that 'something of the same blend of commerce and entertainment' related to both Elizabethan theatre and modern football, and hinting at (though not elaborating upon) 'shared practices and habits-of-mind' (1997: 16). Playing practice over the ensuing decade started to explore some of the ways in which these 'practices and habits-of-mind' manifested themselves at the Globe.

Most obviously, the analogy drew attention to the similarities between Globe audiences and football crowds. Early reviewers made the connection repeatedly, not always in positive terms: the audience of *Henry V* were 'buzzing noisily like a football crowd' (*Observer*, 1 June 1997); 'the atmosphere is one of the football match' (*Time Out*, 11 June 1997); 'the Globe's volatile dynamics' reduced 'the intellectual atmosphere to the level of an Arsenal/Tottenham football derby' (*Time Out*, 3 June 1998). Several of the actors interviewed in Kiernan's *Henry V* Research Bulletin made the same analogy, describing the Globe audience as 'the kind of crowd you get at a football match', the first night 'as if we were all at a football match', and the crowd's reactions to the actors' first appearance as 'like footballers coming out of a tunnel' (Kiernan 1998a: 26, 28, 40). Interestingly, though other sorts of football analogies recur in actor interviews throughout the period, the comparison between Globe and football *spectators* barely returns after 1997, perhaps indicating the gradual shift in audience behaviour discussed above. Conkie analyses this discourse as expressive of a desire to align Globe spectatorship with popular culture and, more worryingly, the 'nationalist-driven xenophobia and heterosexist masculinities' of modern football culture (2006: 70). But it is just as possible to read it in more optimistic terms, as Rylance did in 1997 when he argued that the Globe allowed 'the same easy communication between strangers' as a football crowd, among which he noted it had recently been possible for 'a perfect stranger' to turn to him during play and share 'his full opinion of the quality of the game and what should be done about it' (1997a: 171). In this respect, Rylance's observation recalls Bertolt Brecht's desire for a 'theatre full of experts, just as one has sporting arenas full of experts' (1977: 44). The suggestion seems to be that a more alert, engaged and even critical mode of spectatorship is made possible in the physical and aesthetic context of the Globe auditorium.

The most persistent football analogy in Globe actor interviews, though, is not between crowds and audiences, but between players and actors – most often between teams and ensembles. This seems to have originated largely from Rylance himself, though several other actors and directors used the metaphor. In this context, the likeness emphasizes the importance of both preparedness for improvisation and the role of the ensemble in determining physical focus. Rylance said in 1999 that he felt it was important for actors to have

the right preparation to come out and be able to play in a very live and present way, in a similar way to the way sportsmen are so lucky to be able to do, because they don't know the final score of the match, or the moves of the other players. (Bessell 2000d: 4)

Actor James Garnon explained the metaphor to me as Tim Carroll had to him:

Tim always talks about rehearsing at the Globe as being more like training for a football match. You know, you can't plan how you're going to play a football match. You rehearse set moves, there'll be things you're aiming to get, and if you're in certain positions on the field you do certain things … but the rest of the time, we're trying to keep it as fluid and as light as possible. (Garnon 2006)

In *Different Every Night*, Mike Alfreds extends the metaphor even further, pointing out that like actors, football players have a super-objective ('to be the winning team in their division or in the world'), and 'practise rigorously and develop their skills (their *actions* – dribbling, passing, heading, tackling …) to the peak of their abilities', in order to 'go onto the pitch with all their rules, roles, given circumstances, objectives and possible actions – and *improvise*' (Alfreds 2007: 141–2). In this metaphor, not only performance but also the entire rehearsal process at the Globe is analogous to professional sport.

For Rylance, collective improvisation has a distinctively physical manifestation at the Globe, requiring the ensemble to perform like 'a football team in which each player instinctively knows where to find another, sight unseen' (Day 1996: 271). He explained to the company of 2002's *Twelfth Night* that they should learn to 'pass the story' to one another 'like a ball', keeping their movements collectively focused in order to avoid distracting the audience from the desired point of attention (Ryan 2002a: 31). The same analogy cropped up in actor Jem Wall's description of 'lines being passed like a ball across the stage' in 2002's *A Midsummer Night's Dream*:

If I have a line, to make it work it is up to you to receive the line ... You have to make sure you are always available. You also need to be constantly aware of everything – your actions and movements – because they can either increase or decrease the focus from where it should be. (Ryan 2002b: 8)

This aspect of Globe playing is a direct response to the theatre's particular playing conditions: the actors' bodies do the work normally done by stage lighting in determining visual focus. 'Passing the ball' is a metaphor for the dynamic by which the whole onstage ensemble shifts its physical attention – and thus the audience's – to a new speaker, who must respond to this bestowing of focus immediately before passing it on in turn. It is perhaps for this reason that Marcello Magni has repeatedly likened the Globe performer to a sportsperson, calling the theatre 'an actor-athlete's space' (Bessell 2000c: 15), and noting the importance of warming up in the same way that one would in order to 'get ready to play a football match' (2005: 27 May).

The result of this sort of playing – the theory goes – is to bestow a sense of unpredictability on the theatrical event. The director and teacher Keith Johnstone invented the improvisation form 'Theatresports' in order to find a form of theatrical performance that generated the kind of spectatorial enthusiasm he had witnessed at wrestling matches, noting that the 'excitement of sport is maximized when there's a fifty/fifty toss-up between triumph and disaster' (1999: 1, 67). The playwright Sarah Kane similarly yearned for the kind of thrilling spontaneity in the theatre that she had witnessed at football matches, praising director Vicky Featherstone's 1998 production of her play *Crave* for creating an environment in which the actors could perform like Kane's favourite football team, Manchester United: 'when they fly, they take off together, and when they don't, the collapse is truly ensemble' (1998: 12). Rylance's own desire for football-like theatrical performance can be read in this context: 'even if you have a great production,' he has argued, 'it will not always be great on the night, any more than a great football team will always play well and win' (2008: 107–8). The audience, alert to the possibility of failure, is invited to find the moment-by-moment discovery of storytelling insights and serendipities all the more exciting. This concept assumes, of course, that an audience will be able to intuit that the playing of a scene is being improvised live, rather than repeated from meticulous rehearsal. While this is arguable, I am not sure that spectators *are* always able to tell; this does perhaps account for the importance of the more obviously unplanned moments in Globe performances, such as actors' reactions to birds, planes, or the weather. It may also explain why Rylance invited Britain's leading improvised comedy troupe The Comedy Store Players to perform at the Globe every year from 1998 onwards (a tradition maintained under Dominic Dromgoole); Rylance also engaged one of the troupe's best-known members, Josie Lawrence, to play Benedick at the Globe in 2004's all-female *Much Ado About Nothing*, and appeared with them himself as a guest performer at the Comedy Store in March 2004.

The clowning expert John Wright considers 'the notions of acting as play and theatre as game' fundamental to performance at the Globe (2006: xvi). Wright's own distinction between 'open games' and 'closed games' may be useful in unpicking the different (and perhaps contradictory) ways in which the concept of 'theatre as game' can be seen in practice at the Globe. On the one hand, a 'closed game' is one with set rules, as in Johnstone's Theatresports (Wright 2006: 82). Applied to mimetic drama, this concept of 'game' introduces an element of competition between the actor/characters, and Wright discusses this competition in terms remarkably similar to the post-Stanislavskian terminology discussed in Chapter 2: games, he says, 'give you a simple structure in which to play an objective – and you must play to win' (ibid.: 88). When, in her Foreword to *Different Every Night*, Pam Ferris describes 'the push and pull of battling out a well-written scene with another actor' as being like a 'football match', she is using the metaphor to describe the process of actor/characters with mutually contradictory objectives fighting out a semi-improvised *agon* (Alfreds 2007: xi). Melanie Jessop gives an example from the Globe's *Romeo and Juliet* (2004):

I suppose each character wants to make the play and the story their own. The idea of competitiveness between Lady Capulet and the Nurse is particularly interesting. I think it's a competition the Nurse wins hands down – clearly, Lady Capulet has been involved in an ongoing battle to dominate this member of her household and she has never won. (2004: 9 April)

Rather similarly, Escolme suggests that *Richard II* can be performed as a 'competition for stage presence' between Richard and Bolingbroke in which the king's 'super-objective is a performance objective – to reach the point where his own presence in the theatre is more engaging than those who have set about to reduce his fictional power' (2005: 114, 123–4).

But not all games are competitive – especially in the theatre – and it may be helpful to think of theatrical game-playing not only as a contest between actor/characters but also as open-ended imaginative play between actors and audience. Rylance told the Globe audience in a 1998 programme note, 'If you feel like playing as well, we would love to pass the ball to you, join in' (Shakespeare's Globe 1998b). The metaphor drifts here from one of a competitive game with set rules – professional football – to an altogether different one of gentle collaborative play, something akin to a kickabout in the park. When Carroll describes *Twelfth Night*'s gulling scene (2.5), for example, as 'a game', he is not simply suggesting that Malvolio and the characters tricking him are playing out competing objectives (though they may well be), but that the actors playing them are asking the audience 'to be complicit in accepting something which is literally unbelievable' (2008: 38). Thus, in Carroll's version of the scene, the game of hiding from Malvolio was extended to deliberately ludicrous extremes: Sir Toby, Sir Andrew and Fabian pretended to be birds in order to cover up noises they had made, shuffled the whole box tree closer to Malvolio in order to eavesdrop more closely, and hurried back into it after he made a false exit and re-entrance (Sir Andrew even got his head stuck in it). The game, in this instance, was to ask the audience to accept that Malvolio remained oblivious to the other characters' increasingly obvious self-jeopardizing actions. It was a particularly self-advertising example of the sort of game the Globe regularly asks of its spectators, as actors assert that a bare stage is a moonlit forest, a tempest-tossed ship or a crowded battlefield – a game, in other words, of make-believe. At such moments, in Wright's terms, the game is 'declared' to the audience, and everyone present is aware that the actors are playing it 'so as to have an effect on the audience' (2006: 46).

The dynamics of play

Wright illustrates the dramatic potential of 'declaring the game' with a discussion of Rylance's 1999 performance as Cleopatra. The 'game' of this performance, says Wright, was 'clear right from the start':

> Here was a man dressed in woman's clothes, walking and sounding like a woman, with a face that was palpably that of a man. The key to his 'femininity' was a sable wig that he would occasionally brush away alluringly from his face. It was a rich and satisfying parody at first, and the early scenes of the play were very funny. (2006: 95)

These early scenes invited the audience to notice Rylance/ Cleopatra *playing* at the character's 'infinite variety', as he/ she switched suddenly from self-dramatization, to capricious playfulness, to weeping, to indignation, provoking audience laughter with every change. An ambiguity over who it was that was being so self-consciously performative – Rylance the actor, Cleopatra the character, or both – was, I think, an important part of the performance. Shakespeare's Cleopatra is, after all, a 'player' herself, acutely aware of the performed nature of her identity. She chooses to be 'sick and sullen' in response to Antony's mood, for example (1.3.14), and decides to step back into a different mode of her identity when Antony performs a different version of his: 'since my lord / Is Antony again, I will be Cleopatra' (3.13.191–2). At the same time, the Rylance/Cleopatra stage figure was ever-present in the here-and-now of the playhouse in these early scenes, sharing his/her reactions to the events of the play with the audience, and prompting much laughter.

The performance's climax, however, asked the audience to buy into a sense of the character's interiority. Following the death of Antony, Rylance's Cleopatra appeared onstage in a plain white shift, without her wig. The absence of the wig exposed Rylance's own short hair, which had been partially shaved, in clumps, in an attempt to evoke Plutarch's description of the grief-stricken Cleopatra as 'marvellously disfigured' and having 'plucked her hair from her head' (Bessell 2000a: 18). For the *Evening Standard*'s Nicholas de Jongh, this was both a meta-theatrical exposure of Rylance's masculinity and, paradoxically, a moment of 'authentic emotion' from the character (2 August 1999). Wright describes it as the moment in which the production 'touched tragedy' for the first time: now Rylance 'was Cleopatra with all the beauty, power and dignity that the role demanded' (2006: 95–6). He argues that its power was a direct result of Rylance 'declaring the game' in the earlier acts, and that it is 'unlikely that we would have felt such a sense of loss had we not enjoyed the game of a man having the audacity to play such an iconic figure in the first place' (ibid.: 96).

A particular moment in the production was identified by several reviewers as having facilitated this effect. The spectacle of Rylance's Cleopatra and her women hauling Paul Shelley's dying Antony in a canvas harness up to Cleopatra's 'monument' on the upper stage drew comic attention to the physical exertions involved, and perhaps to the real masculine bodies standing in for the fictional female ones; when Rylance's Cleopatra exclaimed 'How heavy weighs my lord!' (4.15.33), audiences tended to laugh loudly as if it were the punchline to a joke. Michael Billington assumed the moment was 'meant to raise laughs as well as a body' (*Guardian*, 2 August 1999), while John Gross described it as 'a piece of pantomime which solicits laughter from the audience, and receives it' (*Sunday Telegraph*, 8 August 1999). But Jaq Bessell's Research Bulletin for the production suggests that the creative team were initially surprised by the amount of laughter generated by this moment, and that it 'might have been disturbing to the actors, if it were not matched by a tangible pathos that filled the auditorium only seconds later' (Bessell 2000a: 19). Antony dies just moments after he is pulled up into the monument, and Rylance's performance of this scene turned Cleopatra's line 'The crown o' th' earth doth melt' into what Billington described as 'a sky-rending cry of despair' (*Guardian*, 2 August 1999). For Susannah Clapp, it was 'the high, piercing moment of the evening, the point when a switch is suddenly thrown and everyone is for a little while still and shocked' (*Observer*, 8 August 1999). Rylance told the *Evening Standard* that he learned to think of it as an example of the way in which Shakespeare 'opens people's hearts with humour and then plunges the knife in', observing that only seconds after the big laugh, 'the audience is suddenly, absolutely, silent' (31 July 1999). According to James Garnon, Rylance shared this observation with the casts of later seasons, noting that in Shakespeare's plays there was often 'a big laugh just before a major tragic moment, if you can find it' (Garnon 2006).

The impact of a switch from audience laughter to shared silence was observed from the beginning of the Globe project – Kiernan, for example, noted that in the first two seasons, '[a]t moments when the audience is emotionally moved and goes quiet, its participation is as palpable in its still silence as in its animated noisiness' (1999: 36). This effect remained a central tool in the Globe company's inventory for the duration of the Rylance era. In the first of the brothel scenes in Kathryn Hunter's 2005 production of *Pericles*, for example, Marcello Magni's Boult established 'a wild, interactive relationship with the audience', inviting spectators to play along as if they were potential clients and employees for the brothel – as Magni himself observed, at the Globe, 'that kind of involvement is immediately received with pleasure' (2005: 27 May). When he returned to the stage having acquired Laura Rees's Marina, however, the dynamic changed: Rees looked around at the audience as if they were 'quite intimidating' (Rees 2005: 27 May), and the scene took a much darker turn. Boult and the Bawd examined Marina's body in a clowning sequence which, when I saw it, provoked a great deal of laughter from the audience before suddenly silencing them:

> **Bawd** Boult, take you the marks of her, the colour of her hair –
> **Boult** (*peering under her skirt*) Natural.
> **Bawd** Complexion –
> **Boult** (*sniffing her armpit*) Fresh.
> **Bawd** Height –
> **Boult** (*squeezing her breasts*) Pert.
> **Bawd** Her age –
> **Boult** (*kissing her*) Underage.
> **Bawd** With warrant of her – (*Bawd grabs Marina's crotch as Marina screams*) – virginity.
>
> > (4.2.51–3; ad-libs transcribed from
> > Shakespeare's Globe 2005c)

The increasingly disquieting threat to Marina forced the audience, in Magni's words, to 'somehow step back': 'From being the naughty, anarchic servant doorkeeper, Boult becomes ugly and horrible' (2005: 27 May). In the next brothel scene, when he unrolled a rusty toolkit and promised 'she shall be ploughed' (19.170), the audience laughter sounded to me like laughs of horror.

But both the emotional impact and the ethics of such moments require spectators who are able to recognize a shift in tone and respond accordingly, and if they do not, an altogether different effect is achieved. When Hannah Betts reviewed *Pericles* for *The Times*, she complained that,

> when presented with the prospect of a virgin being about to be raped by a blunt instrument, the audience falls about laughing – not edgy, uncomfortable laughter, but great guffaws of hilarity as the child-like victim cowers centre stage. (11 June 2005)

As with the similar controversy over *Measure for Measure* discussed above, such moments are defined just as much by the audience reaction as they are by the stage business itself, and that reaction is only partly within the control of the actors and can differ wildly from performance to performance. I first saw Carroll's *Twelfth Night* in 2002, and then saw it again when it was revived the following summer. The first time I saw the production, I was struck by the poignancy of the moment in the final scene in which Sir Toby Belch (Bill Stewart) rejected Sir Andrew Aguecheek's offer of help, spitting a list of insults at him with spiteful cruelty (5.1.202–3); Sir Andrew (Albie Woodington) physically slumped, and then left the stage slowly, in electrifying silence, betrayed, lonely and unloved. I remember thinking it a stroke of directorial brilliance that refocused the whole climax of the play onto the malevolence and human cost of Sir Toby's mischief-making. The following year, I was surprised and disappointed to find the same moment – played in a very similar way – was now met with a comic 'aah!' from the audience, registering the betrayal as relatively untroubling, and effectively brushing it aside.

Globe performances have also made use of more gradual shifts from laughter to silence over the course of a play. In 2001's *King Lear*, Michael Gould's Edmund fostered an interactive and often comic relationship with the audience.

According to the production's Research Bulletin, Barry Kyle emphasized from the start of rehearsals that 'Edmund belongs to the world of the people, of the yard, not of the court', and directed Gould to begin Edmund's first soliloquy halfway up a pole in the yard, speaking directly to the groundlings around him, and springing up onto the stage as he resolved to take Edgar's land (1.2.16): 'He should come up through the yard to take over the great stage of kings, asking why he should be kept down' (Bessell 2002a: 21). Gould's Edmund remained in dialogue with the audience throughout the performance, identifying 'drunkards, liars and adulterers' amongst the spectators as if he were picking out his fellows (1.2.123–4) and co-opting them into his nefarious plans.[4] As we have seen, Gould played the line 'Which of them shall I take?' (5.1.58) in order to solicit audience responses – but at the end of this speech, as Edmund resolved that 'my state / Stands on me to defend, not to debate' (5.1.69–70), Gould played the conclusion as if he were 'rejecting the audience, telling them I do not want anything to do with them because I am going to be king' (2001: 19 May). This was Edmund's final soliloquy, and the character's refusal to engage with the audience as the play's tragic climax played out produced a dislocating effect: the audience's Vice-like collaborator had put an end to their fun together, and now they had to watch the results of the very actions they had been encouraged to enjoy.

Rylance's Hamlet (2000) provided one of the most sustained and complex examples of this effect at the Globe (Figure 5). In virtually all of his Globe performances, Rylance made use of an uncanny ability to share his subjectivity with the audience; Paul Taylor once described Rylance's characteristic stage persona as 'what psychiatrists would term an "undefended personality"', one who 'renders himself totally vulnerable to the audience and is therefore eminently approachable' (*Independent*, 27 April 2003). At the same time, Rylance has often described his own approach to acting as a dynamic between 'hiding and revealing', as he explained to BBC Radio 4's *Desert Island Discs* in 2015:

Figure 5 *Mark Rylance as Hamlet (2000). Photograph by John Tramper. Shakespeare's Globe: Archive.*

> Acting's a mixture of reaching out to people, which I would call a kind of electric thing – you have to stir and engage their imagination at times – and at other times be more like a magnet and drawing them towards you. (20 February 2015)

This dynamic was a crucial part of his performance as Hamlet, in which he alternately engaged the audience in interactive dialogue and distanced himself from them. As Taylor put it in his review for the *Independent*, Rylance showed himself able to 'create both a magically intimate rapport with the audience and an infinitely subtle sense of the progress of his character's inner life' (12 June 2000).

He started his performance giving little away. Hamlet's first line, 'A little more than kin and less than kind' (1.2.65), was delivered directly to Claudius rather than as an aside, and he began the first soliloquy, just as he had in his career-defining performance in Ron Daniels's production of the play for the

RSC in 1989, with his back to the majority of the audience. 'O that this too too solid flesh would melt' (1.2.129) thus became a private wish, a 'manifestation of inner life', in Escolme's words, 'overheard by the audience, rather than consciously produced in their presence' (2005: 63). When Rylance/Hamlet finally did turn around, halfway through the speech, it became evident that he had been crying; this was a stage figure who wished to *hide* his emotion from the audience, and was relenting only as he started to realize that he needed to explain himself to them – he began shyly, even haltingly. As Rylance explained, 'I found I could begin my first soliloquy with my back to the audience and gradually let them in to the currents of grief, in chaos beneath the surface of the character' (2003: 134). While Escolme and Lois Potter's accounts of the performance note that Rylance turned to take in the audience on the line ''tis an unweeded garden / That grows to seed' (1.2.135–6), in the performance observed by W. B. Worthen, it seems to have been later, on 'no more like my father / Than I to Hercules' (1.2.152–3).[5] The discrepancy suggests that Rylance experimented with different dynamics of hiding and revealing in this speech as the run progressed.

As the play continued, Rylance's Hamlet gained more confidence in his exchanges with the audience. Soon, he was able to address them directly: 'sit still my soul' (1.2.255) was delivered straight to the auditorium, as was his reference to 'this distracted globe' (1.5.97). The long speech beginning 'Now I am alone' (2.2.484–540) became a conversation with spectators in what Michael Coveney described as 'a master-piece of introspection, audience-baiting and sudden impulse' (*Daily Mail*, 23 June 2000). The various written accounts of Rylance's performance of this speech indicate just how open it was to the contingencies of Globe liveness. As Rylance's Hamlet reflected upon his own inaction and compared himself unfavourably with the player who was able to express such grief 'for nothing – / For Hecuba' (2.2.492–3), he approached the groundlings to ask them – and the whole auditorium – 'Am I a coward?' (2.2.506). At this point, his performance would vary depending on audience response: when Worthen saw it, somebody shouted 'No!' (2003: 106); whenever Carroll saw it, the audience remained silent (2008: 40); in the performance attended by Potter, Rylance added an irritated ad-lib, 'Well, *am* I?' (2001: 128); Conkie witnessed both a 'timid "no"' and a more confident 'yes you are' at different performances (2006: 38); audiences in the four performances observed by Escolme both answered back and remained silent (2005: 71). In *Play*, Rylance recalls one performance in particular:

> I remember a boy, no more than 12, only just able to look over the front of the stage from the yard, nodding his head when I asked, 'Am I a coward?'. I had to separate him from the rest as I proceeded to castigate them all for not calling me a coward. (2003: 134)

As Carroll points out, there was 'no doubt that he was really asking the audience', and this fact itself 'lent the situation an electric charge' (2008: 40). Rylance would respond to any interjections with his next line, 'Who calls me villain?' (2.2.507), making eye contact with anyone who answered 'yes', or looking elsewhere for a 'yes' if he heard a 'no'; he would treat an audience silence with contempt, as if the crowd were 'weaklings too frightened to take him on' (Escolme 2005: 71). The speech continued, and soon Hamlet was struck with an idea: 'I have heard / That guilty creatures sitting at a play … have proclaimed their malefactions' (2.2.523–7). Again, accounts of what happened at this moment vary enormously: in Worthen's account, 'Rylance eyes us, and the audience starts to hoot and applaud' (2003: 106); Dobson records an emphasis on the word *sitting*, suggesting 'a moral distinction between those who had paid up to be out of the rain and those who preferred to be closer up in the yard' (2001: 262); Potter, by contrast, remembers Rylance 'barely glancing in our direction' on the line (2001: 128).

Rylance continued to build on this interactivity in the next and most famous of Hamlet's soliloquies, 'To be, or not to be'

(3.1.55–87). Rylance had already discovered the potential of treating this speech as a dialogue with the audience in his 1989 RSC performance (Day 1996: 270). The Research Bulletin shows that for the Globe production, he initially chose to play the speech 'internally', since it was 'contemplative rather than discursive' in tone; when he moved from the rehearsal room to the Globe stage, however, the speech 'seemed much more opened out' and 'had a more reflective and discursive quality than could be seen in the rehearsal hall' (Bessell 2001b: 21). By the end of the run, he had become used to thinking of it as a conversation with the audience:

> [I]f you actually take it step by step, you know, 'to be or not to be, that is the question'; then imagine the audience saying, 'What do you mean, that is the question?' And go on, 'Whether 'tis nobler in the mind to suffer the slings and arrows of outrageous fortune', there is a sense of dialogue with the audience who are playing the role of Hamlet's conscience at that moment. (2008: 107)

By this point in the play, the audience had been rejected, appealed to, confronted, asked for advice, and their own reactions to Hamlet's speeches fed into the moment-by-moment choices Rylance made in moving the story forwards.

Rylance's Hamlet thus built up an intimate rapport with his audiences over the course of the performance, frequently both provoking and responding to loud bursts of laughter – he tended to pause for a moment after he accused the groundlings of being 'capable of nothing but inexplicable dumbshows', for example, allowing room for laughter and playful booing before adding, '... and noise' (3.2.11–12). But as the play neared its climax, his intimacy with the audience began to fall away. Block's production followed the Folio in omitting Hamlet's final soliloquy, 'How all occasions do inform against me' (4.4.31–65), so that for the last two acts of the play, Hamlet had no more sustained dialogues with the audience. Escolme argues that Rylance/Hamlet's retreat from audience interaction for this last section of the performance constituted a 'bereavement for the spectator' in which the audience was forced to 'say goodbye to the complex theatrical subjectivity of Hamlet, as he slips back into a simpler moral frame where there can be no questioning of man's inevitable fate' (2005: 73). Audience response was, by this understanding, no mere by-product of the performance – it was fundamental to the tragic arc of the play.

During its first decade, then, the Globe pioneered a kind of Shakespearean theatre-making that was truly radical in its willingness to open itself up to the contingencies of audience response. Theatrical, architectural and cultural factors combined to make Globe audiences especially receptive to invitations to participate, leading commentators to coin new terms for this new mode of audience behaviour: Kiernan preferred 'audience performance' to either 'response' or 'participation' (1999: 28), while as we have seen, Worthen discussed the phenomenon as 'Globe performativity' (2003: 79–116).[6] Experiments with visible, vocal audiences allowed Globe actors to arrive at a practical understanding of *locus* and *platea* in Shakespeare's dramaturgy that went beyond mere stage positioning, encompassing a dynamic withholding and granting of direct address, and a powerful interplay between audience laughter and silence. This mode of playing moved beyond any sense of a straightforward binary between the there-and-then of the story and the here-and-now of the playhouse, allowing stage figures to be ambiguously both actor and character at once – to quote Potter's description of Rylance's Hamlet, 'both inside and outside the play at the same time' (2001: 128). In this sense, *locus* and *platea* interplay became not so much a stepping in and out of the fiction (as post-Brechtian accounts of Shakespeare's stagecraft have often assumed) as it was a sustained game of imaginative bisociation. Crucially, the game-like nature of playing at the Globe allowed audience response to alter acting choices and play a key role in determining meaning. This did not always 'work', in that audiences often responded in ways that the creative teams – not to mention critics – found distasteful or politically problematic. But the act of foregrounding audience response in this way was itself deeply political, and the next chapter will explore the politics of performance at the Globe in more detail.

4

The Politics of Performance at the Globe

Academic writing on Shakespeare's Globe has tended to be dominated by debates over the politics of performance at the theatre. While this body of analysis is diverse and multi-faceted, it tends to centre on a handful of key questions. Does the Globe invite its audiences to indulge in a nostalgic fantasy of 'authentic' Shakespeare? Is this fantasy rooted in Anglo-centric and imperialist ideals, or does performance at the theatre challenge such uncritical nationalism? Does performance at the Globe, especially in its cross-gender productions, peddle stereotyped and backward-looking notions of masculinity and femininity, or does it reveal the 'performativity' of gender? This chapter will survey some of the academic answers to these questions, alongside the often very different answers suggested by the theatre's own practitioners, before arriving at its own conclusions about the politics of Globe performance.

The theatre was the subject of politicized academic critiques long before it had opened. This was in part due to the Shakespeare Globe Trust's protracted legal battle with Southwark Borough Council in the 1980s. The Labour-controlled council had initially been sympathetic to Wanamaker's project, but in 1982, a more radical group gained control and withdrew its support. The North Southwark

Community Development Group argued that the proposed theatre was an elitist enterprise, and that the land would be better used for council housing. The dispute lasted until 1986, when the matter reached the High Court, and after five days the parties involved finally reached an agreement. In a 1988 essay, John Drakakis characterized the episode as 'a struggle between a self-appointed custodian of high culture (allied with a property developer interested primarily in the commercial potential of the scheme) and a democratically-elected local authority' (1988: 27). He questioned the assumption that the Globe was 'giving Shakespeare back to the people' and accused Wanamaker of 'doing little more than rehearsing that fundamentally hegemonic strategy of constructing a common language and imposing it upon all, "whether cultured or not"' (ibid.: 33, 38).[1] Drakakis aligned the Globe project with other examples of 'reactionary populism' that work 'to obscure historical difference' in the service of 'what is basically a paternalist, aristocratic politics' (ibid.: 26, 33). A similar argument was put forward by Terence Hawkes four years later in his book *Meaning By Shakespeare*: the new Globe's pretensions to 'authenticity', he argued, could encourage spectators to 'forget about change and about the history and politics which produce it', asserting instead a 'true unchanging English culture' (1992: 142).[2] In the same year, Alan Sinfield's book *Faultlines* opened with a discussion of a 1989 issue of *Armed Forces Journal International* that included a full-page image of the 'original' Globe as part of an advertisement for the weapons manufacturer Royal Ordnance. Sinfield's analysis, which does not mention Wanamaker's reconstruction project, nonetheless shows how the iconography of the Globe was being used in the late 1980s as 'a legitimation of imperial enterprise' (1992: 6).

These critiques were written in Thatcher's Britain, before either New Labour's victory or the opening of the finished Shakespeare's Globe in 1997. They have, however, shaped much of the subsequent discourse about the theatre. Crystal Bartolovich's 2001 essay for *Marxist Shakespeares* understands the Globe project as a response to the cultural crises of 1970s Britain and the way in which the politics of the Thatcher years 'relied heavily on a certain celebration of "Englishness" and "tradition"'; the theatre could thus be read, she argues, as

> a made-to-order defence against the identity crisis which has troubled postwar Britain, offering its people a chance to discover, and, above all, possess, once again that ancient and settled national identity that the very name of 'Shakespeare' is supposed to conjure up. (2001: 190)

Like Hawkes and Drakakis, Dennis Kennedy worried that the Globe was glossing over historical difference, smoothing away Shakespeare's 'otherness' in the interests of tourism and 'late capitalism's global homogenizing commodification' (2001: 24–7). W. B. Worthen agreed, seeing the Globe as an example of 'the commodification of "pastness" within the economy of international tourism'; we shall see later in this chapter how he understood the Globe's intercultural performance work as embodying an old-fashioned colonialist attitude that was similarly touristic in its commodification of other cultures (2003: 29). In a 2005 article, Catherine Silverstone claimed that the Globe had 'become a showpiece, like Stratford-upon-Avon, for asserting that British Shakespeare is the most "authentic", where visitors are promised a nostalgic slice of the past for easy consumption in the present' (2005: 32). Her article focuses especially on gender, sexuality and national identity: the theatre's all-male productions tended to reinforce 'conventional associations between anatomical sex and gendered behaviour', she argues, and she cites the xenophobic audience responses to the French characters in *Henry V* as evidence that 'the Globe tends to reinforce rather than undermine such ideological positions' (ibid.: 38, 46). Rob Conkie uses a similar turn of phrase in his 2006 book *The Globe Theatre Project*, in which he argues that the Globe's *Henry V* and *Antony and Cleopatra* 'tended to represent profoundly conservative and unreconstructed perspectives of gendered and sexualised identities' and that the productions staged according to the 'authentic brief' reproduced 'profoundly conservative and pernicious ideological positions' (2006: 54, 221). Even the Globe's most deliberately inauthentic productions, he argues, were 'dehistoricised, mythologised, theatricalised and depoliticised' (ibid.: 216).

The view of the Globe's work that emerges from such critiques is hard to square with Rylance's own politics.[3] In 2002, Rylance became one of the founding patrons of Peace Direct, a charity set up to support non-violent conflict resolution. He campaigned vociferously against the international arms trade, using the platform of the 2002 *Evening Standard* Theatre Awards to speak out against both it and the newspaper's own willingness to print advertisements for the Territorial Army. He is a long-standing supporter of Survival International, a campaigning organization for the rights of indigenous tribal peoples, and of numerous other charities and pressure groups which represent the interests of the global poor. He was a high-profile protestor against the Iraq war from 2003, and in 2005 he deployed the iconography of the Globe in precisely the opposite manner to the 1989 Royal Ordnance advertisement, hosting a fundraising performance at the theatre for Human Rights Watch during which Rylance himself appeared as President George W. Bush in a scene from David Hare's anti-war docu-drama *Stuff Happens*. That a theatre led by such a prominent and prolific activist should be repeatedly accused of making work which was at best toothlessly conservative, and at worst politically oppressive, is a conundrum that needs some unpicking.

The answer might lie in the attitudes towards the politics of theatre most frequently expressed by Rylance and his core team. Asked in a 2005 interview with the 'health and healing' magazine *Caduceus* whether his work was moving 'into a more political arena', Rylance replied that

> [w]e need more people who promote conciliation and honouring of both sides, who question the means by which

they are resolving their issues. In a global village the time has passed for violent resolution of issues. ... Therefore when you ask whether I want to be more political, my answer is that I do, but I don't want to be just another angry person. (Peterson 2005: 9)

Rylance's priority was more spiritual in nature, he said: to 'provide some ritualistic movement to the year, primarily to help people to get a soul's view of what is happening' (2005: 9). For him, politics were inseparable from the spiritual. The 1999 Roman Season was thus 'dedicated to the question of Government both secular and spiritual', and the 2000 Hercules Season to exploring the 'transformational and healing properties of theatre' (Rylance 2000a). This is, perhaps, one of the key points of difference between Rylance and many of the scholars who objected to the Globe on political grounds; Graham Holderness, for example, cited Rylance's interest in mystical practices as evidence that 'an unillusioned grasp of history' was unlikely to be found at the Globe (2001: 102). Cultural materialist critics have tended to reject the notion that Shakespeare's plays are the source of unchanging truths about the human condition, or that Shakespeare's audiences shared an 'Elizabethan world picture' by which they understood the universe and their places in it. Rather, they argue, the plays were sites in which the ideological legitimation of a historically specific political order was both staged and challenged. Rylance thus ran the risk of marking himself out to such critics as a conservative thinker whenever he argued along the following lines, as he did in 1997:

As the first Artistic Director of Shakespeare's Globe, I hope we can provide theatrical experiences that reflect and enrich human nature in its many physical, psychological, spiritual and divine forms. The wide spectrum of the Elizabethan world picture may have assisted Shakespeare in creating drama that has proved universal in application, while remaining firmly rooted in Nature. (1997a: 175)

This belief in the universality of Shakespeare's drama certainly puts Rylance at odds with the majority of politicized academic critics on a philosophical level. Whether it means his theatre practice was necessarily conservative or ahistorical is another question. Conkie has noted Rylance's investment in 'essentialised and de-historicised methods of playing Shakespearean characters' (2006: 52), but this does not seem to me to be an entirely fair description of a practice that routinely sought advice from specialists in historically specific etiquette, clothing and customs. For Bridget Escolme, by contrast, Rylance's 'determination to put historical research into theatrical practice has often cut through the bardolatry that suggests Shakespeare is always our contemporary' (2008: 409).

Rylance and his team tended to shy away from making overtly political statements in their work. The Globe's most provocative move in this respect was to call its 2003 season the 'Season of Regime Change', a title that Rylance explained to audiences in his generic introduction to the season programmes as a reference to James I's accession to the English throne in 1603, but that in 2003 was also inescapably an allusion to Britain's military involvement in Afghanistan and Iraq:

> 400 years after that transition from Tudor to Stuart rule, and faced with a modern world which increasingly turns to violence in order to effect security or regime change, I offer you a season at the Globe which explores power and change on three levels: in our states, in our marriages, and in our relationship to the divine. (Shakespeare's Globe 2003a, 2003b)

In his interview with me, he explained the thinking behind this provocation:

> It wasn't an escape from now, coming to the Globe. We're doing these plays – we're not *interpreting* them, but we're *playing* them – because they resonate. I'm picking this

season because it resonates with the present time. Regime change was an idea that everyone was talking about, so here were a number of plays about how regimes change, for your consideration. (Rylance 2016a)

Any geopolitical parallels were veiled in the productions themselves, and barely referenced in the reviews in the press. The BBC4 television broadcast of *Richard II* on 7 September 2003, however, was prefaced by a series of interviews with the creative team that invited the audience to read the play in political terms without dictating what those readings should be: Master of Play Tim Carroll recognized the season title as 'an extremely provocative one' and alluded obliquely to modern 'parallels', while Master of Theatre Music Claire van Kampen suggested that the play's presentation of a leader precariously surrounded by opposing factions 'doesn't need me to say how relevant that is at the moment'. The next interview did so more explicitly: actor Justin Shevlin recounted that the Foreign Secretary Jack Straw, and Straw's predecessor Robin Cook – who had recently resigned from the government over the invasion of Iraq – saw the production on the same day, and were watched with great interest by the cast. Later, in an interval interview with Razia Iqbal, Carroll mentioned that he had frequently been pleasantly surprised by the modern connections pointed out to him by audience members, and observed that spectators were 'very quick on the uptake about the many ways in which Shakespeare is correspondent with today's events'. The Globe's line was thus fairly consistent: audiences were invited to think politically, but were not presented with a particular thesis.

This is in keeping with the Globe's attitude towards the making of theatrical meaning more generally. As we saw in Chapters 2 and 3, the Rylance-era Globe was home to a theatre practice in which 'fruitful' dramatic situations were played relatively spontaneously before an audience who would shape the way in which those situations played out by contributing their own responses. It is impossible, under such circumstances, for practitioners to fully control the political meanings of a production, dependent as those meanings are on the consensus (or otherwise) of the responding audience. The Globe is an inherently political space, in which crowds of spectators – both British and global – perform group identities by laughing, applauding, or indeed staying silent together. But claims like those cited above that there is any kind of *fixed* politics to Globe performance – for example, that the theatre tends to reinforce rather than undermine hegemonic ideologies – are difficult to support, given that Globe performance is more often a forum for audience expression than it is a one-way conduit for ideology. This chapter will consider two areas in which Globe performance has been the site of political debate – cultural identities, and gender identities – to explore this idea in more detail.

Cultural identities

As we saw in Chapter 1, much of the discourse surrounding the Globe's opening in 1997 was linked to ideas about British national identity, and the choice of *Henry V* as the official opening production appeared to confirm that the Globe itself was keen to encourage the connection. But the charge that the Globe was peddling some sort of regressive nationalistic fantasy of Britain (or perhaps England) would seem to be easily countered by the organization's outward-looking internationalism. Wanamaker had always been keen for the theatre to host visiting productions, drafting plans in 1989 for an annual 'International Shakespeare Festival' featuring 'approximately ten companies from as many countries' (Wanamaker 1989). As it happened, nothing on this scale happened at the Globe until long after Rylance's directorship, when his successor Dominic Dromgoole staged a one-off festival of thirty-seven plays by thirty-seven different international companies as part of London's Cultural Olympiad in 2012. But Rylance was, like Wanamaker, a keen internationalist, and his archive includes multiple boxes full of correspondence with international artists. A number of foreign practitioners were involved in the 1995 Workshop Season, and many of these performers and companies returned to work at the Globe later in the Rylance era. An early example was the Bremer Shakespeare Company, who had brought their all-male, German-language production of *The Merry Wives of Windsor* to the unfinished Globe site in 1993. They returned to lead four workshops during the 1995 season, and they performed a 'specially written masque' to celebrate the unveiling of the heavens over the stage during the 'Festival of Firsts' in 1997. Their co-founder Norbert Kentrup joined the Artistic Directorate in 1994, and learned English in order to play Shylock at the theatre in 1998.

The Globe's most public engagement with the international theatre community was its 'Globe to Globe' programme, a series of visiting productions starting in 1997 and ending in 2001 (before being revived some years later under Dromgoole). Companies were generally invited because Rylance felt that their cultural traditions might have something to teach the Globe about open-air playing, and often in order to tie in with a broader intercultural festival (such as the UK's 'Brazil 500' festival in 2000). The first production, in 1997, was Welcome Msomi's *Umabatha*, a Zulu-language adaptation of *Macbeth* that had originated in South Africa in 1973 and toured the world until 1982 (Figure 6). Set in the early nineteenth-century Zulu Kingdom, *Umabatha* drew upon the history of the warrior king Shaka to tell the tale of Mabatha and his wife Kamadonsela's conspiracy to murder their king Dangane. The production was designed to showcase Zulu culture, replacing the swords and daggers of Shakespeare's play with warrior shields and assegais, and the large cast performed interweaved sequences of drumming and group movement. *Umabatha* was followed in 1998 by the Cuban company Teatro Buendía's *Otra Tempestad*, literally 'Another Tempest', a loose adaptation in which various Shakespearean characters,

Figure 6   *The company of* Umabatha *(1997). Photograph by John Tramper. Shakespeare's Globe: Archive.*

including Shylock, Macbeth, Romeo, Othello and Hamlet, are shipwrecked on Prospero's distinctly Caribbean island, where they encounter female Yoruban goddesses who take the form of characters including Lady Macbeth, Desdemona and Ophelia. This irreverent, tongue-in-cheek production was once again dominated by movement and music, but unlike *Umabatha* it staged a deliberately provocative relationship with the Shakespearean authority of the Globe space (at one point, Hamlet groped the breasts of one of the statues on the *frons scenae*). The Globe to Globe show in 1999 was *Kathakali King Lear*, a translation of Shakespeare's play into the traditional Indian dance-drama form characterized by its highly codified gestural and facial expressions and its elaborate costumes and make-up. Adapted by the French choreographer Annette Leday and the Australian playwright David McRuvie, this was a deeply intercultural production that had been touring internationally for a decade. In 2000, the theatre hosted a carnivalesque *Romeu e Julieta* by the Brazilian troupe

Grupo Galpão that brought stilt-walkers, puppets, clowns and a Volvo onto the Globe stage; the show had originated as a street-theatre production in the early 1990s, and combined an early twentieth-century Portuguese translation with popular songs, circus skills and audience interaction. Like Teatro Buendía, Grupo Galpão had a strong seam of parody running through their production, a clown version of Shakespeare narrating, playing music and stage-managing much of the action. Finally, in 2001, the Globe welcomed not one, but two, Globe to Globe productions: a return of *Umabatha* in April, and a visit from Japan's Mansaku Company in July. The latter performed their *Kyogen of Errors*, the first Globe to Globe production actually to have been conceived with the Globe in mind. This was an adaptation of *The Comedy of Errors* to the form of Kyogen, a Japanese comic tradition based on stock situations and characters. In this production, Syracuse and Ephesus became Shirakusa and Kurokusa, 'white island' and 'black island' respectively, and the show was presided over by a narrator-like 'Lord of Misrule'. Time and budgetary constraints meant that the Globe to Globe programme was suspended from 2002.

To generalize about these five different productions would be misleading and pernicious, but it is worth noting some trends at the levels of programming and reception. Conkie quotes Susannah Howard, the Globe's International Development Officer, on the criteria that the Globe looked for in productions being considered for a Globe to Globe residency in 1999:

They must include a plot true to the original Shakespearean story, ideally presented as an ensemble piece in a style true to artistic, social and cultural traditions of and in the language indigenous to the country of origin. Since the language barrier could be perceived as a problem, experience has taught us that a strong element of physicality is needed, using colour, movement and methods other than speech, such as acrobatics, tricks and mime, to communicate with the audience. Live music is also a must (we don't ask for much!). (Conkie 2006: 147)

Conkie notes the 'competing authenticities' here: productions were asked to be 'true' both to the 'Shakespearean story' and to their own countries' 'cultural traditions', an injunction that in several cases proved entirely self-contradictory (2006: 147). For some companies, the very act of adapting a Shakespearean story compromised the integrity of the traditions upon which they were drawing: Conkie suggests that *Umabatha* was so close to Shakespeare's play that it problematized any notion of 'Zulu authenticity' (ibid.: 166), while Suresh Awasthi has argued that Kathakali's highly culturally specific codes and role-types 'cannot be transferred to characters from the plays of other cultures' and that *Kathakali King Lear* ended up misrepresenting both Kathakali and Shakespeare as a result (1993: 176). The Research Bulletin for *Kyogen of Errors* reveals that the production was a very loose adaptation of the Kyogen form, extending the typical running time of 20 minutes to 105, and importing the production's use of masks and musical accompaniment from the Noh tradition rather than Kyogen. In any case, to which originating cultures were the productions being asked to be 'true'? To try to locate a 'country of origin' for an intercultural experiment like *Kathakali King Lear* is already to misunderstand it. Kate McLuskie argues that *Umabatha*'s own attempt to essentialize 'indigenous' South African culture was a similarly simplistic misrepresentation of the country (1999: 156). Such a notion is reliant on a purist idea of fixed traditions untouched by other cultural influences, an idea which is problematic for all the same reasons as the claims to straightforward historical authenticity that have so often been made on behalf of the Globe itself. Both *Otra Tempestad* and *Romeu e Julieta* found much of their subversive force in a playful staging of *collisions* between cultures; in a preview article in *The Independent*, Judith Palmer described the former as an investigation of 'the space where worlds collide, the confluence of old and new world orders' (22 July 1998).

Globe to Globe's reception in the British press tended to construct the productions in terms of the physical and the exotic, often in rather simplistic terms. The *Evening Standard*, for example, emphasized *Umabatha*'s 'stomping, high-stepping warriors' and 'ullulating, hip-shaking females' (5 August 1997), while readers of the *Independent on Sunday* were told they would not go to see the production 'for its delicate psychological insight or nuanced interpretation of character' but 'for a truly exuberant night out' (10 August 1997). *Kathakali King Lear* was likewise characterized by its 'rhythmic foot stamping' and 'hypnotic drumming and singing', but while the *Evening Standard*'s critic found it 'as sensually invigorating as it is anthropologically edifying' (7 July 1999), *Time Out*'s complained that it proved 'frustratingly resistant to more than a simplistic reading' (14 July 1999). Numerous accounts of *Otra Tempestad* described the production as 'bizarre' and confusing, and many drew an eroticized attention to its topless performers: the *Evening Standard* previewed it under the headline 'Topless *Tempest* crosses Globe' (11 May 1998), while Charles Spencer of the *Daily Telegraph* found himself enthused by its 'highly attractive young women, who are sportingly topless for long sections of the show, cheering up the chaps and annoying the feminists in the audience' (23 July 1998). Several critics, looking for a political angle, found themselves frustrated by the production's refusal to draw clear parallels between Prospero's island and Castro's Cuba.

In his survey of press reviews of the first four Globe to Globe seasons, W. B. Worthen identifies a 'surprisingly uniform' reception in which 'Shakespeare's global visitors are represented as energetic, technically accomplished, visually stunning yet intellectually and/or artistically stunted' (2003: 153). A particular tendency was to marginalize the visiting theatre companies as parochial and behind the times. For the *Independent*'s Paul Taylor, Teatro Buendía's 'vocabulary of movement' was 'a little hackneyed', and their stage pictures, which included swaying poles to represent a storm and red silk for blood, 'scarcely shocking in their novelty' (25 July 1998); Spencer likewise found the use of masks and red silk 'wearily over-familiar' (*Daily Telegraph*, 23 July 1998). Grupo Galpão were similarly charged with having created a production that might 'have some social value' in their native Brazil, but was 'simply visiting exotica' at the Globe, as the *Guardian*'s Michael Billington explained:

> On a global level, ... the circus metaphor is in danger of becoming an exhausted cliché. In Brazil it may still have resonance. But in the west we have seen too many people, from Fellini, Brook and Anthony Newley to every avant-garde group you care to name, colonise it for it to have any residual life. (15 July 2000)

As Worthen points out, the implication of Billington's review is to cast European theatre as the sophisticated centre of global performance as opposed to the 'irreducible *locality*' of the Brazilian company: 'if they were really *global*, they would know that circus was last year's, or last decade's, fad' (2003: 160). Conkie surveys the same set of reviews in the first chapter of his book on the Globe, concluding that 'these acts of condescension work, probably unconsciously, to maintain the hegemonic structure of English, authentic, representational, and internally consistent Shakespeare' over 'Other, hybridised, presentational, and performatively constructed Shakespeare' (2006: 35).

The questionable assumptions behind both the programming and the press reception of Globe to Globe have led critics like Worthen and Conkie to conclude that the festival itself was something of a colonialist enterprise, serving to endorse white, Anglo-centric prejudices about non-Western cultures. His survey of reviewers' responses leads Worthen to assert that the festival was complicit in the 'Disneyfication' of foreign cultures, reducing what is complex and multifaceted in reality 'to a narrow range of metonymic signs' (2003: 157):

the exuberant black body = Africa; exotic flora and fauna and surreal magical realism = politically mysterious Cuba; colourful but inscrutable physical discipline = India (and Asia in general); lively but untutored street performance = Brazil (think Carnaval). (2003: 161)

Thus, for example, the force of the Globe *Umabatha* was 'to confirm European fantasies of Africa, its people, and their cultures, reified against the whitewashed background of tourist privilege, the privilege to decide others' meanings, the privilege of *owning* Shakespeare' (2003: 155). Conkie likewise suggests that 'the Globe-to-Globe programme casts those at the new Globe in the role of imperial patron or benefactor, where, as a reward for taking the authentic Shakespeare to the globe, the globe is allowed to return to the sacred, metropolitan space at the centre' (2006: 146). In his subsequent close analysis of the productions themselves, however, Conkie goes on to contrast *Umabatha*'s attempts to transcend cultural difference with *Otra Temptestad*'s more radical critique of the Globe's 'global pretensions' (ibid.: 161).

It is striking, and I think problematic, that these arguments rely on the reviews in the British press as a gauge of audience response. The assumption that Globe to Globe was inherently colonialist is predicated not only on the notion that British newspaper critics are typical audience members, but also on an assumption that audiences at the Globe are overwhelmingly white, Western and Anglophone. This does, I think, rather underestimate the diverse and international composition of Globe (and especially Globe to Globe) audiences. Tourists were always present in Globe audiences, and some productions, like Grupo Galpão's, drew members of London's own expatriate communities to the theatre in significant numbers. One of the reasons for the programme's shaky press response, in fact, may have been its decentring of the critic as the possessor of all the cultural codes necessary to understand the productions: three of the Globe to Globe shows played without any English-language surtitles, meaning that audience members fluent in the languages concerned had a conspicuous headstart on those who were not. A few critics acknowledged their loss of expert status, Jeremy Kingston, for example, 'craving to be told what lies behind the shifts in misfortune and understand the grace notes that will always escape a synopsis' (*The Times*, 23 July 1998), and Rachel Halliburton admitting that 'as an outsider', it was 'difficult to judge' the performance of *Kyogen of Errors* (*Evening Standard*, 19 July 2001).

Similar problems underlie attempts to pin down the cultural politics of the Globe's in-house productions. As we have seen, the vociferously nationalistic group identities voiced by Globe audiences during its official opening production of *Henry V* provoked consternation amongst many commentators; the French characters were booed and heckled, and spectators tended to cheer jingoistically for Harry, England and Saint George, leading both press and academic critics to conclude that the theatre was complicit in encouraging a backward-looking, uncritical nationalism. Cynthia Marshall, however, argued in *Shakespeare Quarterly* that 'rather than unifying playgoers through shared illusion, this production worked to factionalize the group by emphasizing differences'. She recognized that the production tended to position its audience as Henry's loyal English army: when the King instructed anyone who had 'no stomach to this fight' to depart, one playgoer apparently shouted 'we're with you, Harry!', 'to the delight and apparent approval of most everyone else' (2000: 360). But the Globe audience also tended to include a number of French visitors, some of whom, in the performance attended by Marshall, 'initially spoke out but became more taciturn as the evening proceeded'; Welsh groundlings apparently likewise interjected during the argument between Fluellen and Pistol (an especially loaded exchange, Marshall points out, given the production's context in the run-up to the 1997 referendum on Welsh devolution). 'Because individual spectators were empowered to speak,' she concludes, 'the audience as a whole became aware of the multiple subjectivities it contained' (ibid.). For Yu Jin Ko, meanwhile, the production was better understood as one that pulled its audience in and out of jingoistic responses, in a kind of Brechtian process of alienation. The audience's cheers and boos, he argued, indicated their willingness to 'see a good fight', but their chuckles at Canterbury's 'tortuous' justification for the invasion also acknowledged the 'flimsy grounds of the war' (1999: 115). Throughout the production, he suggested, the audience was 'reminded that it shared a privileged part in this game that Henry was leading it in' (ibid.: 116). When the game turned dark, as it did upon Henry's order to execute the prisoners, or empty, as it did when it became clear that the audience would not get to see any onstage representation of the Battle of Agincourt, Ko felt that 'the deflation of defeated expectations became palpable' (ibid.: 117). In different ways, then, both Marshall and Ko saw the production as one that put group identity into quotation marks, constructed it as something that spectators could slip into and step out of, participate in and problematize. But it is worth noting that once again, all of these conclusions rest upon the readability of audience response: the collective booing, cheering and laughter, the individual heckles, even silences or 'shuffling and looking about' (ibid.: 118). Reading politically at the Globe means reading not a stable performance text, but reading the audience itself.

Rylance was, in fact, keen for his theatre practice to break down what he called the English 'patriotic hold of Shakespeare', and he made a point of casting international actors from the start (*Associated Press*, 12 August 1995). The presence of American accents amongst the cast was a regular feature in early critical discourse about the Globe, and several productions drew from a wider pool of actors: in 1998's *The Merchant of Venice*, for example, Norbert Kentrup's German-accented Shylock shared the stage with an Italian-accented Launcelot Gobbo (Marcello Magni) and a Swiss-accented Jessica (Lilo Baur). In 2005, Kathryn Hunter's production of *Pericles* drew attention to the international composition of its cast, its ad-libbing West African-accented Gower (Patrice

Naiambana) at one moment pointing out the nationalities of each member of the ensemble in turn: 'A Hungarian, an Italian, a Nigerian ... Where are you from, Jules?'. When the actor concerned (Jules Melvin) replied 'Yorkshire!', the Globe audience cheered in response, and Naiambana turned to them to ask, apparently baffled, why it had been *Yorkshire* that got the applause. It was a playful but pointed attempt to problematize the cultural identity created by the shared cheering. Naiambana's Gower repeatedly invited spectators to connect the performance with global politics, interpolating references to Hurricane Katrina, the Middle Eastern refugee crisis, the Make Poverty History campaign and the 2005 G8 conference. The spectator was thus positioned alternately both as a humorously inward-looking Little Englander and as a concerned global citizen (though in reality, of course, they might have been neither). The production seemed to recognize that the Globe offers its audience no single, consistent group identity, but a variety, and that those identities have life only as they are enacted or rejected by spectators.

Gender identities

Perhaps the most strongly political aspect of the Globe's work during the Rylance era was its exploration of cross-gender performance. Six of the 'Original Practices' productions over Rylance's artistic directorship were staged with all-male casts, more-or-less in keeping with what is known of Elizabethan casting practices; as several scholars have pointed out, though, some (if not all) of the female roles would have been played on the early modern stage by boys, so the new Globe's practice of casting adult males was something of a misrepresentation of 'Original Practices'. The new Globe's tradition of all-male casting, which started with *Henry V* in 1997, was controversial within the theatre community, too: there are so few parts for women in the classical repertoire that depriving them of even these was, to many, indefensible. When the Globe staged two further all-male productions in 1999, including Rylance's own performance as Cleopatra, Giles Block warily observed that 'there are so few parts for women anyway, that I don't feel we should repeat the experiment too frequently' (Bessell 2001c: 15). Rylance was sensitive to these concerns, and had in fact been looking for opportunities to repeat 1996's one-off experiment in all-female casting (the Prologue Season's single performance of *Damon and Pythias*). Documents in his archive show that Rylance was developing plans in the run-up to the 1999 season for an all-female *Julius Caesar* to be directed by Kathryn Hunter, but this did not transpire: Hunter ended up directing a mixed-gender *Comedy of Errors*, and *Julius Caesar* became the Globe's second all-male production (Rylance 1998).

The following season, Rylance invited Vanessa Redgrave to play Prospero in a mixed-gender production of *The Tempest*. Rylance told the *Independent* that one of the reasons for this was because he had promised to 're-balance the nicking of Cleopatra' from female actors (19 January 2000). One might point out that a single gender-swapped role (or two, if one counts Geraldine Alexander's Ariel) in a play that is heavily weighted towards male roles even by Shakespearean standards is only a token step, but it was nonetheless a symbolic one. 'We have a lot of women who have had the experience of Michael Gambon,' Rylance observed, 'but there are not any parts for them to play' (19 January 2000). The Globe thus contributed to a growing series of high-profile castings of women in male Shakespearean leading roles, following Fiona Shaw's Richard II at the National Theatre in 1995, and Kathryn Hunter's Lear at the Leicester Haymarket and Young Vic in 1997. The casting of Redgrave led many to anticipate that the production would have a Brechtian edge, given her lifelong political activism and the evident disjunction between actor and role; the appointment of Master of Play Lenka Udovicki, an exile from her native Belgrade as a result of the Yugoslavian wars, seemed to confirm that this would be a production with something political to say. As it transpired, though, the production 'drew only indirectly' on Redgrave and Udovicki's experiences (Bessell 2001a: 5). Redgrave's was a surprisingly benevolent Prospero, and many reviewers were disappointed by the absence of any clear political angle. Paul Taylor, for example, had been intrigued by the prospect of the left-wing activist Redgrave 'impersonating Shakespeare's arch colonialist oppressor', but found the production 'curiously uncompelling' and 'more remarkable for its eccentricities than its political edge' (*Independent*, 30 May 2000).

Following a fourth all-male production in 2002 (*Twelfth Night*), the 2003 'Season of Regime Change' became the most important year in the Globe's ongoing experiment in single-gender performance. Four of the season's five productions were played by single-gender companies. *Richard II* and *Edward II* were all-male, though in both cases there was a consensus in the press that, as Patrick Marmion put in in his review of *Edward II*, this was 'a ruse that brings little insight and needlessly shuts out women' (8 August 2003). The same season's all-female productions of *Richard III* and *The Taming of the Shrew* provided a different story. The season's emphasis on 'Regime Change' has already been discussed above in terms of its nod towards global politics, but it became clear in the all-female productions – especially *The Taming of the Shrew* – that the season title was also inviting its audience to think about gender in political terms. *Shrew* was prefaced by a newly written prologue, in which the speaker reminded the audience that despite the trend for all-male casting, 'Vice-versa's very rare':

> But in this odd piece,
> The girls do get the chance to wear the codpiece.
> Our new production, crammed with female talents,
> May help in some way to redress the balance.

In a rather counter-intuitive decision, the Globe's first female company was led, initially at least, by a male Master of Play,

Barry Kyle. This had not always been the intention: Rylance had originally secured a prominent female director to work on the productions, but had to let her down when it became clear that she did not have the confidence of one of the company's leading actors (Rylance 2016a). Barry Kyle was available, and stepped in to direct both, indicating in an interview he gave to the *Independent* that he was excited by the opportunity in *Richard III* to 'rehabilitate the notion that the female voice is also a voice of history' (8 May 2003). *Richard III* opened to some success, but as rehearsals progressed for *Shrew*, it became evident that Kyle was having difficulties of his own – not connected to the production, but impacting upon it – and two weeks into rehearsals, Rylance had to find another Master of Play to replace him. This was written about repeatedly in *The Times* as if the all-female company had objected to Kyle on grounds of his gender (9 July, 11 August and 16 August 2003), but according to Rylance this was not the case – the 'personal reasons' cited in the press release announcing Kyle's departure were not a euphemism (Rylance 2016a). Rylance approached Phyllida Lloyd, who was a friend of Janet McTeer's (playing Petruchio) and had directed Kathryn Hunter (the 2003 season's Richard III and Katherina) in a *Pericles* for the National Theatre in 1994 in which Hunter had also played cross-gender. Lloyd accepted, and set to work immediately. Reflecting on the production some years later, she told Heather Neill that her experience at the Globe had been revelatory, allowing her to recognize that 'the themes of the plays can be released by a single-gender company, male or female' (Neill 2012). Following her stint at the Globe, Lloyd went on to direct further all-female Shakespeare productions for the Donmar Warehouse, and would revisit *Shrew* with an all-female cast, led once again by Janet McTeer as Petruchio, for the New York Shakespeare Festival in 2016. At the Globe, a second all-female company was assembled for 2004's *Much Ado About Nothing*, reuniting many of the 2003 company, this time under a female Master of Play from the start (Tamara Harvey).

When Globe actors discuss cross-gender performance in interviews, they tend to take a remarkably consistent line: the actor's task is to play the *character*, not the gender, and gender is often only incidental to that task. As Sarah Woodward, a member of 2004's all-female company, put it: 'when you're concentrating on understanding a complete character, their sex seems by the by' (2004: 11 April). Perhaps this philosophy should not be surprising, given the standard Globe approach towards objective-driven playing; indeed, numerous actors express the task of playing cross-gender in precisely these terms. Playing Viola in *Twelfth Night*, Michael Brown was 'consciously not worrying' about 'the challenges in playing a woman', focusing instead on 'what Viola wants, where she is, what obstacles she faces and how she overcomes them' (2002: 1 April). For Paul Chahidi, Maria was 'just another character that I am playing, who happens to be a woman', and all he cared about was 'what she wanted from the scene' (Rylance et al. 2008: 208). Chu Omambala treated *Edward II*'s Queen Isabella in the same way 'as other parts', focusing on things like 'how does this person react to a given circumstance?' and 'this is what I have to do in order to achieve my objective' (2003: 23 June). Hunter likewise approached the role of Richard III 'in the same way I would any other', thinking of him as 'a person slowly learning that it's impossible to operate without a conscience' (*Independent*, 8 May 2003). Her fellow cast member Amanda Harris felt that 'one of the worst things I could do in rehearsals would be to try and "act like a man"', and chose instead to focus 'on my character's intentions and objectives' (2003: 5 May). This is not to say that no concessions were made to gender when it came to characterization: the men playing women in *Twelfth Night* spent some rehearsal time thinking about feminine voice and movement, while Omambala recognized that as Isabella he was 'walking differently' and his voice was 'slightly softer than normal' (2003: 23 June). Playing Lord Stanley in *Richard III*, Penelope Beaumont made 'a conscious effort not to be overly feminine', though she noted that there

was 'a difference between this and trying to be "masculine"'
(2004: 11 April).

Reviewers were split over whether or not the Globe had
succeeded in rendering the actor's gender irrelevant to the
performance. Kiernan concluded after the 1997 season that
'audiences simply believed "Katherine" was a young woman'
(1999: 55), while in 1999 Stephen Fay found the men playing
women in *Antony and Cleopatra* 'consistently convincing'
(*Independent on Sunday*, 1 August 1999). Billington asserted
that Redgrave's Prospero 'transcends gender' and that 'for
most of the time gender seems irrelevant' (*Guardian*, 27 May
2000). Hunter's Richard III apparently made Lyn Gardner
'entirely forget that she is a woman playing a man' (*Guardian*,
13 June 2003), and John Gross found himself similarly
oblivious to gender at the following year's *Much Ado About
Nothing*, noting that '[m]uch of the time you forget (at
least I did) that the male characters are being played by
women' (*Sunday Telegraph*, 6 June 2004). Some reviewers,
on the other hand, found themselves unable to put the actors'
genders out of their minds. For Robert Hewison, Rylance
was 'so determined to avoid contemporary associations with
drag' in his performance as Cleopatra that he seemed 'not to
transform himself at all' (*Sunday Times*, 8 August 1999). The
men playing women in 2003's productions were, for some,
'obtrusively manly' (*Daily Telegraph*, 16 May 2003) and
'strikingly masculine' (*Sunday Telegraph*, 3 August 2003);
there were complaints that the actors' conspicuous masculinity set up 'distracting sexual reverberations' (*Evening
Standard*, 1 August 2003) and raised 'questions about sexual
identity that make few useful intellectual inroads' (*Daily
Telegraph*, 16 May 2003). Reviewers unimpressed by the
cross-gender experiment tended to reach for unflattering
comparisons with pantomime, drag comedy and school plays.
Thus, for example, both Rylance's Cleopatra and Omambala's
Isabella were compared with the drag performer Danny La
Rue (*Evening Standard*, 2 August 1999; *Spectator*, 9 August
2003); Redgrave was accused of 'pranc[ing] around the stage

like a Principal Boy who has stumbled into the wrong theatre' (*What's On*, 7 June 2000); many of the older male actors playing women were likened to Widow Twankey or Charley's Aunt. The laziest and most persistent gibe was to compare the single-gender productions with school plays, an analogy that cropped up occasionally in relation to the all-male companies but with a frequency bordering on the offensive, given the implications of immaturity and amateurishness, in reviews of the all-female productions.[4]

These accounts of cross-gender performance at the Globe rather understate the extent to which some of these productions explored the performativity of gender itself. Actors in the all-female companies evidently anticipated that the disjunction between the male characters they were playing and their own female voices and bodies would have a significant bearing on the way the productions made their meanings, and would show cultural norms about masculinity in an ironic light. Hunter told the *Independent* that she expected a battle scene between female performers to have a dislocating effect on the audience, exposing the hollowness of some of the myths of patriarchal culture:

> All that recent argument about the war in Iraq being a necessary war. Here, seeing a bunch of women going to war, with all the implications that brings, won't it be hard not to think differently, to question whether it really was a necessary war? (8 May 2003)

Harris likewise felt that Buckingham and Richard's political skulduggery would be 'made funnier by the fact that we are two women playing two men', adding 'another layer' – presumably an ironic one – to the story of 'two men playing the political game so coldly and viciously' (2003: 23 May). This approach became more overt when Lloyd took over *The Taming of the Shrew* and encouraged her cast to see the play as a satire on masculinity. Whereas Kyle had steered the company away from 'stereotypes or characterizations', according to Yolanda Vazquez, Lloyd invited her cast 'to do caricatures of these men' (Rylance et al. 2008: 202). Janet McTeer explained in an interview in the programme that 'as a group of women we can gently satirize men by exaggerating male behaviour' (Shakespeare's Globe 2003b); as Meredith MacNeill pointed out in one of her 'Adopt an Actor' interviews, 'when you've got a play that deals with female obedience staged by an all-female cast, it does lend itself to that sort of take' (2003: 23 May). Reviewers certainly picked up on this aspect of the production, noting that 'the male ego is satirised and male pretension gently mocked' (*The Times*, 23 August 2003) and that the cast made 'satirical fun of the way men walk, talk and misbehave' (*Evening Standard*, 22 August 2003).

For all the actors' claims to be playing the character rather than the gender, there was an implicit recognition of the performativity of gender in most of the cross-dressed productions at the Globe. The rehearsal processes tended, for example, to involve exercises in gendered movement. James Gillan, who played Iras in 1999's *Antony and Cleopatra*, found himself wishing that he had been given a 'crash course' in 'walking, talking, sitting and standing as a woman' earlier on in the rehearsal process (Bessell 2000c: 15). The men playing women in 2002's *Twelfth Night* were offered precisely this, sharing a session with Master of Dance Siân Williams on 'the different physiognomies of men and women' and 'how that affects their movement', following which they concluded that, in general, 'very stereotypical male movement occurs in straight lines and angles' whereas 'women move in curves on stage' (Rylance et al. 2008: 207–8). This generalization seems to have been adopted by other Globe personnel: Master of Movement Glynn MacDonald taught actor Jem Wall that, in order to play a 'high class woman', he must 'never walk in a straight line, always in curves' (Ryan 2002b: 7). MacDonald offered the same advice to the men playing female roles in *Richard II* the following year, adding that '400 years ago, a woman's clothing would have meant that she couldn't take huge strides, but instead had to walk using very small steps so as not to fall over her dress' (Shorey 2003: 18 April). She wrote in the production's programme that while a straight-forward demonstration of 'femininity' by the male actors would have been 'either comic or embarrassing', she hoped that she had helped them to achieve 'a level of subtle under-standing of womanly grace helped by precise attention to gesture and moving on released curves' (Shakespeare's Globe 2003a). The all-female companies worked in a similar way on 'masculine' movement, being encouraged to 'take up more space' and open out their shoulders (MacNeill 2003: 23 May). Marcello Magni worked with the cast of *The Taming of the Shrew* on the movement of male archetypes, while the following year, the Tudor Group encouraged the cast of *Much Ado About Nothing* to think about the ways in which Elizabethan masculinity was signified differently from modern masculinity, emphasizing 'control and refinement rather than suppressed power' (Ogbomo 2004: 25 April). In many cases, actors found their performances of gender dictated by their costumes, and those playing female characters often found it helpful to wear practice corsets and farthingales during rehearsals. Playing Katherine in *Henry V*, Toby Cockerell discovered that his dress caused him to 'glide across the floor' and made it hard for him to breathe (Kiernan 1998a: 25), while Paul Chahidi as Maria in *Twelfth Night* felt 'totally dominated' by his (Gray 2002: 7). These discoveries were not confined to male actors, of course: Meredith MacNeill, playing Lady Anne in the all-female *Richard III*, found herself learning how to move in an Elizabethan farthingale from the actors in the male company (2003: 15 May).

The gender politics of these experiments are thus highly complex. On the one hand, some Globe practices seem to have demonstrated a tendency to essentialize gender perfor-mance, distilling innately 'masculine' or 'feminine' behaviours, and, by repeating them, implying that those behaviours are simply natural and unchangeable. But by the same token, one could argue that such performances *historicized* the performance of gender, making it seem provisional, alien and culturally specific. The tyrannical restrictions placed on female characters' movements by their historically accurate costumes were plain to see, and forced the bodies of male and female actors alike to move in ways that seemed odd and unnatural. Many of the OP productions were drawing on early modern courtesy manuals for their movement styles, meaning that actors were taking on the often rigid and prescriptive gendered characteristics of the Elizabethan upper classes. MacNeill's Lady Anne, whose movement had been partly learned from male performers and partly determined by her costume, was described by one critic as 'confusingly got up to look like a drag-queen' (*Evening Standard*, 12 June 2003), while Lois Potter, reviewing the production for *Shakespeare Quarterly*, found it odd 'to see women playing men more convincingly than they played women' (2004: 451). There was surely no danger that 'conventional associations between anatomical sex and gendered behaviour' were being reinscribed here (Silverstone 2005: 38).

The academic debates surrounding the gender politics of the new Globe are neatly encapsulated in James C. Bulman's edited collection *Shakespeare Re-Dressed*. The essays in this book are multifaceted, but those dealing with the Globe can, broadly speaking, be divided into two camps. On the one hand, scholars like Melissa D. Aaron, Roberta Barker and Rob Conkie tend to understand Globe performance as having given expression to conservative views of gender (though it is perhaps significant that these critics consider only the Globe's all-male productions).[5] For Aaron, all-male performance at the Globe is guilty of 'toying with homoerotic *frisson* while making it safe for the tourists because it's "historically authentic" – even if it's *not* historically authentic' (2008: 151). Barker concurs, arguing that the Globe's veneer of 'authenticity' protects its spectators from becoming involved 'in an erotic encounter that challenges the boundaries of their definitions of self, desire, or morality', and she contrasts all-male performance at the Globe with productions like

Cheek by Jowl's *As You Like It* (1991), which she considers to have been more radical in this respect (2008: 67–8). Of the three, Conkie discusses the Globe at the greatest length, arguing that 'performances at the new Globe, especially those labelled authentic … are more likely to rehearse, maybe even to endorse and naturalize, unreconstructed ideologies of the early modern period' (2008: 191).[6] For Conkie, the Globe's 1999 production of *Antony and Cleopatra* 'revealed a stereotyped femininity constructed by a series of masculine perspectives', and made no attempt to resist or subvert early modern England's 'most blatant female stereotypes' (2008: 191, 194).

On the other side of the argument are those who see the Globe's cross-gender performances as more subversive in nature. In *Shakespeare Re-Dressed*, this perspective is represented by Elizabeth Klett, Judith Rose and James C. Bulman.[7] Klett is the only critic in the book to examine the work of the Globe's all-female companies, and she argues that in both Hunter's performance as Richard and McTeer's as Petruchio, the actors 'used their bodies to denaturalize gender' (2008: 168). Hunter's Richard, suggests Klett, was 'constantly striving to perform the part of a swaggering, cocky, sexually successful man', and he shared his difficulties in successfully performing this role with the audience (2008: 177). McTeer's Petruchio, meanwhile, was a more consummate masculine performer, but the 'simultaneous presence of both masculine and feminine signifiers' in her performance 'made it difficult to read McTeer's body as exclusively either male or female' (2008: 181) (Figure 7). Rose reads 2002's *Twelfth Night* in similar terms, suggesting that Jenny Tiramani's award-winning costume design was at the heart of the production's gender signification. The play's female characters (and Sebastian too) were presented in white make-up and silk wigs, and their costumes restricted their movements in some of the ways described above. The male performers were thus conspicuous beneath these highly artificialized signifiers of gender, which 'brought the performative aspect of gender in sharp relief';

Figure 7 *Janet McTeer as Petruchio in* The Taming of the Shrew *(2003). Photograph by John Tramper. Shakespeare's Globe: Archive.*

in Rylance's 'gliding, white faced Olivia', for example, 'the masquerade of femininity was fully apparent' (2008: 212, 221). Bulman's analysis of the same production tends to concur, noting the pre-show sequence during which actors could be seen inside the tiring house donning their make-up and costumes for the forthcoming performance and 'practising the prim gestures and gliding walks that would mark them as feminine'. This metatheatrical display, he argues, provided 'a mutual reinforcement of theatrical and gender artifice Brecht would have approved' (2008a: 234). Bulman agrees with Aaron and Barker that the Globe's transvestism was 'rendered safe by the distancing device of historical recuperation', but unlike them he argues that

> calling the use of an all-male cast an 'original practice' is in fact a tactical ruse by which Rylance coaxes audiences to divest themselves of essentialized notions of gender and sexuality and, if only for the duration of the play, to entertain queer thoughts. (2008a: 233)

Bulman saw the reception of *Twelfth Night* as an indication of a progressive cultural turning-point in which same-sex attraction could be publicly celebrated. The enthusiastic applause of the Globe spectators at the end of the play, he suggests, 'indicated that they were complicit in the sexual politics of the performance, revelling in the ambiguities of gender role-play and accepting with pleasure the homoerotic potential of the final couplings' (2008a: 241).

Both Rose and Bulman focus on a particular moment in *Twelfth Night*, and it is with an analysis of this moment that I would like to conclude this discussion of the Globe's gender politics. As they rehearsed the scene in which Orsino and Viola (disguised as Cesario) listen to Feste sing 'Come away, death', Master of Play Tim Carroll and actors Liam Brennan and Michael Brown realized that the scene could lay the groundwork for Orsino's decision to marry Viola upon his realization of her true identity in the play's final scene (Ryan 2002b: 16). Carroll asked Brennan and Brown to think about 'the manner in which the music affects Cesario' and to draw parallels with 'the beginnings of a love affair' (Ryan 2002a: 26). This led to a sequence charged with homoerotic tension. The scene up until Feste's song made liberal use of silences as the two made, and broke, eye contact with one another, Orsino presumably registering on some level the double meaning behind Cesario's admission of love for someone 'Of your complexion' and of 'About your years' (2.4.26, 28). As they sat upon a centre-stage bench to listen to the song, Orsino clasped Cesario's hand in a gesture of comradely fellow-feeling, a moment of physical contact that transformed, almost imperceptibly, into something more overtly romantic: a softening of the posture of both figures, a hesitant turn inwards, another moment of broken eye contact. At the end of the song, Orsino demanded in a sudden outburst to be left alone with Cesario, and moments later, as Cesario asserted 'Ay, but I know – ' (2.4.103), he (or she) seemed on the verge of declaring his (or her) love. Another charged pause followed, after which Cesario began his/her tale of a sister who pined

away with unrequited love. When Cesario revealed that he/
she was 'all the daughters of my father's house, / And all the
brothers too' (2.4.120–1), he/she broke down in tears and
Orsino comforted his page with a hug. The hug lingered a
little too long to remain entirely platonic, culminating in a
moment in which the two seemed on the verge of kissing one
another, before Cesario broke away (to audience laughter)
with 'Sir, shall I to this lady?' (2.4.122) (Figure 8).

The scene was picked up by press and academic critics alike
as a highlight of the production. For Roger Foss, it was 'a
breathtaking moment of sexual danger' (*What's On*, 29 May
2002); Ben Brantley described it as a 'sexy, uncomfortable
and highly disorienting' sequence in which 'different levels of
perception swim in and out of focus' (*New York Times*, 29
August 2002). We have seen above that various critics found
the sexual tension of cross-gender performance at the Globe
'distracting', but here we see its radical potential. The reader
will have noticed that in my account of the bench scene, I

Figure 8   *Liam Brennan as Orsino and Michael Brown as Viola/
Cesario in* Twelfth Night *(2002). Photograph by John Tramper.
Shakespeare's Globe: Archive.*

was unable to decide whether to use the masculine or the feminine pronoun in my description of Viola/Cesario. This is because the scene was a perfect example of the kind of theatrical bisociation discussed in Chapter 3. Michael Brown, Viola and Cesario were 'swimming in and out of focus' in the exchange, sometimes distinguishable as the actor, his character and her assumed identity, but blurring at other times into a single stage figure of ambiguous gender with desires that were impossibly both hetero- and homoerotic at once. For Silverstone, the moment admitted 'the possibility of a range of desires and sexual identifications between actors, characters and spectators which do not invite easy categorization as homo- or heteroerotic' (2005: 41).

Under such circumstances, a straightforwardly Brechtian reading of the cross-dressed stage figure, in which the character signifies one thing while the actor signifies its opposite, becomes untenable – though of course the gap can open and close over the course of the performance. Thus, for example, while Janet McTeer's conspicuous identity as a female performer made it possible to read her Petruchio as a parody of macho posturing, there were moments when McTeer and Petruchio collapsed into a single, androgynous stage figure who was attractive, as Kate Bassett suggested in her review, because his/ her 'unladylike performance' was 'so liberated and natural' (*Independent on Sunday*, 31 August 2003). In a similar way, Klett found it impossible as she watched Vanessa Redgrave's Prospero 'to fix Redgrave as either father or mother, male or female, at any particular moment' (2009: 97). Escolme argues that 'what was significant' about the Globe's cross-gender performances was the way in which 'gender was intermittently denaturalised and placed in quotation marks on this stage' – 'intermittently', she points out, because 'it was often possible to forget' the actors' genders (2008: 410). This was, I would suggest, because Globe performance blurred the boundaries separating actor from character much more frequently than other modern theatres. When a cross-dressed character addresses *us*, co-opting us into his or her fictional erotic desires, actor and character, and therefore masculine and feminine, collapse into one liminal figure.

Reading the audience

It is worth remarking that virtually all of the competing claims considered in this chapter and elsewhere in this book for the politics of performance at the Globe rely in some way upon the interpretation of audience response. Laughter, applause, cheering, shuffling and silence have all been cited as evidence of the ideological effects of Globe performance upon its spectators. This is a dangerous game to play: the dominant audience reaction will tend to obscure divergent responses, and even something as tangible as shared laughter can mask a variety of different attitudes (delight, scorn, surprise, approval, ridicule, discomfort). In the absence of qualitative data about the responses of Globe spectators to performance at the theatre, academic critics have often turned to press reviews (this book itself is no exception). This is, perhaps, unavoidable, but it should be recognized that newspaper critics are a very small subsection of the Globe's wider audience, and may not be typical. Indeed, it is significant that one of the first doctoral research projects to be co-supervised by the Globe was Penelope Woods's *Globe Audiences: Spectatorship and Reconstruction at Shakespeare's Globe*, a project in which Woods collected and examined a wide range of audience feedback relating to the ways in which spectators interacted with performance at the theatre (Woods's excellent project post-dates the Rylance era, hence its absence from the present study).

The Globe is an inherently political space. Its shared light auditorium and enthusiastic audiences mean that the group identities expressed within its walls are much more visible and audible than their equivalents at most other theatres. During the Rylance era especially, the provisionality of the productions themselves, and their receptivity to the vagaries of audience response, meant that audiences could have a palpable effect on the ways in which the stage action unfolded. In making meaning from the performance, spectators would read not just the stage, but the reactions of their fellow spectators. Nicholas Le Prevost, who played Autolycus in 1997, recognized this aspect of spectatorship at the theatre, noting that '[h]ere it's a social, public, political experience to watch a play' (Miller-Schütz 1998: 46). But Le Prevost evidently found his experience at the Globe dissatisfying in this respect, remarking that though he loved 'being with the audience ... I only wish it was a different audience' (ibid.: 47).

Le Prevost's impatience with the audience is telling. An inherently public auditorium like the Globe's can expose, to use Conkie's term, the 'ideological faultlines' within the crowd it contains (2006: 75). One last example from *The Taming of the Shrew* will suffice as an illustration. In one scene, Hunter's starving Katherina was reduced to attempting (in vain) to steal a bone from Petruchio's dog. One critic recorded the audience's laughter at this sequence as having been the loudest of the night (*Evening Standard*, 22 August 2003), and another agreed that the moment was 'hilarious' (*What's On*, 27 August 2003). For others, it was 'not quite so funny' (*The Times*, 23 August 2003) and 'uncomfortably close to domestic abuse' (*Jewish Chronicle*, 29 August 2003). Jane Edwardes's review for *Time Out* reveals the complexity of the wordless debate that was being played out within the audience here:

> It's at this point – as Hunter looks so vulnerable onstage – that I began to wonder why the women in the audience weren't standing up for her more. The Globe is notorious for the volubility of its groundlings and if ever there was a case for booing this must be it. Instead, the ironic cheers of the men what all that could be heard.

Lloyd and her cast, concluded Edwardes, 'have found many ways of enlightening the play, but if anything they've made it even harder to watch' (27 August 2003). What is striking here is that Edwardes gives over the last part of her review not to the production, but to a critique of the audience themselves.

Attempts to label the politics of performance at the Globe as either progressive or conservative thus rather miss the point. Nobody involved in performance at the Globe would deny that the theatre has sometimes been a forum in which audiences have felt empowered to give expression to troubling social and cultural attitudes. Equally, the Globe has housed progressive responses that challenged previously dominant cultural norms, as we have seen in Bulman's analysis of the cheering at the end of *Twelfth Night*. But what is clear is that at the Rylance era Globe, the audience reactions *made* the politics. It was a democratic space, complete with all of the problems that democracy entails.

5

An Interview with
Mark Rylance

*STEPHEN PURCELL: One of the things that my
research for this book is uncovering is that the kind
of theatre you were making at the Globe was so
responsive, so live, that what you can't do is pin it
down, and say of a production, 'This thing always
happened at this particular point.'*

MARK RYLANCE: No. We were talking directly with
the audience, and giving the audience enormous power.
And a lot of what the audience needed to do was to
express their rage at being suppressed for so long. In
the initial press conference when I was made Artistic
Director, there was a question thrown at me about,
'Would it be alright for the audience to throw things?' I
said, 'I don't say no to it; I want them to come and do
whatever they feel like doing'. And of course everyone
picked up on that and then that became the headline.
But we were very near a marketplace, as it would
have been originally, and people came with bags of
vegetables and greens.

I remember when we were doing *Henry V* that the
French, young Christian Camargo and the others,
were very, very angry and upset that their scenes were

dominated by vegetables flying in on them. I came off
stage once and I saw Rory [Edwards] sitting there with
a big sword, and armour, furious. I said, 'Rory, are you
alright?' He said, 'They're only fucking doing it because
they know we can't fucking get them!' I thought he
was going to jump off the stage, he was really furious.
So we had a big company meeting the next day, and
Richard [Olivier] was very unnerved about it too, and
sensitive about the criticisms of pantomimic coarsening
of the plays. It was a really seminal moment, actually.
He said, 'I will go and try and deal with it in the yard.'
'Would you, please?' we all said. The next night, the
vegetables started again, and Richard wades through
the yard, which is difficult, a very crowded yard, and
finds a woman with a paper bag of vegetables. She's
taken a wide stance and is reaching into the bag, and
she's hurling them at the French, and she's crying, I
think. He said, 'What could I do? It was a completely
authentic, legitimate response. She wasn't trying to
undermine us, she was completely caught up. It would
have been against all my objectives as a director to stop
her having that relationship with the play.' Shakespeare
wrote for a much more empowered audience than our
modern theatres allow.

So we struggled on and we struggled on and we said,
'Well, what can we do about it?' Eventually, wonderful
old William Russell, who was playing the King of
France, and was very quiet and listening to all this,
he said, 'Well, what do you expect? They're English.
Merde.' That night, the Dauphin came out, and when
the audience started to howl and hiss, he went forward
and stole one of their baseball caps from the front
of the yard and put it on and said the lines about,
'Tomorrow I'm going to walk over your dead heads
and your dead bodies,' and he engaged with them.
They pulled out of him a performance of arrogance and
pride and superiority that he had not found before that.

So we all started to see that the audience were fellow actors and that they were being liberated like we were, and they were also learning how to play this ancient theatre instrument. To suppress them, as the press were saying we should, would have been completely the wrong reaction. Yes, it was wild, and eventually we had to determine that if something is offered to you from the audience that is helpful to the story, then respond, but if it isn't, then play on. Because there were sometimes responses that were just actually to do with anger about the cultural position of Shakespeare as a repressive, frightening force that is used in tests, and means that some people get better positions in schools and other people don't. There is a lot of anger about it, and all kinds of things that are unconscious that needed to be expressed, but were not necessarily part of the particular story we were telling. They were another story about society's relationship to this phenomenon of Shakespeare, which is really banged into us all the time. The greatest thing that England has ever done, and if you don't like it and don't love it then you're kind of subhuman. That's a pretty frightening thing for people.

SP: *This has in many ways really beautifully and eloquently answered one of the questions that I was going to ask, which is, was it a political theatre? I think what you've just explained to me is that it was political in the sense that it was inviting the audience into something, an institution, a culture, that had previously excluded them, that had previously been uninterested in their voices.*

MR: The building was political. The project is led by the architecture. All the activities are in response to the architecture. Some theatre makers sought to learn from the architecture, others sought to dominate and even eradicate its challenges. I know what Sam wanted us to do. He wanted us to learn something new and hopefully valuable from the architecture. He hoped we would change. That meant letting go of our familiar tricks, lighting, amplified sound, actors talking to themselves when they soliloquize. And it meant learning new tools, live acoustic music, for instance. We had six-person bands on every show. Many actors and directors were too frightened to let go of what they did well, or believed was right. Learning something new meant our work was chaotic, necessarily, at times. We stumbled and got lost at times, as any work that explores new territory must. We had to learn to speak differently, using the floor of the stage. The relationship between our characters and the audience was the most challenging and enjoyable thing to learn.

The question of how much as a theatre performer, theatre director, theatre actor, you try and control the audience to behave in the ideal way, is an important question for me. We are storytellers, so we are steering the experience, but how much should we limit the response of the listeners? By chance, some evening I will have what I believe to be an ideal performance of a play I am in, and then I'll get fixated: 'That was the greatest one, because I swung them this way, then they swung back that way, then I got them with that surprise in the story there.' Then the next night I'll try and swing them that way, and they won't want to go that way, and I'll be frustrated. Then I'll warp the performance to try and do that. If you are acting *with* the audience, they must be free to express their half of the conversation. They are not the same people as the night before. Early on in my career, Mike Alfreds was always trying to get me to let go of the idea of an ideal performance, and accept that the *present*, even *chaotic* performance was the ideal: to be present and not try to over-control. It's not helpful, really, to over-control what an audience experiences, whether you are a director or an actor, as you lose presence and spontaneity. In the end it is all about trying to be in the same room with the audience. Tim [Carroll] and Claire [van Kampen] were always saying to me that when I was least prepared was when they most enjoyed what I was doing.

SP: Because you're vulnerable then?

MR: Yeah, and I'm more with that audience that night. It's a hard one, because there is a structure to a text, to a play. It isn't chaos, it isn't soup. There is a structure, and when it does land, when you do feel that you are in harmony with that structure and the audience is in harmony with you in that structure, there is an added, deeper harmonic kind of delight that is hard for me not to be addicted to and be aiming at. Actually that kind of happening is a matter of grace.

SP: We were talking about those confrontational relationships with the audience that happened in the early seasons – those very robust, noisy, vigorous interactions between the audience and those on the stage. It seems to me that audiences became less combative over the period. Is that right? That in earlier seasons there was a lot of booing, a kind of power tussle, almost, between stage and audience, and then in later seasons it felt perhaps a bit more harmonious, a bit like everyone had understood the expectations that the space conferred upon them.

MR: Yes, that did happen. That did happen. I think both groups, both the audiences and the actors, got better at how to play that space, if I can apply the word 'play' to audiences as well. I think there was an initial cultural story about the reconstruction of the Globe theatre after so many years, and as I was saying, the intellectual love of Shakespeare overshadowing the other loves of Shakespeare, and those other more subconscious, sensual, emotional, irrational responses to Shakespeare having been really dominated by the presentation of interpreted moments on stage and the audience being held in the dark, and by many actors also complaining about the audience making any noise. I remember during my time there reading about actors being very angry about audiences not paying attention. I thought, it's up to *us*, you know? So I think it [that initial audience reaction] was a swing back, but it burnt up rather quickly. It did burn up.

SP: Did the introduction of the Masters system [in 1999] profoundly change the way in which the Globe worked, or was it more of an accommodation to a system that was already emerging?

MR: That's a good question. It's hard to know if it profoundly changed anything; it's hard to have any kind of perspective on that. I think the directors were aware of it. I mean, it was me, certainly, as a member of the acting company, saying, 'I want myself and my fellows to have three hours a week, of the hours that I am budgeting you for rehearsing this play, dedicated to our craft, in the way that ballet dancers have classes in the morning'. It meant that the directors were having to accept my requests for how they worked their rehearsal period – particularly Giles Block – in terms of the idea of having a character like a conductor in opera, who was only listening to the relationship of the actors to the words. Eventually, the directors saw that it was an incredible tool, when they needed to focus on all the emotional and different qualities in the final weeks of rehearsals and in previews, that there was Giles coming to us and saying, 'Is that really helping you, to stress that word, or to land on that word?' Or, 'Can you not connect those? You're breaking those two lines into four statements; what happens if you move through those statements and land here?' So underneath the Master of Play's role, the Master of the Words was doing fundamentally good work on the spontaneity and the speed and liveliness of the speech. Giles and I shared the objective of the sound of spontaneous speech that had never been said before.

But the Master of Play was the captain of the ship. It wasn't direction by committee. He or she absolutely decided when a decision was required. My explanation to them was, 'You must decide what's best for the story'. So that's the ruling thing: the story. Sometimes a Shakespeare production will tell a story *about* the story, rather than just tell the story. This kind of thing is admired in some circles. These are called ground-breaking productions! At the Globe, if you weren't telling the story, as if it had never happened before, you lost the audience. There were very bad cameras that we used to film the productions, early on. By accident, we discovered when we were searching forward to find a certain bit of a production, that the yard would be moving all around, and then suddenly they would be still. And so we said, 'What's happening when they're still?' And we saw that it was where the story had gripped them. Then there were other moments when I started to see, 'Ah, they're not actually just playing the story as if it's present, they're doing a kind of *take* on the story.' So that was one of the first lessons the Globe taught me: that a lot of the meaning was in the story, was in the twists and turns, or the zigzags, as John Dove [who directed *Measure for Measure* and *The Winter's Tale* in 2004 and 2005] came to call them. You really needed the story in there to keep that big mob of people concentrated. That was a specific discovery the Globe gave me: the important structure to Shakespeare's storytelling was a necessity in the amphitheatre.

SP: *There is often an assumption that a production has to have a political or social thesis; that it's asserting something, either consciously or unconsciously, about war, or gender, or love, or whatever, and that it's a conduit via which that message travels to the audience. I think that's a misrepresentation of what happens at the Globe, because as you've just been saying, meaning gets created by that strange alchemy that happens between audience and actor.*

MR: I enjoy productions that are like that sometimes, if they're well acted. But certainly Tim [Carroll] identified for me a very dead limb in Shakespeare performance, which is how I was taught to play at the RSC early on, which was working for the meaning of a scene and then working out a construct of how you felt that meaning would be performed. (Scenes in life don't mean anything. They just are.) And then that construct being stuck to, or 'frozen', as they call it in America. 'Blocked'. The words give away what is going on. So you get these static moments that *calcify*. They maybe work in rehearsal, the first time you find them, and everyone is excited about this discovery; but then they become calcified, and they are absolutely dead, and you sit in the audience and there is nothing to do with life, because life isn't played that way. It becomes like going to a tennis match where neither John McEnroe nor Borg want to win, but they want to display the best tennis match, and so they fake it: they hit the ball, they practise for ages this one thing, but the rest of it is dull, it's just dead. Shakespeare plays are an experience on many levels, not an examination question or essay. All thesis or message productions are a reduction of something much more wild and vital.

I have to say, it was identified to me even earlier when I was trained at RADA by the great Hugh Cruttwell, who trained so many of us. Hugh did not appreciate Lord Olivier's work, and I asked him once why, and he said, 'It's because I could see that he had worked out something in every performance that the critics could write about very eloquently within twenty minutes.' He said, 'I got fed up with it. I could see he was manipulating or offering something to them.' Now, I never saw him perform live, and I expect those things were still rather thrilling, but I could see that what Hugh was identifying was endemic, and was not just Olivier.

SP: I noticed that all of a sudden in 2003 and 2004 the vast majority of productions were OP, having had none in 2001. Why was there that sudden shift towards doing lots of OP in those two years especially?

MR: The 2001 season was *Cymbeline*, *Macbeth* and *King Lear*. They were all free-hand productions. Barry Kyle's [*King Lear*] was an RSC-type production. *Macbeth* was very modern and very experimental. *Cymbeline* was very modern and experimental too, but had a lot of OP-type things: one suit of clothing, and you moved quickly. None of them employed lighting or amplification. They all employed live music. They all did something to the *frons scenae*. But the radical thing about that season was the idea of re-rehearsal. That we would do less, better. So we would only do three productions, and after they had played for a while we would see if a re-rehearsal period would enable the company to take on board what they were experiencing with the audience, and adjust the production from what they learnt whilst playing.

   Then what happened was *Twelfth Night* and the invitation to the Middle Temple Hall [in 2002], and the experience of playing in an actual surviving Elizabethan building where Shakespeare and his fellows had acted. Jenny [Tiramani] made a great push forward, from the natural hair of Cleopatra to the silk wigs and the stylized makeup of the two boys. I would say with *Julius Caesar* and *Antony and Cleopatra* [in 1999] she was still learning, and some of the clothing choices in *Julius Caesar* were still really raw and rough and confusing for critics and audiences, and for the actors too. But with *Twelfth Night* she really hit her stride, in that it was stunningly beautiful, and it was accurate. Tim arrived too, with his rigour and his wit, and a group of actors who emerged and stayed for a while – who were born in the *Macbeth* experience and then came into *Twelfth Night*.

So that was the Cupid and Psyche season [2002], which stands out to me as really the high point of my time there, I think, with the big inclusion of *The Golden Ass* and Mike [Alfreds] doing *A Midsummer Night's Dream*. There were only three shows again. So by the time we got to 2003, we hadn't done a lot of OP, but we'd discovered with *Twelfth Night* that for the first time, the critics approved of OP. They saw what we were hunting for and had been struggling to find for a while, and it manifested in a very popular show.

So a lot of different things came together and then, yes, it did feel it was time. The 2003 season was a complete reinvestment in OP. We also took off the walls of the tiring-house, and in a kind of nod to the research aspect of what we were doing, we started to share the dressing room. We'd done it at Middle Temple Hall, and found the audience loved it, seeing the authentic makeup we were using and seeing us being laced and all the detail that was underneath the clothing, which had initially been mocked, that we were wearing handmade underwear and stuff like that. But it was Jenny trying to say that this is a reconstruction.

SP: 2003 was also the experiment with single gender companies. You had the all-female and the all-male companies.

MR: That's right, that's right. And what a delight that was. Deborah Warner had said when she saw me play Cleopatra that the thing about gender is it demands that we take an active imaginative role as an audience: 'You're not doing it all for us. You do enough, and it's best when you do as little as required to charm our imagination to take part. We become willing, playful contributors, imaginatively.' She said, 'That's when the space works for me'. When the audience experience is creative, I came to understand, is when it's at its best. That stayed with me, actually, even into film acting now. I can now find Brando and Cagney and other people talking about that too. Leave room for the audience to create: don't do it all for them, or they'll just sit back passively and they don't get the same buzz. The really subtle buzz they get is when they've made it happen too, by lending and by creating it with their imaginations.

It was fun though. It was daring. It was frightening at times. You must have read that story about the man in the yard who confronted us during a performance? He said, 'What's wrong with real women, why do we have to watch these fucking fairies?' to Danny Sapani and James Gillan and me. We all came offstage and had all had the same thought when he said that: 'But we *are* women. The poor man, he's insane.' It's very rare you get an audience angrily, emotionally, actively defying the illusion that you're creating. Going straight for the under-core, the under-nature of what is going on. Not saying 'Take the money, fat man' to Shylock, or some of those comments, but going right at you. Our defences were so complete that we immediately forgave him and assumed he was mad.

*SP: Well, he's the single voice who's saying that in a
theatre full of people who are playing along.*

MR: Yeah, he soon became the victim actually, the one
in trouble, and I soon became the one calming the rest
of the audience and saying 'Queen Cleopatra says you
can have your money back', swallowing him into our
reality. We realized that we had all the power, because
we had a reality that they had paid money for us to
prepare, and they had come to take part in it. This was
the radical thing for me. I'd always projected criticism
onto the audience, and my own fears that they were in
judgement, and protected myself from that and put up
a fourth wall. Gradually, as I looked more at them and
started to speak not *to* them or *at* them but *with* them,
I saw that they, even more than us, were invested in it
being good. They really wanted to be taken out of their
lives, and everything you felt you lacked, sometimes,
as an actor – your motivation to play – was there, for
free, in their eyes. Not in all of them: you could also
find people who were like *[pulls a blank expression]*,
but you could just move away from them and find
someone else. Or if you were playing Hamlet, and
you hated yourself, you could look for those ones that
hated you, and say, 'Why haven't you hit me in the
face and pulled my beard? Why have you been letting
me go on like this for so long?' The interaction became
so valuable.

SP: How would you describe the Globe's core mission?

MR: That's a really good question. I don't think anywhere
else in the world has anyone managed to galvanize the
scholastic, theatrical and financial communities into
a really rigorous reconstruction of an early theatre
tool, and a very, very particular one, which was one of
the spaces where Shakespeare's plays were first heard
and was, therefore, clearly in the imagination of the

author when he imagined his plays. As much as when Spielberg imagines a film script he imagines the camera and the equipment and the screen which will convey it to an audience. So it's a very, very resonant – and I dare even to say important – development in the life of Shakespeare since the death of Shakespeare. A really radical step which Poel and other people had tried.

Research, rigour about materials, rigour about craft, and a hope that the space therefore describes as closely as we can manage, and more than any other space in the world, the relationship that the audience and actors had in there. That's the core mission, to be led by the architecture, and the development over twenty-five years of how that architecture was constructed, and then to apply those same techniques to the productions and to that relationship. At least occasionally – not always, but at least once a year – to try and reconstruct that. An exploration of original playing practices.

As you say, it had an effect on the audiences, their willingness to suspend belief, their willingness to sit and stand physically and be able to look at each other and listen to the play and enjoy that as well. So it is, and was, and will again be developing appreciation of Shakespeare in all the different modes that human beings can appreciate anything. Intellectually, emotionally, soulfully, sensually. That's the core mission.

EPILOGUE: LEGACY AND RETURN

In late 2000, the Globe's Artistic Directorate expressed a wish for Mark Rylance to continue as Artistic Director until at least 2004. Some of them, however, indicated that they were not entirely satisfied with the quality of the work produced under his leadership so far, and that they hoped to see something closer in style to the work of other major British theatre companies. In his report to the AD that November, Rylance resisted the premise that the Globe's productions compared badly with such work, and he took the opportunity to reflect upon what he considered to have been the Globe's unique strengths:

> As an actor and sometimes director my career is guided by a love for experiment and risk. I love this theatre for its experimental nature. I think it is the most experimental and challenging theatre there is at present. I joined the AD, as I expect all of you did, because it seemed there was a possibility to make something different at the Globe. Something different for actors, something different for audiences, something different for Shakespeare. (Rylance 2000b)

The Globe, he continued, was a building and an organization in which the hierarchies of other theatres had been replaced by a spirit of 'striving in friendship, of friendship in strife, between all the people who are necessary to make a play and theatre company'. It was in that spirit, he wrote, that he intended to continue (ibid.).

By summer 2004, however, Rylance had begun to feel, as he later put it, 'out of joint' with the Globe. His duties as Artistic Director were leading him in a different direction from his inclinations as an artist, as he explained in an interview with the *Pittsburgh Post-Gazette* the following year:

> [T]o be an actor, you're trying always to be present, to convince people it's happening for the first time – spontaneous and playful. As artistic director, you're separate from the group – you have to climb up a hill, look ahead and think where there'll be food 12 months ahead. (4 December 2005)

He reflected upon this further in his interview with me:

> The constant distraction about risk assessment and the five-year plans and the avoidance of risk was so counter to the search for spontaneity and the search for risk, radical risk, that I can see now that it was schizophrenic. It was dividing me. (Rylance 2016a)

There were also more specific problems. A debate in 2003 between members of the theatre's Board about the length of his remaining term as Artistic Director had left Rylance feeling demoralized. The discussion had involved a conversation between the Globe Board's Chairman, Sir Michael Perry, and the Artistic Directorate, during which it had become clear that Rylance no longer enjoyed their full support. As he explained in an email to me, the episode led him into a 'deep depression':

> To be honest, I was burnt out with the struggle and relentless work. I was being attacked for my openness to the authorship question, for my political support for the anti-war movement, and finally for the work in the theatre, by the majority of the AD, who didn't seem to understand or appreciate anything we had achieved. (Rylance 2016b)[1]

Rylance was finding himself at odds with the increasingly corporate culture of the Globe's management and frustrated by what he perceived as their tendency to undervalue the theatre's work as the organization's core activity. From his perspective, the theatre company was being used to subsidize the organization's other work, an arrangement that placed the burden of funding the Education department on the shoulders of Shakespeare audiences and artists (through higher ticket prices and lower wages) rather than on government or philanthropy. While Rylance recognized Globe Education as 'the oldest department of the project and doing wonderful work', he felt that this state of affairs was forcing him to schedule reliably commercial Shakespeare productions at the expense of visiting international productions, plays by Shakespeare's contemporaries, and even the less popular Shakespeares (Rylance 2016b).[2] In a letter to Perry and the Globe's General Director, Peter Kyle, in August 2004, Rylance explained that unless they could find some way to free the theatre department from this financial obligation, the 2005 season would have to be his last. He reiterated that he had come to the Globe 'because of my love for risk and exploration and my belief that great productions are born from a great ensemble', and he cited 2002's *Twelfth Night* as an example of such a production. The Globe, he wrote, had 'turned out to be every inch as radical a space as Sam imagined', one that was 'challenging almost everything about Shakespearean performance if not general theatregoing at present'. He listed some of the theatre's successes: its affordability, its revival of 'an appreciation of sound in speech and music', its 'sense of social inclusion', its 'honest storytelling dynamics', its focus on actors' skills, its challenge to the 'conceits' of twentieth-century 'director's theatre', and above all, its encouragement of actors and audience 'to meet face-to-face in the shared light and imagination of the Globe'. 'All of this,' he concluded, 'is hard won and is now in peril' (Rylance 2004b).

In his resignation letter to staff the following month, Rylance wrote that he hoped that his successor would continue to experiment with Original Practices and explore the possibility of a 'classical youth theatre'. He still believed, he assured them, that 'we have the most exciting theatre space in the world,' and he hoped 'to be welcomed as part of the company and as part of the wider circle of advisors and volunteers'. He also expressed a hope that he might, depending on the wishes of the new Artistic Director, return to the theatre as an actor (Rylance 2004c). His subsequent correspondence with Dominic Dromgoole, who was announced as the Globe's new Artistic Director in May 2005, shows a genial and mutually supportive handover. Dromgoole invited Rylance back as an actor for the 2007 season, but Rylance expressed a feeling that it was too soon for him to return, since it would be the first season for which Dromgoole had had the benefit of a full year's experience (Rylance 2006). Several of the 2005 Globe company subsequently worked with Rylance on his own play, *I Am Shakespeare*, an anarchic comedy about the Shakespeare authorship debate, in 2007; in the same year, Rylance, Claire van Kampen and Jenny Tiramani were jointly given the Sam Wanamaker Award for their pioneering work over the theatre's opening decade. Rylance planned to revive Phoebus Cart, the company he had run prior to his time at the Globe with van Kampen and Tiramani, and to stage an Original Practices production of either *Othello* or *Richard III* with them under the direction of Tim Carroll. As it happened, Rylance spent much of 2007 and most of 2008 in the West End and Broadway revivals of Marc Camoletti's farce *Boeing-Boeing*; he performed shorter runs of Ibsen's *Peer Gynt*, Beckett's *Endgame* and David Hirson's *La Bête* between 2008 and 2011, and from 2009 until early 2012 spent long periods playing the role of Johnny 'Rooster' Byron in Jez Butterworth's play *Jerusalem*, a landmark performance for which he was the recipient of multiple awards. It was not, therefore, until 2012 that Rylance, van Kampen, Tiramani and Carroll reunited for their Original Practices *Richard III*, which played at the Globe alongside a revival of *Twelfth Night*. Both productions subsequently transferred to the

West End and Broadway, his performance as Olivia winning Rylance his third Tony Award. In 2015, Rylance returned to the Globe to star in van Kampen's play *Farinelli and the King* at the newly opened Sam Wanamaker Playhouse, the indoor theatre whose outer shell had been awaiting the necessary funds for completion throughout Rylance's own artistic directorship. He was acknowledged, alongside van Kampen and a few others, with a Senior Research Fellowship at the Globe later in 2015.[3]

Under Dromgoole's leadership, the theatre continued to flourish in ways that both built upon and departed from Rylance's artistic directorship. Prices remained low, especially in the yard, and the theatre continued to attract full and diverse audiences. Dromgoole's Globe was, like Rylance's, characterized by vigorous interaction between actor and audience, and some of the Dromgoole-era productions were even more adventurous than their predecessors in their use of the yard. Dromgoole revived Globe to Globe, staging an ambitious six-week festival of thirty-seven Shakespeare plays in thirty-seven different languages in 2012, inviting two or more international companies to the Globe for residencies every subsequent year, and sending a small-scale production of *Hamlet* to 197 different countries between 2014 and 2016. Dromgoole also developed the Globe as a home for new writing, the Rylance-era director John Dove working on many of the new plays. While Dromgoole maintained Rylance's investment in rigorous historical research – the construction of the candlelit Sam Wanamaker Playhouse would not have been possible without it – he ceased to distinguish 'Original Practices' productions from those allowed a 'free hand'. The experiment in single-sex casting was not revived until Rylance's return in 2012. Productions were increasingly design-led, often completely covering over the *frons scenae* and extending the stage into the yard. Perhaps understandably, given that Dromgoole is a director rather than an actor, the theatre under his leadership also saw a substantial shift in power back towards the director, and what Tim Carroll described to me as 'a more conventional approach to "solving" the play than I was ever interested in' (Carroll 2016).

Dromgoole handed over to Emma Rice in 2016, whose first season indicated a continued interest in interactive and playful productions, and a more radically irreverent and postmodern sensibility than either Rylance's or Dromgoole's. But Rice's directorship also took a further step towards putting the semiotics of the Globe space back under the control of directors and designers: productions in her first season made use of lighting rigs and amplified sound, and for the first time in the Globe's history, spectators at evening performances were allowed to fade into darkness as the sun set. This shift in the Globe's practices proved to be a step too far for the theatre's Board, who concluded after a 'productive debate concerning the purpose and theatrical practice of the Globe' that the theatre should return to a programme that was 'structured around "shared light" productions without designed sound and light rigging' (Shakespeare's Globe 2016). The decision led to the announcement that Rice would be stepping down as Artistic Director following the 2017–18 Winter Season, and a controversy in the press and on social media that tended to simplify the disagreement as if it were a straightforward contest between progressive forces (represented by Rice) and reactionary ones (represented by the pre-Rice Globe and the spectre of 'historical authenticity'). The debate reawakened some of the clichés about the theatre that had been dormant since the Rylance era: when Lyn Gardner, for example, complained that the decision sent out a message that 'the Globe is not really a theatre but part of the heritage industry and a plaything for academic researchers', her words directly echoed some of the reviews of the theatre's opening seasons (*Guardian*, 25 October 2016).[4] This characterization of the Board's decision tended to ignore the ways in which Rice's use of lighting and sound technology had moved the Globe's theatre practice closer to the conventions of the modern mainstream theatre, making it in some ways *less* experimental than the work of her predecessors, for all of its innovations in other respects. In reverting to such a binary understanding of the Globe's practices, many in the theatre community seemed to be overlooking the extent to which Rylance and Dromgoole's 'shared light' work had itself been radical and groundbreaking.

Rylance's ten years at the helm of the Globe had a major impact on modern British theatre. Opening to reviews that often dismissed the theatre's work as eccentric, lightweight, unsubtle and populist, under his leadership the Globe became one of Britain's leading classical theatres, winning the *Evening Standard*'s Special Award in 2002 and garnering multiple Olivier Award nominations for *Twelfth Night* in 2003 (Best Revival, Best Actor for Mark Rylance, and Best Costume Design for Jenny Tiramani, going on to win the latter). With 600 £5 tickets available for every show, the theatre's affordable pricing set a new standard for accessibility that rival theatres with subsidies could not ignore: when Nicholas Hytner became Artistic Director of the National Theatre in 2003, he introduced a new annual £10 ticket season; the Royal Shakespeare Company introduced a £5 ticket scheme for 16- to 25-year-olds the following year. Rylance's Globe was, for a few years in the late 1990s, the only major British theatre to regularly produce plays by Shakespeare's contemporaries, and this programming must have helped to provoke the revived interest in these plays that since 2012 has driven Gregory Doran's artistic directorship of the RSC. The Globe was influential, too, as the country's most prominent example of a galleried auditorium with a thrust stage, and its success presumably galvanized the building of the Rose Theatre at Kingston, which hosted performances in its unfinished shell from 2003 before opening officially in 2008, and the redevelopment of Stratford's Royal Shakespeare Theatre, which was announced in 2004 and completed in 2010. The RSC's Artistic Director Michael Boyd explained the latter in terms that clearly evoked the Globe, without mentioning it by name:

Most major new theatres of the last century have moved away from the 'us and them' of the 19th century proscenium 'picture frame' in search of spaces which celebrate the inter-action cinema can't achieve. Our commitment to bring an immediacy and clarity to Shakespeare means we need to bring the audience to a more engaged relationship with our actors. The best way we can achieve this is in a bold, thrust, one-room auditorium – a modern take on the courtyard theatres of Shakespeare's day. (RSC 2004)

But it was the Globe's foregrounding of the audience's role in the making of theatrical meaning that was its major influence. In a post-show talk in 2005, Tim Carroll spoke about what he described as the Globe 'virus' – actors from Globe productions going on to work at other theatres and taking with them the Globe's more interactive style of performing. Indeed, Jonathan Slinger, who was a member of the Globe's Opening Season company before going on to greater success at the RSC, said in 1997 that he felt sure he would take the 'openness' he had learned at the Globe 'to whatever I do next', and that 'just because an audience is not visible doesn't mean that they become invisible' (Miller-Schütz 1998: 56). In 2004, Michael Billington observed that it had been 'fascinating to see how an actor like Jasper Britton, who has worked at the Globe, used its audience-contact techniques when he played Fletcher's *The Tamer Tamed* at the Royal Shakespeare Company' (*Guardian*, 20 September 2004). When I interviewed Carroll in 2016, we discussed the RSC's 2015 production of *Henry V*, in which the audience in the centre stalls had remained lit, and were addressed frequently throughout by Alex Hassell's Henry (Hassell himself is an alumnus of the Rylance-era Globe). Carroll suggested that the Globe had played a role in this 'increased willingness to keep the audience in the game' (Carroll 2016). It was part of a wider cultural shift in this respect, and Rylance has contextualized his work as part of a movement that also includes companies like Kneehigh and Punchdrunk (2008: 109).

The Globe's work has been radical for those of us who write about performance, too, because it challenges the dominant ways in which both press and academic critics tend to understand the making of theatrical meaning. Newspaper critics, scholars and even theatre marketing departments often want a Shakespearean production to be attributable to a director as an author-figure, to be a fixed text that communicates some sort of thesis on the play. Rylance's Globe steadfastly refused to play that game and has been repeatedly misunderstood as a result. Billington wrote in 2004 that he hoped Rylance's successor would turn away from 'old-fashioned, actor-driven' productions and opt instead for 'intellectually challenging, director-led reinterpretations of Shakespeare', though he went on to cite Mike Alfreds's *Cymbeline* as the sort of work he would like to see more of (*Guardian*, 20 September 2004) – a rather ironic example, because, as Trevor Rawlins points out, *Cymbeline* was one of the most 'actor-driven' of all the Rylance-era productions (2012: 441).

It seems fitting to give the last word to Rylance himself. In a 2002 newsletter to friends of Shakespeare's Globe, he suggested that 'the major discovery of the first years of the Globe' had been that of 'the modern Shakespearean audience':

My fellow actors and I are constantly amazed by the level of imagination given to us by audiences in the Globe. I have often heard reactions to lines, or seen an expression in someone's face, which has taught me something I hadn't realised about the character I am playing. For the first time in centuries actors are regularly seeing and hearing the great friendship audiences feel for Shakespeare and theatre. This architecture is reviving an old friendship between actors and audience, which years of television, film, and stuffy darkened theatres, has undermined. I think this friendship inspires honesty, truth, and good humour in our theatre.

APPENDIX

Productions at Shakespeare's Globe, 1996–2005

Season	Title	Author	Director / Master of Play	Notes
1996: Prologue season	*The Two Gentlemen of Verona*	William Shakespeare	Jack Shepherd	Modern practices, mixed gender
	A Midsummer Night's Dream	William Shakespeare	Barrie Rutter	Visiting production from Northern Broadsides
	Damon and Pythias	Richard Edwards	Gaynor McFarlane	Visiting production from a new all-female company
1997: Opening season	*Henry V*	William Shakespeare	Richard Oliver	Original practices, all-male
	The Winter's Tale	William Shakespeare	David Freeman	Modern practices, mixed gender
	A Chaste Maid in Cheapside	Thomas Middleton	Malcolm McKay	Modern practices, mixed gender

Season	Title	Author	Director / Master of Play	Notes
	The Maid's Tragedy	Francis Beaumont and John Fletcher	Lucy Bailey	Modern practices, mixed gender
	Umabatha: the Zulu Macbeth	Welcome Msomi	Welcome Msomi	Globe to Globe production from the Johannesburg Civic Theatre, South Africa
1998: 'Season of Justice and Mercy'	*As You Like It*	William Shakespeare	Lucy Bailey	Original practices, mixed gender
	The Merchant of Venice	William Shakespeare	Richard Oliver	Original practices, mixed gender
	The Honest Whore	Thomas Dekker (with Thomas Middleton)	Jack Shepherd	Modern practices, mixed gender
	A Mad World, My Masters	Thomas Middleton	Sue Lefton	Modern practices, mixed gender
	Otra Tempestad	Raquel Carrió	Flora Lauten	Globe to Globe production from Teatro Buendía, Cuba

Season	Title	Author	Director / Master of Play	Notes
	Venus and Adonis	John Blow	Ian Caddy	Opera using 'recreated seventeenth-century staging and gesture'
1999: 'Anniversary Season' / 'Roman Season'	*Julius Caesar*	William Shakespeare	Mark Rylance	Original practices, all-male
	The Comedy of Errors	William Shakespeare	Kathryn Hunter	Modern practices, mixed gender
	Antony and Cleopatra	William Shakespeare	Giles Block	Original practices, all-male
	Augustine's Oak	Peter Oswald	Tim Carroll	Modern practices, mixed gender
	Kathakali King Lear	David McRuvie and K. Marumakan Raja (trans.)	Annette Leday and David McRuvie	Globe to Globe production from Annette Leday/ Keli Company, India/France
2000: 'Hercules Season'	*The Tempest*	William Shakespeare	Lenka Udovicki	Modern practices, mixed gender (including a female Prospero)
	Hamlet	William Shakespeare	Giles Block	Original practices, mixed gender

Season	Title	Author	Director / Master of Play	Notes
	Two Noble Kinsmen	William Shakespeare and John Fletcher	Tim Carroll	Modern practices, mixed gender
	The Antipodes	Richard Brome	Gerald Freedman	Modern practices, mixed gender
	Romeu e Julieta	Onestaldo de Pennafort (trans.)	Gabriel Villela	Globe to Globe production from Grupo Galpão, Brazil
2001: 'Celtic Season'	*King Lear*	William Shakespeare	Barry Kyle	Modern practices, mixed gender
	Macbeth	William Shakespeare	Tim Carroll	Modern practices, mixed gender
	Cymbeline	William Shakespeare	Mike Alfreds	Modern practices, mixed gender (six actors)
	Umabatha: the Zulu Macbeth	Welcome Msomi	Welcome Msomi	Globe to Globe production from the Johannesburg Civic Theatre, South Africa
	The Kyogen of Errors	Yasunari Takahashi	Mansai Nomura	Globe to Globe production from the Mansaku Company, Japan
2002: 'Season of Cupid & Psyche'	*Twelfth Night*	William Shakespeare	Tim Carroll	Original practices, all-male

Season	Title	Author	Director / Master of Play	Notes
	A Midsummer Night's Dream	William Shakespeare	Mike Alfreds	Modern practices, mixed gender
	The Golden Ass	Peter Oswald	Tim Carroll	Modern practices, mixed gender
2003: 'Season of Regime Change'	Richard II	William Shakespeare	Tim Carroll	Original practices, all-male
	Richard III	William Shakespeare	Barry Kyle	Original practices, all-female
	Dido, Queen of Carthage	Christopher Marlowe	Tim Carroll	Modern practices, mixed gender
	Edward II	Christopher Marlowe	Timothy Walker	Original practices, all-male
	The Taming of the Shrew	William Shakespeare	Phyllida Lloyd	Original practices, all-female
	Twelfth Night	William Shakespeare	Tim Carroll	Original practices, all-male (revival of 2002 production)
2004: 'Season of Star-Crossed Lovers'	Romeo and Juliet	William Shakespeare	Tim Carroll	Original practices, mixed gender (some 'original pronunciation' performances)

Season	Title	Author	Director / Master of Play	Notes
	Much Ado About Nothing	William Shakespeare	Tamara Harvey	Original practices, all-female
	Measure for Measure	William Shakespeare	John Dove	Original practices, mixed gender
2005: 'Season of the World and the Underworld'	*The Tempest*	William Shakespeare	Tim Carroll	Modern practices, all-male (three actors)
	Pericles	William Shakespeare	Kathryn Hunter	Modern practices, mixed gender
	The Winter's Tale	William Shakespeare	John Dove	Original practices, mixed gender
	The Storm	Peter Oswald	Tim Carroll	Modern practices, mixed gender
	Man Falling Down	Jack Shepherd and Oliver Cotton	Jack Shepherd and Oliver Cotton (devisers)	Modern practices, mixed gender
	Troilus and Cressida	William Shakespeare	Giles Block	Modern practices, mixed gender (original pronunciation)
	Measure for Measure	William Shakespeare	John Dove	Original practices, all-male (revival of 2004 production for US tour)

NOTES

Introduction

1   Rylance introduced a mid-season re-rehearsal period for the 2001 productions, but did not repeat the experiment.

2   Indeed, Gurr subsequently described 'ideas such as making the actors enter through the yard and up non-Shakespearean steps onto and off the stage' as 'betrayals of the design features inherent in the Globe' (2008: 120).

3   As it transpired, original pronunciation would not be explored until 2004; young men (though not boys) were cast in female roles in productions in 1997, 1999, 2002, 2003 and 2005.

4   The number of 'original practices' productions rises to eight if one counts the 2003 revival of 2002's *Twelfth Night*. See Chapter 5 for Rylance's explanation of the thinking behind the increase in OP programming.

5   There were two 'original practices' productions in 2005 if one counts the revival of the previous year's *Measure for Measure*.

6   See, for example, Michael Coveney, *Daily Mail*, 23 May 2002; Maddy Costa, *Guardian*, 24 May 2002; Georgina Brown, *Mail on Sunday*, 2 June 2002; Ben Brantley, *New York Times*, 29 August 2002.

Chapter 1

1   Ko 1999; Marshall 2000. These perspectives are discussed further in Chapter 4.

2   Participants at the end-of-season conference discussed 'ways of bringing in some form of audience during rehearsals', a

suggestion that would be acted upon during rehearsals for the following year's *Julius Caesar*.

3 See Crystal 2005 for details.

4 Globe Education's programme of staged readings of plays by Shakespeare's contemporaries, however, continued throughout the era and beyond; a full catalogue is given in Carson and Karim-Cooper 2008: 243–54.

5 Kentrup re-articulated his thoughts about the need for a permanent company during the Artistic Directorate's 2000 meeting (Shakespeare's Globe 2000).

Chapter 2

1 Jessica Ryan's Research Bulletin for *Twelfth Night* gives the most detailed account of the Tudor Group's work at the Globe (2002a: 4–12).

2 See for example Chahidi 2002: 1 April, 22 April; Hassell 2004: 27 April; and Gale 2004: 18 April.

3 It is perhaps worth noting that Sam Wanamaker's own acting technique was derived from the 'Method' and relied heavily on improvisation (Day 1996: 51).

4 This advice was also given as a talk to the Globe company in 1997 (Rylance 1997b).

5 When Shepherd returned to the Globe after a long absence in 2005, he directed and co-devised a new play, *Man Falling Down*, in the strikingly non-realistic idiom of masked physical theatre. His programme notes remind the reader that he had, in fact, used masks for the bandits in Act 5 of his inaugural production of *The Two Gentlemen of Verona* (Shakespeare's Globe 2005b).

6 Trevor Rawlins notes that Alfreds ascribes this exercise to the American teacher Viola Spolin, whose book *Improvisation for the Theatre* describes the 'point of concentration' as a 'chosen agreed object (or event) on which to focus; a technique to achieve detachment; … a vehicle that transports the player' (Spolin 1963: 388; Rawlins 2012: 439).

7   See, for example, Miller-Schütz 1999b: 42; Best 2001: 28 May;
    Howey-Nunn 2002: 50; and Brennan 2003: 11 April.

Chapter 3

1   Rylance used the same terminology in a 2015 interview on
    BBC Radio 4 (see p. 148). He told me during our interview in
    2016 that the idea had been explained to him by the Globe's
    Master of Voice, Stewart Pearce.

2   The *Daily Telegraph*'s Charles Spencer did not agree: when an
    'American lady' in the audience answered Edmund's question
    with 'Take 'em both!', Spencer apparently 'felt like ramming
    her programme down her throat' (24 May 2001). Benedict
    Nightingale likewise complained of the moment's 'trivialising
    effect' (*Times*, 24 May 2001).

3   For further details, see Day 1996: 285 and Conkie 2006: 67–8.

4   Gould even learned a few lines in Japanese so that he could
    achieve a similar effect when the production played at the
    Tokyo Globe (Gould 2001: 24 September).

5   See Escolme 2005: 64; Potter 2001: 128; and Worthen 2003: 106.

6   Where Kiernan's 'performance' suggests something that
    originates from the audience themselves, Worthen's
    'performativity' implies an identity produced by *discourse* – in
    this case, theme parks, living history restorations, the media,
    and the Globe's own marketing. He borrows the word from
    Judith Butler (among other thinkers), for whom performativity
    is 'that aspect of discourse that has the capacity to produce
    what it names' (Osbourne and Segal 1994: 23).

Chapter 4

1   Subsequent critics, including Egan (1999: 15) and Prescott
    (2013: 205–6), have argued that Drakakis's account is
    something of a simplification of the various disagreements
    within the groups on both sides of this debate.

2   Issue 1 of the Globe's in-house magazine, *Around the Globe*,
     features an abridged version of Hawkes's piece from *Meaning
     by Shakespeare* in which he 'voices his reservations about the
     rebuilding of the Globe' (Autumn 1996).

3   Or, for that matter, with those of Wanamaker, who had been
     a member of the Communist Party in his youth and remained
     committed to progressive causes throughout his life.

4   Surveying the reviews collated in *Theatre Record*, I found
     examples of the analogy in six different reviews of *Richard
     III*, a further six reviews of *The Taming of the Shrew*, and a
     further five reviews of *Much Ado About Nothing*.

5   Another version of Conkie's article appears in his book *The
     Globe Theatre Project: Shakespeare and Authenticity* (2006).

6   It is worth noting that all three of these critiques highlight the
     Globe's claims to 'authenticity', a term from which, as we have
     seen, Rylance was in fact keen to distance himself.

7   Another version of Bulman's article appears in the Blackwell
     Companion to Shakespeare and Performance, edited by
     Barbara Hodgdon and W. B. Worthen (2005). This collection
     also features a second essay on cross-gender performance at the
     Globe, by G. B. Shand.

Epilogue

1   Following his departure from the Globe, Rylance became
     more public in voicing his doubts about the authorship of
     the works of Shakespeare, helping to launch the 'Declaration
     of Reasonable Doubt' in 2007 and appearing in Roland
     Emmerich's authorship conspiracy film *Anonymous* in 2011.

2   As he put it in an email to me:

     Was the Globe primarily a theatre or an education centre,
     or were they equal partners? Surely the ability of the theatre
     to provide quality Shakespeare for no more than £5 to 700
     people, many of them young, was an educational act in
     itself. (Rylance 2016b)

3   The other fellowships were awarded to Andrew Gurr, Jon

Greenfield, Franklin J. Hildy, Peter McCurdy and Martin White.

4 Compare, for example, Benedict Nightingale's relief when 1997's *The Winter's Tale* confirmed that the Globe was 'not going to be a theme-park for trippers or a playpen for academics' (*Times*, 6 June 1997), or Paul Taylor's worry that the theatre might become a 'tourist-trap-cum-playpen-for-cranky-academics' (*Independent*, 9 June 1997). As Paul Prescott has pointed out, the image serves to 'infantilize academic spectators' (2005: 370).

REFERENCES

Aaron, Melissa D. (2008), '"A Queen in a Beard": A Study of All-Female Shakespeare Companies', in James C. Bulman (ed.), *Shakespeare Re-Dressed: Cross-Gender Casting in Contemporary Performance*, 150–65, Madison, NJ: Fairleigh Dickinson University Press.

Alfreds, Mike (2007), *Different Every Night: Freeing the Actor*, London: Nick Hern Books.

Awasthi, Suresh (1993), 'The Intercultural Experience and the Kathakali *King Lear*', *New Theatre Quarterly* 9 (34): 172–8.

Barker, Roberta (2008), 'Acting against the Rules: Remembering the Eroticism of the Shakespearean Boy Actress', in James C. Bulman (ed.), *Shakespeare Re-Dressed: Cross-Gender Casting in Contemporary Performance*, 57–78, Madison, NJ: Fairleigh Dickinson University Press.

Bartolovich, Crystal (2001), 'Shakespeare's Globe?', in Jean E. Howard and Scott Cutler Shershow (eds), *Marxist Shakespeares*, 178–205, London: Routledge.

Beaumont, Penelope (2004), 'Leonato played by Penelope Beaumont', *Adopt an Actor*, Shakespeare's Globe, http://www.shakespearesglobe.com/discovery-space/adopt-an-actor (accessed 15 November 2016).

Beaumont, Penelope (2005), 'Paulina played by Penelope Beaumont', *Adopt an Actor*, Shakespeare's Globe, http://www.shakespearesglobe.com/discovery-space/adopt-an-actor (accessed 15 November 2016).

Bessell, Jaq (2000a), 'Findings from the Globe 1999 Season: *Antony and Cleopatra*', *Shakespeare's Globe Research Bulletin* 14, http://www.shakespearesglobe.com/uploads/files/2015/02/antony_and_cleopatra_1999.pdf (accessed 15 November 2016).

Bessell, Jaq (2000b), 'Findings from the Globe 1999 Season: *Julius Caesar*', *Shakespeare's Globe Research Bulletin* 15, http://www.shakespearesglobe.com/uploads/files/2015/02/julius_caesar_1999.pdf (accessed 15 November 2016).

Bessell, Jaq (2000c), 'Interviews with the White Company: 1999 Season', *Shakespeare's Globe Research Bulletin* 15a, http://www.shakespearesglobe.com/uploads/files/2016/03/interviews_1999.pdf (accessed 15 November 2016).

Bessell, Jaq (2000d), 'Interviews with the Red Company: 1999 Season', *Shakespeare's Globe Research Bulletin* 15b, http://www.shakespearesglobe.com/uploads/files/2016/03/interviews_1999_red_.pdf (accessed 15 November 2016).

Bessell, Jaq (2001a), 'The 2000 Globe Season: The Red Company, *The Tempest*', *Shakespeare's Globe Research Bulletin* 16, http://www.shakespearesglobe.com/uploads/files/2015/02/the_tempest_2000.pdf (accessed 15 November 2016).

Bessell, Jaq (2001b), 'The 2000 Globe Season: The White Company, *Hamlet*', *Shakespeare's Globe Research Bulletin* 17, http://www.shakespearesglobe.com/uploads/files/2015/02/hamlet_2000.pdf (accessed 15 November 2016).

Bessell, Jaq (2001c), 'Actor Interviews 2000: Red and White Companies', *Shakespeare's Globe Research Bulletin* 18, http://www.shakespearesglobe.com/uploads/files/2015/02/actor_interviews_2000.pdf (accessed 15 November 2016).

Bessell, Jaq (2001d), 'The 2000 Globe Season: The Red Company, *Two Noble Kinsmen*', *Shakespeare's Globe Research Bulletin* 19, http://www.shakespearesglobe.com/uploads/files/2015/02/the_two_noble_kinsmen_2000.pdf (accessed 15 November 2016).

Bessell, Jaq (2002a), 'The 2001 Globe Season: The White Company, *King Lear*', *Shakespeare's Globe Research Bulletin* 21, http://www.shakespearesglobe.com/uploads/files/2015/02/king_lear_2001.pdf (accessed 15 November 2016).

Bessell, Jaq (2002b), 'The 2001 Globe Season: The Rose Company, *Cymbeline*', *Shakespeare's Globe Research Bulletin* 22, http://www.shakespearesglobe.com/uploads/files/2015/02/cymbeline_2001.pdf (accessed 15 November 2016).

Bessell, Jaq (2002c), 'The 2001 Globe Season: The Red Company, *Macbeth*', *Shakespeare's Globe Research Bulletin* 23, http://www.shakespearesglobe.com/uploads/files/2016/03/macbeth_2001_bulletin.pdf (accessed 15 November 2016).

Bessell, Jaq (2002d), 'Interviews with Company Members from the 2001 Theatre Season: The Celtic Season', *Shakespeare's Globe Research Bulletin*, Annex to issues 21, 22, 23, http://www.

shakespearesglobe.com/uploads/files/2015/12/2001_interviews. pdf (accessed 15 November 2016).

Bessell, Jaq (2012), 'The Actors' Renaissance Season at the Blackfriars Playhouse', in Pascale Aebischer and Kathryn Prince (eds), *Performing Early Modern Drama Today*, 85–103, Cambridge: Cambridge University Press.

Best, Eve (2001), 'Lady Macbeth played by Eve Best', *Adopt an Actor*, Shakespeare's Globe, http://www.shakespearesglobe.com/ discovery-space/adopt-an-actor (accessed 15 November 2016).

Block, Giles (2013), *Speaking the Speech: An Actor's Guide to Shakespeare*, London: Nick Hern Books.

Bourne, Bette (2004), 'Nurse played by Bette Bourne', *Adopt an Actor,* Shakespeare's Globe, http://www.shakespearesglobe.com/ discovery-space/adopt-an-actor (accessed 15 November 2016).

Brecht, Bertolt (1977), *Brecht on Theatre*, trans. J. Willett, London: Eyre Methuen.

Brennan, Liam (2001), 'Macduff played by Liam Brennan', *Adopt an Actor*, Shakespeare's Globe, http://www.shakespearesglobe. com/discovery-space/adopt-an-actor (accessed 15 November 2016).

Brennan, Liam (2003), 'Bolingbroke played by Liam Brennan', *Adopt an Actor*, Shakespeare's Globe, http://www. shakespearesglobe.com/discovery-space/adopt-an-actor (accessed 15 November 2016).

Brennan, Liam (2004), 'Angelo played by Liam Brennan', *Adopt an Actor*, Shakespeare's Globe, http://www.shakespearesglobe.com/ discovery-space/adopt-an-actor (accessed 15 November 2016).

Brennen, Paul (2001), 'Edgar played by Paul Brennen', *Adopt an Actor*, Shakespeare's Globe, http://www.shakespearesglobe.com/ discovery-space/adopt-an-actor (accessed 15 November 2016).

Britton, Jasper (2001), 'Macbeth Played by Jasper Britton', *Adopt an Actor*, Shakespeare's Globe, http://www.shakespearesglobe. com/discovery-space/adopt-an-actor (accessed 15 November 2016).

Brown, Michael (2002), 'Viola played by Michael Brown', *Adopt an Actor*, Shakespeare's Globe, http://www.shakespearesglobe. com/discovery-space/adopt-an-actor (accessed 15 November 2016).

Bulman, James C. (2005), 'Queering the Audience: All-Male Casts in Recent Productions of Shakespeare', in Barbara Hodgdon and W. B. Worthen (eds), *A Companion to Shakespeare and Performance*, 564–87, Chichester: Blackwell.

Bulman, James C. (2008), 'Unsex Me Here: Male Cross-Dressing at the New Globe', in *Shakespeare Re-Dressed: Cross-Gender Casting in Contemporary Performance*, 231–45, Madison, NJ: Fairleigh Dickinson University Press.

Burke, Tom (2004), 'Romeo played by Tom Burke', *Adopt an Actor*, Shakespeare's Globe, http://www.shakespearesglobe.com/discovery-space/adopt-an-actor (accessed 15 November 2016).

Carroll, Tim (2008), 'Practising Behaviour to His Own Shadow', in Christie Carson and Farah Karim-Cooper (eds), *Shakespeare's Globe: A Theatrical Experiment*, 37–44, Cambridge: Cambridge University Press.

Carroll, Tim (2016), interview with the author, 16 January.

Carson, Christie and Farah Karim-Cooper (eds) (2008), *Shakespeare's Globe: A Theatrical Experiment*, Cambridge: Cambridge University Press.

Chahidi, Paul (1999), 'Angelo played by Paul Chahidi', *Adopt an Actor*, Shakespeare's Globe, http://www.shakespearesglobe.com/discovery-space/adopt-an-actor (accessed 15 November 2016).

Chahidi, Paul (2002), 'Maria played by Paul Chahidi', *Adopt an Actor*, Shakespeare's Globe, http://www.shakespearesglobe.com/discovery-space/adopt-an-actor (accessed 15 November 2016).

Chekhov, Michael (2002), *To The Actor*, London and New York: Routledge.

Conkie, Rob (2006), *The Globe Theatre Project: Shakespeare and Authenticity*, New York: The Edwin Mellen Press.

Conkie, Rob (2008), 'Constructing Femininity in the New Globe's All-Male *Antony and Cleopatra*', in James C. Bulman (ed.), *Shakespeare Re-Dressed: Cross-Gender Casting in Contemporary Performance*, 189–209, Madison, NJ: Fairleigh Dickinson University Press.

Cordner, Michael (1998), 'Repeopling the Globe: The Opening Season at Shakespeare's Globe, London 1997', *Shakespeare Survey* 51: 205–18.

Cornford, Tom (2012), 'The Importance of How: Directing Shakespeare with Michael Chekhov's Technique', *Shakespeare Bulletin* 30 (4): 485–504.

Crouch, Tim (2011), *Plays One: My Arm, An Oak Tree, ENGLAND, The Author*, London: Oberon Books.

Crystal, David (2005), *Pronouncing Shakespeare: The Globe Experiment*, Cambridge: Cambridge University Press.

Day, Barry (1996), *This Wooden 'O': Shakespeare's Globe Reborn*, London: Oberon Books.

Dessen Alan C. (1998), 'Globe Matters', *Shakespeare Quarterly* 49 (2): 195–203.

Dobson, Michael (2001), 'Shakespeare Performances in England, 2000', *Shakespeare Survey* 54: 246–82.

Drakakis, John (1988), 'Theatre, Ideology, and Institution: Shakespeare and the Roadsweepers', in Graham Holderness (ed.), *The Shakespeare Myth*, 24–41, Manchester: Manchester University Press.

Dyer, Peter Hamilton (2002), 'Feste played by Peter Hamilton Dyer', *Adopt an Actor*, Shakespeare's Globe, http://www.shakespearesglobe.com/discovery-space/adopt-an-actor (accessed 15 November 2016).

Edström, Per (1990), *Why Not Theaters Made For People?*, trans. C. Forslund, Värmdö: Arena Theatre Institute Foundation.

Egan, Gabriel (1997), 'London's New Globe Opens', *Speech and Drama* 46 (1): 18–24.

Egan, Gabriel (1999), 'Reconstructions of the Globe: A Retrospective', *Shakespeare Survey* 52: 1–16.

Escolme, Bridget (2005), *Talking to the Audience: Shakespeare, Performance, Self*, London and New York: Routledge.

Escolme, Bridget (2008), 'Mark Rylance', in John Russell Brown (ed.), *The Routledge Companion to Directors' Shakespeare*, 407–24, London: Routledge.

Forbes, Peter (2005), 'Polixenes played by Peter Forbes', *Adopt an Actor*, Shakespeare's Globe, http://www.shakespearesglobe.com/discovery-space/adopt-an-actor (accessed 15 November 2016).

Freedman, Gerald (2001), 'A Summer of Directing Dangerously', *American Theatre* 18:10. Reproduced at https://www.tcg.org/publications/at/2001/summer.cfm (accessed 15 November 2016).

French, Andrew (1998), 'Gratiano played by Andrew French', *Adopt an Actor*, Shakespeare's Globe, http://www.shakespearesglobe.com/discovery-space/adopt-an-actor (accessed 15 November 2016).

Gale, Mariah (2004), 'Hero played by Mariah Gale', *Adopt an Actor*, Shakespeare's Globe, http://www.shakespearesglobe.com/discovery-space/adopt-an-actor (accessed 15 November 2016).

Garnon, James (2004), 'Mercutio played by James Garnon', *Adopt an Actor*, Shakespeare's Globe, http://www.shakespearesglobe. com/discovery-space/adopt-an-actor (accessed 15 November 2016).

Garnon, James (2006), interview with the author, 6 March.

Gostelow, Harry (2005), 'Cleon, Fisherman, Pandar played by Harry Gostelow', *Adopt an Actor*, Shakespeare's Globe, http:// www.shakespearesglobe.com/discovery-space/adopt-an-actor (accessed 15 November 2016).

Gould, Michael (2001), 'Edmund played by Michael Gould', *Adopt an Actor*, Shakespeare's Globe, http://www.shakespearesglobe. com/discovery-space/adopt-an-actor (accessed 15 November 2016).

Gray, Zoe (2002), 'This Season's Night Wear', *Around the Globe* 21.

Greenfield, Jon (1997), 'Design as Reconstruction/Reconstruction as Design', in J. R. Mulryne and Margaret Shewring (eds), *Shakespeare's Globe Rebuilt*, 81–96, Cambridge: Cambridge University Press.

Gurr, Andrew (1995), 'Staging at the New Globe: A 1995 View', Shakespeare's Globe, http://www.rdg.ac.uk/globe/Articles/ GurrArt.htm (accessed 17 June 2004).

Gurr, Andrew (1997), 'Staging at the Globe', in J. R. Mulryne and Margaret Shewring (eds), *Shakespeare's Globe Rebuilt*, 159–68, Cambridge: Cambridge University Press.

Gurr, Andrew (2008), 'Sam Wanamaker's Invention: Lessons from the New Globe', in Frank Occhiogrosso (ed.), *Shakespearean Performance: New Studies*, 110–28, Madison, NJ: Fairleigh Dickinson University Press.

Harris, Amanda (2003), 'Buckingham played by Amanda Harris', *Adopt an Actor*, Shakespeare's Globe, http://www. shakespearesglobe.com/discovery-space/adopt-an-actor (accessed 15 November 2016).

Hassell, Alex (2004), 'Claudio played by Alex Hassell', *Adopt an Actor*, Shakespeare's Globe, http://www.shakespearesglobe.com/ discovery-space/adopt-an-actor (accessed 15 November 2016).

Hawkes, Terence (1992), 'Bardbiz', in *Meaning By Shakespeare*, 141–53, London: Routledge.

Holden, Michael (1995), 'The Quick Forge and Working House of Thought', Newsletter of the International Shakespeare Globe

Centre, Summer 1995. Reproduced at http://www.rdg.ac.uk/globe/Articles/HoldenArt.htm (accessed 26 June 2004).

Holderness, Graham (2001), *Cultural Shakespeare: Essays in the Shakespeare Myth*, Hatfield: University of Hertfordshire Press.

Hornby, Richard (1997), 'Historic Theatres', *The Hudson Review* 49 (4): 645–51.

Howey-Nunn, Sam (2002), 'The 2002 Globe Season: The Rose Company, *The Golden Ass*', *Shakespeare's Globe Research Bulletin* 27, http://www.shakespearesglobe.com/uploads/files/2015/02/the_golden_ass_2002.pdf (accessed 15 November 2016).

Jessop, Melanie (2004), 'Lady Capulet played by Melanie Jessop', *Adopt an Actor*, Shakespeare's Globe, http://www.shakespearesglobe.com/discovery-space/adopt-an-actor (accessed 15 November 2016).

Jeynes, Elin and Jessica Ryan (2002), 'The 2001 Globe-to-Globe Season: The Welcome Msomi Company, *Umabatha*', *Shakespeare's Globe Research Bulletin* 25, http://www.shakespearesglobe.com/uploads/ffiles/2012/03/891356.pdf (accessed 15 November 2016).

Johnstone, Keith (1999), *Impro for Storytellers*, London: Faber & Faber.

Kane, Sarah (1998), 'Drama with Balls', *Guardian*, 20 August, p. 12.

Kennedy, Dennis (2001), 'Globe Tourism', *Around the Globe* 18.

Kennedy, Dennis (2009), *The Spectator and the Spectacle: Audiences in Modernity and Postmodernity*, Cambridge: Cambridge University Press.

Kentrup, Norbert (1998), 'Shylock played by Norbert Kentrup', *Adopt an Actor*, Shakespeare's Globe, http://www.shakespearesglobe.com/discovery-space/adopt-an-actor (accessed 15 November 2016).

Kerrigan, Patricia (2001), 'Goneril played by Patricia Kerrigan', *Adopt an Actor*, Shakespeare's Globe, http://www.shakespearesglobe.com/discovery-space/adopt-an-actor (accessed 15 November 2016).

Kiernan, Pauline (1995), 'Findings from the 1995 Workshop Season', *Shakespeare's Globe Research Bulletin* (unnumbered), http://www.shakespearesglobe.com/uploads/files/2016/03/1995_workshop_finding.pdf (accessed 15 November 2016).

Kiernan, Pauline (1996a), 'Findings from the Globe Prologue Season 1996', *Shakespeare's Globe Research Bulletin* 5, http://www.shakespearesglobe.com/uploads/files/2015/10/globe_findings_no.5_1996.pdf (accessed 15 November 2016).

Kiernan, Pauline (1996b), 'The Star of the Show', *Around the Globe* 2.

Kiernan, Pauline (1998a), 'Findings from the Globe Opening Season: *Henry V*', *Shakespeare's Globe Research Bulletin* 2, http://www.shakespearesglobe.com/uploads/files/2015/02/henry_v_1997.pdf (accessed 15 November 2016).

Kiernan, Pauline (1998b), 'Findings from the Globe 1998 Season: The Merchant of Venice', *Shakespeare's Globe Research Bulletin* 7a, http://www.shakespearesglobe.com/uploads/files/2015/02/the_merchant_of_venice_1998.pdf (accessed 15 November 2016).

Kiernan, Pauline (1998c), 'Findings from the Globe 1998 Season: The Honest Whore', *Shakespeare's Globe Research Bulletin* 7b, http://www.shakespearesglobe.com/uploads/files/2015/02/the_honest_whore_1998.pdf (accessed 15 November 2016).

Kiernan, Pauline (1998d), 'The Review Conference 1998', *Shakespeare's Globe Research Bulletin* 6, http://www.rdg.ac.uk/globe/research/1998/Rev98Morning.htm (accessed 24 June 2004).

Kiernan, Pauline (1999), *Staging Shakespeare at the New Globe*, Basingstoke: Macmillan.

Kirimi, Kananu (2004), 'Juliet played by Kananu Kirimi', *Adopt an Actor*, Shakespeare's Globe, http://www.shakespearesglobe.com/discovery-space/adopt-an-actor (accessed 15 November 2016).

Klett, Elizabeth (2008), 'Re-dressing the Balance: All-Female Shakespeare at the Globe Theatre', in James C. Bulman (ed.), *Shakespeare Re-Dressed: Cross-Gender Casting in Contemporary Performance*, 166–88, Madison, NJ: Fairleigh Dickinson University Press.

Klett, Elizabeth (2009), 'Gender in Exile: Vanessa Redgrave's Prospero in *The Tempest* (2000)', in *Cross-Gender Shakespeare and English National Identity: Wearing the Codpiece*, 87–114, Basingstoke: Palgrave Macmillan.

Ko, Yu Jin (1999), 'A Little Touch of Harry in the Light: *Henry V* at the New Globe', *Shakespeare Survey* 52: 107–19.

Koestler, Arthur (1976), *The Act of Creation*, London: Danube.

Lanier, Douglas (2002), *Shakespeare and Modern Popular Culture*, Oxford: Oxford University Press.

Leonard, Mark (1997), *Britain™: Renewing Our Identity*, London: Demos. Reproduced at http://www.demos.co.uk/files/britaintm.pdf (accessed 15 November 2016).

Mackintosh, Iain (1993), *Architecture, Actor & Audience*, London: Routledge.

MacNeill, Meredith (2003), 'Lady Anne, Young Elizabeth played by Meredith MacNeill', *Adopt an Actor*, Shakespeare's Globe, http://www.shakespearesglobe.com/discovery-space/adopt-an-actor (accessed 15 November 2016).

Magni, Marcello (2005), 'Helicanus, Simonides, Boult played by Marcello Magni', *Adopt an Actor*, Shakespeare's Globe, http://www.shakespearesglobe.com/discovery-space/adopt-an-actor (accessed 15 November 2016).

Magni, Marcello (2010), interview with the author, 9 June.

Mamet, David (1998), *True and False: Heresy and Common Sense for the Actor*, London: Faber & Faber.

Marshall, Cynthia (2000), 'Sight and Sound: Two Models of Shakespearean Subjectivity on the British Stage,' *Shakespeare Quarterly* 51: 353–61.

McLuskie, Kate (1999), '*Macbeth/uMabatha*: Global Shakespeare in a Post-Colonial Market', *Shakespeare Survey* 52: 154–65.

McMullan, Gordon (2008), 'Afterword', in Christie Carson and Farah Karim-Cooper (eds), *Shakespeare's Globe: A Theatrical Experiment*, 230–3, Cambridge: Cambridge University Press.

Menzer, Paul (2006), 'Afterword: Discovery Spaces?', in *Inside Shakespeare: Essays on the Blackfriars Stage*, 223–30, Selinsgrove, PA: Susquehanna University Press.

Miller-Schütz, Chantal (1997), 'The Opening Season Review at Shakespeare's Globe', http://www.rdg.ac.uk/globe/research/1997/ReviewOS.htm (accessed 24 June 2004).

Miller-Schütz, Chantal (1998), 'Findings from the Globe Opening Season: *The Winter's Tale*', *Shakespeare's Globe Research Bulletin* 3, http://www.shakespearesglobe.com/uploads/files/2015/02/the_winters_tale_1997.pdf (accessed 15 November 2016).

Miller-Schütz, Chantal (1999a), 'Findings from the 1998 Season: *As You Like It*', *Shakespeare's Globe Research Bulletin* 10, http://www.shakespearesglobe.com/uploads/files/2015/10/

findings_from_the_1998_season_as_you_like_it.pdf (accessed 15 November 2016).

Miller-Schütz, Chantal (1999b), 'Interviews of the Red Company Cast Members (1998)', *Shakespeare's Globe Research Bulletin*, Annex to issues 10 and 11, http://www.shakespearesglobe. com/uploads/files/2015/10/interviews_with_red_company_ cast_members_1998_annex_to_10_and_11.pdf (accessed 15 November 2016).

Miller-Schütz, Chantal (2000), 'Findings from the Globe 1997–1998 Season: Shakespeare's Contemporaries at the New Globe (1997–1998): *The Maid's Tragedy, A Chaste Maid in Cheapside, A Mad World, My Masters*', *Shakespeare's Globe Research Bulletin* 12, http://www.shakespearesglobe.com/ uploads/files/2015/02/shakespeares_contemporaries_1997_8.pdf (accessed 15 November 2016).

Mulryne, J. R. and Margaret Shewring (eds) (1997), *Shakespeare's Globe Rebuilt*, Cambridge: Cambridge University Press.

Mulryne, J. R. and Margaret Shewring (1997), 'The Once And Future Globe', in *Shakespeare's Globe Rebuilt*, 15–26, Cambridge: Cambridge University Press.

Neill, Heather (2012), 'Director Phyllida Lloyd introduces her all-female Julius Caesar', *Theatre Voice*, 18 December, http:// www.theatrevoice.com/audio/director-phyllida-lloyd-introduces- her-all-female-julius-caesar/ (accessed 15 November 2016).

Ogbomo, Ann (2003), 'Duke of Norfolk, Murderer 1, Sir William Catesby played by Ann Ogbomo', *Adopt an Actor*, Shakespeare's Globe, http://www.shakespearesglobe.com/discovery-space/ adopt-an-actor (accessed 15 November 2016).

Ogbomo, Ann (2004), 'Claudio played by Ann Ogbomo', *Adopt an Actor*, Shakespeare's Globe, http://www.shakespearesglobe.com/ discovery-space/adopt-an-actor (accessed 15 November 2016).

Olivier, Richard (2015), 'What We Do', Olivier Mythodrama, http://www.oliviermythodrama.com/whatwedo.asp (accessed 15 November 2016).

Omambala, Chu (2001), 'Malcolm played by Chu Omambala', *Adopt an Actor*, Shakespeare's Globe, http://www. shakespearesglobe.com/discovery-space/adopt-an-actor (accessed 15 November 2016).

Omambala, Chu (2003), 'Aumerle played by Chu Omambala', *Adopt an Actor*, Shakespeare's Globe, http://www.

shakespearesglobe.com/discovery-space/adopt-an-actor (accessed 15 November 2016).

Orgel, Stephen (1998), 'What's the Globe Good For?', *Shakespeare Quarterly* 49 (2): 191–4.

Osbourne, Peter and Lynne Segal (1994), 'Gender as Performance: An Interview with Judith Butler', *Radical Philosophy* 67: 32–9.

Peterson, Sally (2005), 'Art and Soul', *Caduceus* 66, Spring, 6–9.

Potter, Lois (1999), 'A Stage Where Every Man Must Play a Part?', *Shakespeare Quarterly* 50 (1): 74–86.

Potter, Lois (2001), 'This Distracted Globe: Summer 2000', *Shakespeare Quarterly* 52 (1): 124–32.

Potter, Lois (2004), 'English and American Richards, Edwards and Henries', *Shakespeare Quarterly* 55 (4): 450–61.

Prescott, Paul (2005), 'Inheriting the Globe: The Reception of Shakespearean Space and Audience in Contemporary Reviewing', in Barbara Hodgdon and W. B. Worthen (eds), *A Companion to Shakespeare and Performance*, 359–75, Chichester: Blackwell.

Prescott, Paul (2013), 'Sam Wanamaker', in Cary M. Mazer (ed.), *Great Shakespeareans: Poel, Granville Barker, Guthrie, Wanamaker*, 151–210, London and New York: Bloomsbury Arden Shakespeare.

Proudfoot, Richard (1999), 'The 1998 Globe Season', *Shakespeare Survey* 52: 215–28.

Purcell, Stephen (2009), *Popular Shakespeare: Simulation and Subversion on the Modern Stage*, Basingstoke: Palgrave Macmillan.

Ramm, John (2002), 'Bottom played by John Ramm', *Adopt an Actor*, Shakespeare's Globe, http://www.shakespearesglobe.com/discovery-space/adopt-an-actor (accessed 15 November 2016).

Rancière, Jacques (2007), 'The Emancipated Spectator', *Artforum* 45 (7): 271–80.

Rawlins, Trevor (2012), '"Disciplined Improvisation" in the Rehearsal and Performance of Shakespeare: The Alternative Approach of Mike Alfreds', *Shakespeare Bulletin* 30 (4): 431–47.

Rees, Laura (2005), 'Marina played by Laura Rees', *Adopt an Actor*, Shakespeare's Globe, http://www.shakespearesglobe.com/discovery-space/adopt-an-actor (accessed 15 November 2016).

Rose, Judith (2008), 'Performing Gender at the Globe: The

Technologies of the Cross-Dressed Actor', in James C. Bulman (ed.), *Shakespeare Re-Dressed: Cross-Gender Casting in Contemporary Performance*, 210–30, Madison, NJ: Fairleigh Dickinson University Press.

RSC (2004), 'RSC outlines plan for renewal of theatre', press release, 22 September, http://www.rsc.org.uk/press/420_1700.aspx. (accessed 26 November 2005).

Ryan, Jessica (2002a), 'The 2002 Globe Season: The White Company, *Twelfth Night*', *Shakespeare's Globe Research Bulletin* 26, http://www.shakespearesglobe.com/uploads/files/2015/02/twelfth_night_2002.pdf (accessed 15 November 2016).

Ryan, Jessica (2002b), 'Interviews with Company Members from the 2002 Theatre Season: The Season of Cupid and Psyche', *Shakespeare's Globe Research Bulletin* (unnumbered), http://www.shakespearesglobe.com/uploads/files/2015/02/actor_interviews_2002.pdf (accessed 15 November 2016).

Rylance, Juliet (2005), 'Perdita played by Juliet Rylance', *Adopt an Actor*, Shakespeare's Globe, http://www.shakespearesglobe.com/discovery-space/adopt-an-actor (accessed 15 November 2016).

Rylance, Mark (1996), notes for talk at Shakespeare Institute, 14 March, Mark Rylance Papers, SGT/AD/1, London: Globe Archive.

Rylance, Mark (1997a), 'Playing the Globe: Artistic Policy and Practice', in J. R. Mulryne and Margaret Shewring (eds), *Shakespeare's Globe Rebuilt*, 169–76, Cambridge: Cambridge University Press.

Rylance, Mark (1997b), notes for talk to Globe company (undated), Mark Rylance Papers, SGT/AD/1, London: Globe Archive.

Rylance, Mark (1998), 'Thoughts for the 1999 Season', 6 June, Mark Rylance Papers, SGT/AD/1, London: Globe Archive.

Rylance, Mark (2000a), artistic plans (undated), Mark Rylance Papers, SGT/AD/1, London: Globe Archive.

Rylance, Mark (2000b), report for November meeting of Artistic Directorate, Mark Rylance Papers, SGT/AD/1, London: Globe Archive.

Rylance, Mark (2001a), 'Posthumus, Cloten, Cornelius played by Mark Rylance', *Adopt an Actor*, Shakespeare's Globe, http://

www.shakespearesglobe.com/discovery-space/adopt-an-actor (accessed 15 November 2016).

Rylance, Mark (2001b), letter to *Twelfth Night* company, 26 November, Mark Rylance Papers, SGT/AD/1, London: Globe Archive.

Rylance, Mark (2003), *Play: A Recollection in Pictures and Words of the First Five Years of Play at Shakespeare's Globe Theatre*, London: Shakespeare's Globe.

Rylance, Mark (2004a), 'Vincentio played by Mark Rylance', *Adopt an Actor*, Shakespeare's Globe, http://www.shakespearesglobe.com/discovery-space/adopt-an-actor (accessed 15 November 2016).

Rylance, Mark (2004b), untitled letter to Sir Michael Perry and Peter Kyle, August, Mark Rylance Papers, SGT/AD/1, London: Globe Archive.

Rylance, Mark (2004c), untitled letter to colleagues and friends, 19 September, Mark Rylance Papers, SGT/AD/1, London: Globe Archive.

Rylance, Mark (2006), untitled and undated letter to Dominic Dromgoole, Mark Rylance Papers, SGT/AD/1, London: Globe Archive.

Rylance, Mark (2008), 'Research, Materials, Craft: Principles of Performance at Shakespeare's Globe', in Christie Carson and Farah Karim-Cooper (eds), *Shakespeare's Globe: A Theatrical Experiment*, 103–14, Cambridge: Cambridge University Press.

Rylance, Mark (2012), *I Am Shakespeare*, London: Nick Hern Books.

Rylance, Mark (2016a), interview with the author, 7 May.

Rylance, Mark (2016b), email to the author, 22 November.

Rylance, Mark, Yolanda Vazquez and Paul Chahidi (2008), 'Discoveries from the Globe Stage', in Christie Carson and Farah Karim-Cooper (eds), *Shakespeare's Globe: A Theatrical Experiment*, 194–210, Cambridge: Cambridge University Press.

Sanders, Rachel (2004), 'Don John played by Rachel Sanders', *Adopt an Actor*, Shakespeare's Globe, http://www.shakespearesglobe.com/discovery-space/adopt-an-actor (accessed 15 November 2016).

Shakespeare's Globe (1993a), Draft Artistic Board Policy, Mark Rylance Papers, SGT/AD/1, London: Globe Archive.

Shakespeare's Globe (1993b), programme for *Tackling Shakespeare*, London: Globe Archive.

Shakespeare's Globe (1995), 'The Shakespeare's Globe Workshop Season in Detail', electronic document, London: Globe Archive.

Shakespeare's Globe (1997), programme for *Festival of Firsts*, SGT/DEV/EV/218, London: Globe Archive.

Shakespeare's Globe (1998a), programme for *As You Like It*, SGT/COMM/PUB/1, London: Globe Archive.

Shakespeare's Globe (1998b), programme for *The Merchant of Venice*, SGT/COMM/PUB/1, London: Globe Archive.

Shakespeare's Globe (1998c), video recording of *The Merchant of Venice*, SGT/ED/LIB/REC/1998/MOV, London: Globe Archive.

Shakespeare's Globe (2000), minutes of September meeting of Artistic Directorate, Mark Rylance Papers, SGT/AD/1, London: Globe Archive.

Shakespeare's Globe (2001), programme for *Cymbeline*, SGT/COMM/PUB/1, London: Globe Archive.

Shakespeare's Globe (2002), programme for *Twelfth Night*, SGT/COMM/PUB/1, London: Globe Archive.

Shakespeare's Globe (2003a), programme for *Richard II*, SGT/COMM/PUB/1, London: Globe Archive.

Shakespeare's Globe (2003b), programme for *The Taming of the Shrew*, SGT/COMM/PUB/1, London: Globe Archive.

Shakespeare's Globe (2003c), programme for *Twelfth Night*, SGT/COMM/PUB/1, London: Globe Archive.

Shakespeare's Globe (2005a), programme for *Pericles*, SGT/COMM/PUB/1, London: Globe Archive.

Shakespeare's Globe (2005b), programme for *The Persephone Projects*, SGT/COMM/PUB/1, London: Globe Archive.

Shakespeare's Globe (2005c), video recording of *Pericles*, SGT/ED/LIB/REC/2005/PER, London: Globe Archive.

Shakespeare's Globe (2016) 'Statement regarding the Globe's future Artistic Direction', 25 October, http://blog.shakespearesglobe.com/post/152286922818/statement-regarding-the-globes-future-artistic (accessed 15 November 2016).

Shand, G. B. (2005), 'Guying the Girls and Girling The Shrew: (Post)Feminist Fun at Shakespeare's Globe', in Barbara Hodgdon and W. B. Worthen (eds), *A Companion to Shakespeare and Performance*, 550–63, Chichester: Blackwell.

Shaughnessy, Robert, ed. (2000), *Shakespeare in Performance: Contemporary Critical Essays*, Basingstoke: Palgrave Macmillan.

Shaughnessy, Robert (2011), *The Routledge Guide to William Shakespeare*, Abingdon/New York: Routledge.

Shorey, Peter (2003), 'Duchess of York played by Peter Shorey', *Adopt an Actor*, Shakespeare's Globe, http://www.shakespearesglobe.com/discovery-space/adopt-an-actor (accessed 15 November 2016).

Silverstone, Catherine (2005), 'Shakespeare Live: reproducing Shakespeare at the "new" Globe Theatre', *Textual Practice*, 19 (1): 31–50.

Sinfield, Alan (1992), *Faultlines: Cultural Materialism and the Politics of Dissident Reading*, Oxford: Clarendon Press.

Smallwood, Robert (1997), 'Shakespeare Performances in England, 1996', *Shakespeare Survey* 50: 201–24.

Smallwood, Robert (1998), 'Shakespeare Performances in England, 1997', *Shakespeare Survey* 51: 219–55.

Smallwood, Robert (1999), 'Shakespeare Performances in England, 1998', *Shakespeare Survey* 52: 229–53.

Spolin, Viola (1963), *Improvisation for the Theatre: A Handbook of Teaching and Directing Techniques*, Illinois: Northwestern University Press.

Stanislavski, Constantin (1989 [1936]), *An Actor Prepares*, trans. Elizabeth Reynolds Hapgood, New York: Theatre Arts Books.

Stanton, Philippa (2002), 'Hermia played by Philippa Stanton', *Adopt an Actor*, Shakespeare's Globe, http://www.shakespearesglobe.com/discovery-space/adopt-an-actor (accessed 15 November 2016).

States, Bert O. (1985), *Great Reckonings in Little Rooms: On the Phenomenology of Theatre*, Berkeley: University of California Press.

Thompson, Ann (2012), 'Staging Plays at Shakespeare's Globe: Then and Now', *Alicante Journal of English Studies* 25: 137–49.

Thompson, Sophie (2004), 'Isabella played by Sophie Thompson', *Adopt an Actor*, Shakespeare's Globe, http://www.shakespearesglobe.com/discovery-space/adopt-an-actor (accessed 15 November 2016).

Trinder, Simon (2002), 'Philostrate, Puck played by Simon Trinder', *Adopt an Actor*, Shakespeare's Globe, http://www.

shakespearesglobe.com/discovery-space/adopt-an-actor (accessed 15 November 2016).

Tucker, Patrick (2002), *Secrets of Acting Shakespeare: The Original Approach*, London: Routledge.

Vazquez, Yolanda (1999), 'Adriana played by Yolanda Vazquez', *Adopt an Actor*, Shakespeare's Globe, http://www.shakespearesglobe.com/discovery-space/adopt-an-actor (accessed 15 November 2016).

Vazquez, Yolanda (2004), 'Beatrice played by Yolanda Vazquez', *Adopt an Actor*, Shakespeare's Globe, http://www.shakespearesglobe.com/discovery-space/adopt-an-actor (accessed 15 November 2016).

Violanti, Heather and Jessica Ryan (2002), 'The 2001 Globe-to-Globe Season: The Mansaku Nomura Company, *Kyogen of Errors*', *Shakespeare's Globe Research Bulletin* 24, http://www.shakespearesglobe.com/uploads/files/2015/02/kyogen_of_errors_2001.pdf (accessed 15 November 2016).

Wade, Alan (2000), 'A *Theatre Annual* Interview with Theatre de Complicite's Lilo Baur and Marcello Magni', *Theatre Annual* 53: 69–78.

Walker, Timothy (2002), 'Malvolio played by Timothy Walker', *Adopt an Actor*, Shakespeare's Globe, http://www.shakespearesglobe.com/discovery-space/adopt-an-actor (accessed 15 November 2016).

Wanamaker, Sam (1989), 'International Shakespeare Festival plans', Mark Rylance Papers, SGT/AD/1, London: Globe Archive.

Weimann, Robert (1978), *Shakespeare and the Popular Tradition in the Theatre: Studies in the Social Dimension of Dramatic Form and Function*, Baltimore and London: Johns Hopkins University Press.

Woods, Penelope (2012), 'Globe Audiences: Spectatorship and Reconstruction at Shakespeare's Globe', PhD thesis, Queen Mary, University of London & Shakespeare's Globe.

Woodward, Sarah (2004), 'Dogberry played by Sarah Woodward', *Adopt an Actor*, Shakespeare's Globe, http://www.shakespearesglobe.com/discovery-space/adopt-an-actor (accessed 15 November 2016).

Worthen, W. B. (2003), *Shakespeare and the Force of Modern Performance*, Cambridge: Cambridge University Press.

Wright, John (2006), *Why Is That So Funny?: A Practical Exploration of Physical Comedy*, London: Nick Hern Books.

All references to the works of Shakespeare are to the Arden Third Series edition where this exists, and otherwise to the Arden *Complete Works* (eds Richard Proudfoot, Ann Thompson and David Scott Kastan).

All newspaper articles are cited parenthetically rather than listed in the References section.

INDEX